John Hare was the last recruit to j............ ....seas Civil Service as an administrative officer in northern Nigeria, and spent seven years in some of the remotest parts of West Africa. He later worked for the BBC and in publishing before returning to Africa to work for the United Nations Environment Programme in Nairobi. His practical experience of camels in both Nigeria and Kenya led to his selection to join the expeditions described in this book. He is also working on an environmental awareness-raising campaign for China with Jane Goodall, using the Lop Nur Nature Sanctuary as a pilot project.

John Hare has written over thirty-five books, mainly for children, many of which have environmental or conservation themes. When not lecturing or travelling, he lives in Kent.

THE
LOST CAMELS
OF
TARTARY

A QUEST INTO FORBIDDEN CHINA

John Hare

An *Abacus* Book

First published in Great Britain in 1998
by Little, Brown and Company
This edition published in 1999 by Abacus

A CIP catalogue record for this book
is available from the British Library.

ISBN: 0 349 11146 4

Typeset in Bembo by M Rules
Printed and bound in Great Britain
by Clays Ltd, St Ives plc

Abacus
A Division of
Little, Brown and Company (UK)
Brettenham House
Lancaster Place
London WC2E 7EN

For Pippa, Charlotte, Hetta,
Suso and Emily

Contents

Acknowledgements

I could not have travelled to the deserts in Xinjiang without the help and encouragement of my friend, Professor Yuan Guoying, an inspirational leader and a fine administrator. And no one should attempt to go into the Gashun Gobi without a guide of the experience and resilience of Lao Zhao, and someone with the strength of character and unfailing good humour of Professor Yuan Guoying's son, Xiao Yuan. My thanks go out to all the other members of our various expeditions in China, especially interpreter, Xiao Zhao; zoologist, Li Weidong; and to Mr An Huimin and Mr Xie Zhiqiang of the Xinjiang Environmental Protection Institute for unfailing support. Also in China, Dr Tony Marsh of Shell and Adam Williams of Jardine Fleming have given both encouragement and practical help, while Nancy Nash in Hong Kong has provided further inspiration. Particular thanks are due to Professor Peter Gunin of the Russian Academy of Sciences, without whom I would not have embarked on the wild camel quest at all; Russian–Mongolian expedition leader, Dr Anna Lushchekina; interpreter, Mikail Samsonov; and Mongolian scientist, Dr Sarantuya, all of whom gave invaluable assistance in the Mongolian

Gobi, where Debbie Atkins from Kenya did prodigious work and put up with great hardship during the winters of 1994 and 1995. In Islamabad, Chargé d'Affaires Mikko Pyhälä and his unassuming wife Pia of the Finnish Embassy provided unstinting hospitality at the beginning and end of each expedition into Xinjiang, while in Nairobi, Cyrie Sendashonga, Nooriya Koshen and in particular Zhou Xuejun of the United Nations Environment Programme (UNEP) gave unfailing support and encouragement. David Day-Wilson was a great companion on camel walkabouts in northern Kenya, and his wife Görel another generous and hospitable supporter.

Back in England, Katie Lee and Fiona McConnon of the Great Britain–China Centre; James MacEwen of the International Trust for Nature Conservation; the Royal Geographical Society; the National Geographic Society; Doreen Montgomery of Rupert Crew; Roddy Dunnett, Mike Davies, and Peter and Kathleen Hopkirk have all given much-needed encouragement and help at different times.

In the United States, the unfailingly good-natured Jenny Lawrence of the Natural History Museum, New York, has been an invaluable link. Shell, China; Cable & Wireless, UK; the Kadoorie Foundation, Hong Kong; the Robert Schad Foundation, Canada; the Ernest Kleinwort Charitable Trust, UK; C. Hoare & Company; Cluff Mining and numerous individuals all over the world have provided greatly valued financial support.

But final and particular thanks must go to Jane Goodall for persistent encouragement and support; Jasper Evans of Kenya, a good friend and a great camel lover; Kathryn Rae, who has freely donated huge amounts of time and personal effort to make both the Lop Nur Nature Sanctuary and this book a reality; and to Pippa, who has uncomplainingly allowed me to wander off into the Gashun Gobi and who has put up with much else besides.

Foreword

As a child I loved to read books about eighteenth-century explorers. How courageous they were: trekking off into the absolute unknown where, inevitably, they were beset by all manner of dangers – hostile tribes, disloyal partners, wild animals and sickness. But when they returned, what amazing tales they had to tell. I felt sad that those days had gone – but, fifty years later, I met a modern version of those old adventurers: John Hare. Accompanied by a small team of Chinese colleagues, John set out to explore one of the most hostile and desolate regions on Earth, the Gashun Gobi desert in the Xinjiang Province of China, where there is no fresh water at all in an area three-quarters the size of Germany. This is the home of the mysterious, shy and fast-vanishing wild Bactrian camels.

This is a book rich in adventure, filled with fascinating historical facts and legends, shrewd observations about the people encountered and their way of life, and vivid descriptions of landscapes as alien to most of us as the surface of the Moon. Each expedition brought its share of excitement, hardship and danger; indeed, the adventures of John and his companions were every bit as amazing as those I had read about with such awe as a child.

John's expeditions were not financed by some wealthy society; he struggled for funding, and for permission from the Chinese, on his own. He was successful partly because of his ability to establish such excellent relations with the Chinese. He gained high-level support and became the first foreigner to receive permission to enter that portion of the Gashun Gobi which had been closed for nuclear testing in the early 1950s. John became involved with the plight of the Bactrian camels because of his love for adventure, not because he was passionate about camels. But as the team learned more and more about these magnificent beasts, with their aloof faces and twin humps, he became increasingly concerned about their survival. The wild Bactrian is one of the most endangered species in the world – more so than the giant panda. There are, of course, many domestic Bactrians, but new research indicates that they are genetically different from their wild forebears. There are no more than 1,200 wild Bactrian camels in the world today; probably less than 800. Of these, 650 are to be found in China, divided into three separate groups each of which is severely threatened by hunting, mining and the despoiling of their habitat. Water is continually scarce. To save these camels is a race against time.

John Hare's expeditions furnished compelling evidence of the need for swift action if the camels were to be protected. So well was this evidence presented, and so compelling the arguments, that the Chinese government has agreed in writing to create the Lop Nur Nature Sanctuary. This huge refuge for the wild Bactrians will cover 107,768 square kilometres in remote north-west China. It will protect a unique and quite unspoilt desert eco-system, with its diversity of life-forms, as well as saving the wild Bactrian camels living there. And this decision comes only just in time, since with the suspension of nuclear tests the area is under increasing threat from hunters and miners. The government will maintain the sanctuary for a minimum of ten years; John must find the money for the infrastructure.

And so this sanctuary will exist because of one dedicated and utterly determined individual. How wonderful to know that people like John Hare still exist in the materialistic and greedy Western world. The Bactrian camels and their desert environment are fortunate in their champion. And I feel honoured to know John, and that he asked me to write this introduction to his book. When you have read it, you will understand why I feel this way. I hope you will recommend it to friends, too, not only because raising awareness will help John help the camels, but because it reaffirms one's faith in human nature, and the fact that, with imagination, courage, diplomacy, dogged tenacity, self-confidence – and a wonderful sense of humour – it is still possible to accomplish the impossible.

JANE GOODALL
March 1998

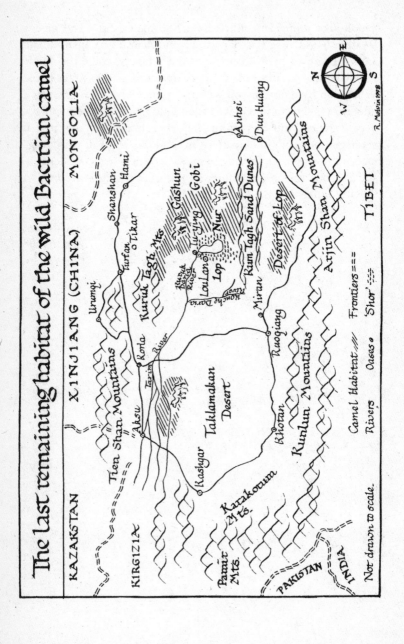

The last remaining habitat of the wild Bactrian camel

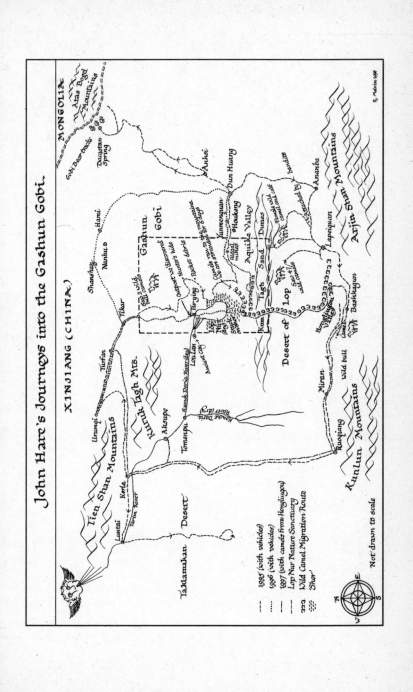

John Hare's Journeys into the Gashun Gobi

Prologue:
How the Camel
Quest Began

A journey of a thousand miles begins with one step
Chinese proverb

'Walk?' exclaimed Professor Yuan. 'Where to?'

I got out of the jeep and pointed towards a barrier of sand dunes that stretched out interminably in front of us.

'There,' I said. 'I want to walk there.'

'Impossible,' came the reply. 'We can't walk over those dunes.'

I could understand his reluctance. We were tired, dirty and thirsty and had been travelling for hours through the Chinese Desert of Lop, described by Marco Polo as 'fearful' and the scholar and traveller, Hsuan Tsang, as the 'haunt of poisonous imps and fiends'. Finally, we'd reached the truly formidable range of the Kum Tagh sand dunes, spreading 400 kilometres east to west and forming a forbidding barrier south of the dry lake of Lop Nur. Admittedly, it didn't look inviting, but I was undeterred.

The Professor and his team followed reluctantly, muttering and grumbling at my utter stupidity. I closed my ears to their mumbled protests and, as though mindlessly possessed, strode on ahead. We tramped on through a howling, dusty gale for about five kilometres, then, just as I rounded a massive dune, I saw the most extraordinary sight. Standing directly in front of me was a wild camel. The beast didn't move, and at first I thought that it must be sick and dying. Moments later, I spotted what looked like a discarded sack at its feet. It was a young camel, no more than a few hours old. A female had just given birth.

The camel calf struggled unsteadily to its feet and began to suckle. All the disappointments and hardships of the previous weeks were forgotten as we watched, completely absorbed by the miracle of new life in one of the most desolate places on earth. We knew that there was no recorded witness of such a scene.

'You must have second sight,' whispered the Professor.

I had nothing of the sort. It was just another inexplicable link in a chain of events that had propelled me into the desert to search for the wild Bactrian camel.

It may seem odd, but I'm not a camel fanatic. I don't, for example, feel that all-embracing fanaticism that grips many devotees of horses. It can at times be quite difficult to like camels. They can be as obstinate as any mule and as bloody-minded as an unbroken colt. They can bite and kick as well as any horse. I knew a Mongol herdsman who was quite literally scalped by a bull camel and a Kenyan girl who was beaten black and blue by sustained blows from a camel's long neck. In addition, unlike horses, camels have the unpleasant habit of regurgitating their food and spitting it all over you. But in spite of all these unpleasant character faults I am a great camel admirer. This admiration started when I first used the animals for transport south of Lake Chad on the Nigerian–Cameroon border. Unlike African porters, who had head-carried my kit from one place to another, my camels didn't complain about the distance or their wages. They didn't get roaring drunk on pay-days, seduce the chief's daughter or need their feet dusting every day with DDT to prevent jigger fleas from laying eggs under their toe-nails.

I also discovered that camels could go where porters couldn't. They could push forward for days through wilderness and wasteland on a minimum of food and water. Unlike the porters, they didn't have to reach a village before nightfall to ensure their contentment. A thorn bush would suffice for food, no matter how long and sharp the thorns. The porters were often very good companions, but a camel could keep me warm on a freezing desert night if I had smeared enough kerosene over my body to keep its greedy parasitical ticks away. I ended those days of West African bush travel with great respect for the cheerfulness and stoic qualities of the porter, but with an unreserved admiration for the camel.

Years later, in northern Kenya, I discovered that camels could take me to places where the toughest and most sophisticated four-wheel-drive vehicles could not go. They are able to cross the sharp, brittle lava flows south of Lake Turkana, a terrain that would instantly lame a horse and shred the tyres of a vehicle. When I was almost on my knees they cheerfully withstood the great heat of the Suguta Valley, and, in the soft sand of river-bed 'luggas', they glided along at five kilometres an hour while I struggled behind to keep up with them. It seemed, as one plodded after them over rocky outcrops and watched their lower hind legs contract and extend, that they had been blessed with natural shock absorbers. From time to time, urine would dribble down their hind legs to provide their bodies with an in-built cooling system.

Those days and nights of travel and travail in Africa were in the company of the dromedary, the single-humped camel that has been extinct in the wild for over 2,000 years. However, in the Gobi deserts of Mongolia and China, the single-humped camel's double-humped cousin, the Bactrian camel (*Camelus bactrianus ferus*), still survives as a truly wild creature in some of the most inhospitable country in the world. We believe that there could be less than a thousand of them, and that they are more endangered than the giant panda. Their principal enemy is man, who hunts them, prospects for oil in the desert wastes where they struggle to survive, conducts nuclear tests in the heart of their homeland and poisons their limited grazing by using potassium cyanide in a search for gold.

In my quest for this timid and elusive creature, I have been led into some of the most breathtakingly beautiful yet hostile country imaginable. I have travelled through areas closed for over forty years, made a first crossing of the Gashun Gobi from north to south and been fortunate to stumble across a lost outpost of the ancient city of Lou Lan. I've taken camels over the forbidding Kum Tagh sand dunes and crossed the 200-kilometre-long dried-up lake-bed of Lop Nur. Whether walking behind the single or double-humped domestic variety or scanning the skyline for their wild relative, the camel has enabled me to do what I like doing best: exploring.

I am neither a qualified naturalist nor a scientist, but have always had the instincts of an explorer. I marvel at the links in the chain of events that have, in only three years, enabled me to visit the four enclaves in the Gobi in China and Mongolia where the wild Bactrian camel still survives.

The trail begins in neither of those two countries but in Moscow where, in 1992, I had arrived to stage an exhibition of environmental photographs in the Polytechnic Museum. In 1992, Moscow held diverse attractions for an adventurer. At night the city was a dangerous place. Communism had collapsed and, with it, law and order. I witnessed the torching of private-enterprise wooden shops and heard the sounds of street shoot-outs. The KGB men still stood in hotel and office lobbies reading their newspapers upside-down, my room telephone was bugged and I couldn't persuade a persistent caller that my name was not Roger. Taxi drivers were as likely to rob you as to take you where you wanted to go, and the Metro, though still a model of efficiency, had been turned into a market place. I watched chickens being killed, plucked, eviscerated and sold at the top of the premier Metro station's escalator, and scanned the sad faces of women, young and old, who lined the station environs and offered for sale anything from a toddler's shoe to a cucumber. I also survived a rather frightening confrontation with a rough Muscovite, full of vodka, who, thankfully, slumped to the ground at my feet before he could relieve me of my wallet.

It was at a post-photographic exhibition party that I turned to a burly Russian, dressed in an ill-fitting brown serge suit and sporting a Stalin look-alike moustache, and asked him how he was managing to survive in lawless Moscow. At that moment, camels, the desert and the Gobi could not have been further from my mind, but the man's soft blue eyes with a far-away look should have given me a clue.

'I work for the Russian Academy of Sciences,' Peter Gunin replied in hesitant English. 'I lead the joint Russian–Mongolian expeditions to the Gobi desert. That takes me away from Moscow every year, and so I manage to survive.'

He said this as though it were of absolutely no significance. He might have been telling me that he was a lottery-seller in the Moscow Metro who occasionally managed to take a day off.

This was clearly no longer a moment for small talk. 'Do you ever take foreigners on your expeditions?' I asked. 'I'd give my right arm to go with you.'

Peter Gunin stroked his bushy moustache. 'There's no market in Moscow for a foreigners' right arm,' he said with a smile, 'even the Mafia aren't interested in them. However, if you could find some foreign exchange . . .' Since the collapse of communism, the Russian Academy of Sciences' finances had clearly reached crisis levels. 'What can you do?' he continued. 'Are you a scientist?'

'Unfortunately not,' I replied, searching desperately for something relevant to say. 'I could take photos. I could come as your cameraman.' My ability as a photographer is very modest but Canon, the sponsor of the photographic exhibition, had recently presented me with a new camera. I had yet to learn how to use it.

'My colleague, Anatoly, is coming on the next expedition as the official photographer,' Peter replied.

'I could publicise the work you're doing in Mongolia. I could take a video?'

'That would be a help, but it's not really enough. Is there nothing you can do that has a scientific background? I will have to justify your inclusion to the Academy.'

I realised that I was at the bottom of a barrel being scraped and that Professor Peter Gunin must be very short of funds.

'Do you use camels on your expeditions?' I asked. 'I've had experience working with camels in Africa.'

Gunin's face lit up immediately. 'That's it,' he cried.

'I don't understand.'

'Camels! We need a camel expert. We need someone to under-take a survey of the wild camel population in the Mongolian Gobi.'

'I know nothing about the wild camel,' I said. 'Nothing at all. I didn't even know there was such an animal.'

'You will learn all about the wild Bactrian camel if you come with us,' Peter said. He gave me a broad wink, 'Provided you can get the foreign exchange.'

'How much do you want?'

'Fifteen hundred dollars plus your air fare.'

'I'll try to find it,' I said without the slightest hesitation. I had no idea how, or even whether I would get leave of absence from my job with the Information Service of the United Nations Environment Programme (UNEP). I only knew that this oppor-tunity was too good to miss.

Peter suddenly became serious. 'I can't offer you a formal invi-tation to join us until I have tested your camel credentials,' he said with the utmost gravity. My heart sank. I knew quite a lot about the camel's behaviour patterns, but if I was to be quizzed on scien-tific detail, I was sunk.

'Please, tell me why it is that the genital organ of the male camel points backwards, whereas in all other animals it points forward?'

Remembering an old Arab story, I told Peter that when God created the first animals He soon realised that He was going to have unending trouble replicating them when they died. So He sculpted an assortment of reproductive organs and summoned the newly created animals to a fitting session.

'You must be a naturalist after all,' Peter said with a smile. 'I am obviously getting a very scientific answer.'

'The first to come was a donkey,' I continued. 'He went off with the biggest organ that God had made, although he was definitely not the biggest animal. Then all the other animals made their choice, until only one organ was left. It was long and thin and had been poorly and hastily constructed. "Why have we got a spare organ?" asked God. "There must be an animal who hasn't come forward to be fitted." "It's the camel," the donkey replied smugly. "We've told him to come, but he just lifts up his long neck and looks down his nose. He says that he can't be bothered to come for a fitting and that he's got better things to do." "He must come," God commanded. At last the camel came, looking very grumpy and making a number of grumbling camel noises. Holding his head high, he said, "I don't want it." Then he turned his back on God and walked away. As you can imagine, God was very angry. "You will have it whether you want it or not," God shouted, throwing the last organ at the camel as it started to walk away. It landed the wrong way round, and that's the answer to your question, Professor Gunin. May I join your expedition as the camel expert?'

Peter burst into laughter. 'To the Gobi!' he shouted, holding up his glass of vodka.

'To the Gobi,' I echoed as we tossed the vodka down in one.

'To the wild camel.'

'To Mongolia.'

'To the Sciences of Russian Academy.'

'To the joint Russian–British expedition to the Gobi.'

'What about the Mongolians?'

'The Mongolians,' we solemnly intoned.

'To . . .' Our bonhomie blossomed on an ocean of vodka.

Peter needed that foreign exchange. Two weeks later the invitation reached me in Kenya, signed by the very distinguished Academician Sokolov of the Russian Academy of Sciences. I accepted, even though I still had to find the money and, more importantly, the time. Peter wanted me to arrive in Ulan Bator in under six months, on 3 August 1993.

I made it, via an Aeroflot flight, only one day late. I had found the foreign exchange by tapping an unallocated resource in a friendly UNEP bureaucrat's budget, and the time by taking the trip out of unspent home leave in England. Aeroflot stewardesses are renowned for their unsmiling countenances, but on this flight they grimly dispensed large quantities of vodka which eventually diverted the attention of the more nervous passengers from the poor condition of the plane. Across the aisle from me sat three noisy Spaniards who were rapidly drinking themselves into a stupor to celebrate the fact that they had managed to buy permission from the Mongolians to shoot the rare and highly-endangered snow leopard. I asked my travelling companion, a high-powered American lawyer who had been employed by the Mongolian government to try to sort out the country's chaotic land laws, how much they would have had to pay.

'Twenty-five thousand dollars is the going rate,' he replied. 'In Mongolia you can buy permission to do anything, except bring the Russians back.'

I looked out of the window. Lake Baikal, with its polluting cellulose factory and the surrounding vast expanse of forest, had given way to treeless steppe. The green rolling landscape was criss-crossed with vehicle tracks.

'A nomad can't keep to a straight road,' said the lawyer, reading my thoughts. 'The Mongolians drive their vehicles and ride their motorbikes in exactly the same way as they ride their horses – anywhere they want. It's not surprising when you realise that there are just over two million Mongols and more than seven million horses. They're used to having a horse at hand to take them anywhere.'

The Spaniards started to sing. The vodka bottles were empty. There wasn't a stewardess in sight.

'That's the oldest game reserve in the world,' said my companion, pointing to a forest of straggly trees on a hilltop. 'The Mongols care about animals.'

'Unless you have dollars,' I commented wryly.

The sky was a brilliant blue and the strong scent of wild flowers hung on the pure cool air as we alighted at Ulan Bator airport. Three Mongolian ancients wearing dark-blue cloaks and knee-length boots with upturned toe-caps squatted outside the airport entrance. They stared as my Russian interpreter, Mike Samsonov, rushed forward, hand outstretched.

'Welcome, John. Welcome to Mongolia. Peter's in the car.'

Mike gave me a hug. He had been my interpreter in Moscow during the photographic exhibition. In his late fifties, a minor KGB official and an ex-military officer, he was out of a regular job and as thankful as I to be in Mongolia. He might have been planted to keep an eye on me, but that didn't really matter in post-Soviet Mongolia. His soulful, sentimental rendering of Russian folk songs would enliven many a star-encrusted Gobi night, just as they had done in his apartment block in the outer suburbs of Moscow. Peter greeted me with yet another friendly hug and we drove off into the city.

'I've found accommodation for you in an apartment,' Peter said. 'But first I want to take you to our expedition base, where you can pick up any clothing and equipment that you need.'

We drove past row upon row of fenced-off tents, the traditional round felt tent of the Mongol, or *ger*. These urban *gers* – rooted, numbered and immovable – were a partial solution to the capital's housing problem, and infinitely preferable to an apartment in a soulless, concrete building.

'I'd rather stay in one of those,' I said, pointing to a tent set apart from the others and guarded by a large black dog with an upturned bushy tail.

'That dog wouldn't allow you to get within spitting distance of the front door,' Peter said with a laugh. 'Mongolian dogs are noted for their ferocity.'

Ulan Bator is not a pretty place, dominated as it is by two decrepit power stations and surrounded by crumbling concrete blocks of apartments, another dismal legacy of the Marxist architecture that can be found from Alma Ata to Zanzibar. As we passed one half-completed concrete building, Peter said, 'That was to have been our permanent scientific base and expedition centre. Unfortunately, with the introduction of the market economy and the cutting of the ties with Russia, the Mongolians have seized it and put it up for sale on the open market.'

I realised that the Mongolians were catching on to the free market system as quickly as the Russians. Our driver turned sharply to the left, we drove through a huge puddle which tested the water-resistant qualities of our Russian-made jeep, and entered a compound of ramshackle wooden huts.

'You can see why we needed a new centre,' said Peter ruefully. I could indeed. The place was falling to pieces.

A small, dark-haired woman wearing military fatigues scuttled up to us.

'Hallo, I'm Anna.' She paused for a moment, and then added, 'And I'm the boss.' She gave a meaningful glance over my shoulder towards Peter.

I looked into Anna's sad eyes and care-worn face. I'd been told by Peter that she was a leading expert on jerboas and gerbils. She seemed to me to resemble a related species, the hamster.

'I'm even the boss of Peter,' Anna continued, anxious to establish her position in the expedition hierarchy.

'Everyone is number two to Anna,' said Peter with a smile.

Anna rarely smiled. She gave me a rather wistful glance and waved towards a dilapidated hut. 'Our store,' she said with a sigh. 'Go and pick up anything you need. It's full of ex-army equipment.'

The Russians had been expeditioning to the Gobi for over thirty years and knew exactly what to take. I was given a thick and well-padded sleeping bag and a metal folding bed. Ten minutes later I was standing in front of a cracked and dirty mirror, laughing at the reflected image of a middle-aged Russian conscript.

I went outside to meet the other members of the expedition and was introduced to them one by one. There was wiry, willing, camera-festooned Doctor Anatoly Prischeper, Peter's deputy, who was a geographer, a specialist in dry lands and the expedition photographer. Professor Nikolai Nikolayevich, a good-natured bear of a man who was a leading botanist from Leningrad University. Nikolai was also the expedition's quarter-master. He insisted that cabbages, onions and tomatoes be sliced to his own meticulous standards, and no vehicle could be loaded, no box unpacked, without his watchful presence.

Peter's brother, also named Anatoly, was an ex-army colonel who Peter had said was in need of a job. I never quite grasped what his expedition 'job' was, although when we returned to Ulan Bator he seemed to be skilled at selling off our surplus stores and equipment.

Drivers Vasily, Eugenie and Vanya completed the male contingent of the party. They were a trio of sharply contrasting personalities. Vasily, sombre and dour, thought only in terms of days, hours on the job and money; Eugenie was unaware of a world that existed outside his driver's cab, except when it made an appearance disguised as a bottle of vodka; and Vanya, the smiling, singing, whistling, wild onion-picker and obsessive vehicle polisher, delighted in venturing into the Gobi.

There were also two Mongolian women: Sarantuya, a student of Peter's whose name translates to Moonlight Dream, and Dashzeveg (Dasha), who was named after a Tibetan God. Sarantuya was never without a smile and seemed to be in a permanent state of happy intoxication. She confided, with a giggle, that her husband was very cross that she had left him to travel with the expedition. In complete contrast, the expressionless Dasha seldom smiled and, although loosely termed 'a scientist', she appeared much more concerned with the state of her nails than with scientific data. Neither Sarantuya nor Dasha conformed to the traditional Mongolian ideal of a woman, who should be 'wonderfully fat, and she who has the least nose is considered the most beautiful'.

As the expedition progressed I had the uncomfortable feeling that Moonlight Dream and Dasha had been brought along more for their ability to peel potatoes and wash up than for their scientific qualifications. The bilateral 'jointness' of the expedition had a somewhat hollow ring.

Times had, however, changed. The Mongolians were the masters now and, after years of being treated as second-class citizens in what was virtually a colony of Russia, resentment of the continued and overt Russian presence was rife. Russian soldiers had recently been asked to leave and their base ransacked. All the scientific equipment had been stolen from Peter's expedition base at Eikhyin Gol. Our team was definitely in Mongolia under sufferance. There was now a different foreign presence in Ulan Bator. The capital was awash with personnel from the UN and other international organisations. Many were Americans, who saw Mongolia and its vast rolling steppes in terms of Montana in the 1880s.

I spent the night in a spacious flat which Peter had hired. There were 'girlie' calendars in the sitting-room and pictures of Chinese factory workers on three of the four walls surrounding my bed.

11

The windows looked out on to rows of identical crumbling concrete blocks. The double doors to the flat could only be unlocked with three keys. 'They are all drunks and thieves,' Mike had whispered to me before saying good-night. 'Take great care.' The thieves I didn't encounter, but the drunks were audible. The night was punctuated with the crash of broken bottles and sounds of splintering glass. I had already been told about Mongolian drinking habits and how the tippler is encouraged to drink more and more until he eventually topples to the ground in a stupor. This, it is thought, is the best way to keep him from committing mischief. Not a foolproof system, I concluded, as I listened to much noisy and drunken mischief-making. Most of the early travellers to the court of the Great Khan from Genghis onwards commented how high Mongolian officials, and even the Great Khan himself, were frequently to be found in a state of complete intoxication.

However, next morning, when we visited the Vice-Minister for Nature, Dr Tserendulamyn Shiirevdamba, he was completely sober. We were given tea, and faced him across a table on which was placed a large and very dusty bowl of faded pink plastic tulips. Peter told him what we intended to do and precisely where we intended to go. The Vice-Minister nodded, smiled and wished us luck.

Later that morning, we picked up a very distinguished hitchhiker, George Schaller, the renowned American naturalist, who, because of the acute shortage of petrol, which was strictly rationed, had no other method of travelling to the Gobi. At 11.30 a.m., with driver Vanya at the wheel of our Russian army jeep, we drove south out of Ulan Bator. Behind us, two Russian-made Gaz 66 trucks followed, one laden with petrol and water, the other with foodstuffs and camp equipment. The tall chimneys of Ulan Bator's two ageing power stations belched forth thick, black, acrid smoke in farewell salute.

'To the Gobi!' shouted Vanya, his eyes twinkling. 'Perezd.'

'Gobi, Gobi. Perezd. Perezd,' we echoed in response. I turned up the flaps of my Russian army hat and pinched myself to make sure that it wasn't all a dream.

1
Between the Dragon
and the Bear

The Great Way is very easy, but all love the by-paths
Chinese proverb

'Those are the Bogd Ula mountains, the oldest game reserve in the world,' commented George Schaller, pointing towards the lush, green, heavily wooded hilltops that I had seen from the air. 'In the late seventeenth century, an enlightened successor of Genghis Khan declared them a protected area. They contain many species of antelope and . . .'

My mind wandered. The Bogd Ula mountains held more sensational associations. They had been the out-of-town retreat of the Living Buddha of Mongolia, the Bogd Khan, reincarnated over the years from the spirit of Genghis, whose debauched last representative came to grief in the 1920s after the brief and bloody reign of Major-General Baron Roman Fyodorovich von Ungern-Sternberg, known to posterity as the Mad Baron.

I once met a woman in Kenya who knew a young Ungern-Sternberg. 'I think he's in the export/import business,' she told me. 'He's a nice man, very quiet, calm and efficient. What I remember most about him is his eyes, they're bright blue and very striking.' The Mad Baron's eyes, according to a contemporary source, 'glared out, like those of an animal from a cave'.

The 'quiet, calm and efficient' contemporary Ungern-Sternberg's psychopathic relative fought in the Great War with a heroism bordering on lunacy, and the victory of Bolshevism in Russia found him firmly in the opposing camp. He collected together a motley army of desperate men of different nationalities with the aim of founding a vast Asiatic Empire, just as Genghis Khan, with whom the Baron claimed affinity, had done. He then planned to lead his conquering horde into Europe to defeat the Bolsheviks. His recruitment methods were novel. Going down a line of potential recruits, he would stop before each man in turn, look him in the face, hold his gaze for a few minutes and then scream, 'To the army!', 'Back to the cattle!' or, simply, 'Liquidate!'

Between 31 January and 3 February 1921, the Mad Baron and his rag-tail army of 1,700 defeated the 12,000 soldiers of General Hsu Shu-tseng, a Chinese warlord whose oppressive regime had been holding the Bogd Khan prisoner in the Bogd Ula mountains for non-payment of taxes.

Discarded mutton bones have a peculiar usage in Mongolia. When they are dried in ashes, the resulting cracks foretell the future. This is an age-old method of divination. A thirteenth-century traveller had written that 'he [a Mongol servant] does nothing in the world without consulting the bones'. The Mad Baron used the same method for forward planning and the disposition of his units when he launched his attack on the Chinese in the Bogd Ula mountains. Following a mutton-bone diagnosis on the best time to advance, a small force of 300 men climbed up the thickly-wooded mountain slopes, burst into the palace, seized the blind old Bogd Khan, hoisted him on to a horse and galloped away with him as fast as they could. Soon, the rest of the Baron's men were engaging the Chinese on three fronts. Before long the battle had become a massacre. Ungern-Sternberg's mutton-bone plan of action resulted in an overwhelming victory which convinced the Mongolians that the Mad Baron was a reincarnation of the God of War, sent from heaven to lead them. One of his followers, Alioshin, described the scenes after this defeat:

Mad with revenge and hatred the conquerors began plunder-
ing the city. Drunken horsemen galloped along the streets
shooting and killing at their fancy, breaking into houses, drag-
ging property outside into the dirty streets, dressing
themselves in the rich silks found in the shops. In front of the
Chinese banks, lines were formed, where each man was given
the right to plunge his bloody hand inside the strong boxes
and get what his luck would bring him. Some were fortunate
enough to drag out gold coins and bullion. Some were less
fortunate and got silver, while many found only paper currency and bank notes, which they immediately threw into the
street as worthless.

[For three terrible days] innumerable men, women and
children of all ages, races and creeds were hacked to bits and
bayoneted and shot and strangled and hanged and crucified
and burnt alive. It was remarkable that nobody paid the slightest attention to their wounds; whether the excitement was too
great or they had become used to cuts and bruises, I do not
know . . . the mob attacked Jews, and all of them perished in
agony. The humiliation of the women was so awful that I saw
one of the officers run inside the house with a razor and offer
to let the girl commit suicide before she was attacked. With
tears of gratitude she thanked him in a few simple words and
then cut her throat . . . The drunken mob invented a new
sport of killing men on the streets by striking them direct in
the face with thick wooden blocks. There was one Cossack
who was killing his own men right and left, until someone
shot him . . . Many women offered to sell themselves to save
the lives of their husbands and brothers. But, as often as not,
they were cheated in the end . . .

The delighted Bogd Khan, the Living Buddha, 'a stout old man
with a heavy shaven face resembling those of the Cardinals of
Rome' and 'wide-open, blind eyes', was proclaimed Emperor of all
Mongolia, with the Baron doubling in the roles of Military Adviser
and God of War.

In return, the Baron initiated a bus service, introduced electricity, had bridges constructed, set up a veterinary laboratory and generally cleaned up the capital. These constructive measures were achieved by operating a regime, backed by Japanese money and intrigue, of terror and massacre for which it would be hard to find a parallel. Contemporary accounts abound in tales of baker's boys being baked alive in their own ovens, of prisoners being fed to the Baron's private pack of wolves, of innumerable men, women and children of all ages, races and creeds put to death by every imaginable method, wherever possible in the presence of the Mad Baron himself.

But when the Baron began his crusade into Russia to liberate the people from the Communist revolutionaries, he provided the excuse the Red Army needed for their invasion of Mongolia. On 6 July 1921, 10,000 Soviet troops marched into the capital, at that time called Urga, and established a new Mongolian National Government under a lama called Bogdo, who became the Prime Minister. A local revolutionary, Sukhe Bator, who had gone to Moscow to seek Soviet intervention, was made Minister of War. Two months later the Mad Baron was captured and sent to Novosibirsk in Russia. There, he was tried for, among other things, attempting to restore the monarchy, and was executed by firing-squad. He reportedly told his accusers that, 'For a thousand years the Ungers have given orders. We have never taken orders from anyone. I refuse to accept the authority of the working class.'

After the death in 1924 of the 54-year-old Bogd Khan, Outer Mongolia was once and for all declared a People's Republic and became the first, and for many years the only, Soviet satellite. The Mad Baron's bloody intervention had indirectly saved Mongolia from the fate of Tibet, which fell disastrously into Chinese hands.

Later, under the Soviet regime, the Bogd Ula mountains housed a secret hideaway for Communist Party bosses. By 1993 they had reverted to their ancient status as a protected animal reserve, with the addition of tourist 'facilities' in the form of props from the film of the life of Genghis Khan.

We were passing through rolling steppe. The lush green landscape sprawled to the far horizon in every direction. Overhead the sky was a bright, cloudless, deep blue. Small herds of horses roamed everywhere and one stallion, to my amazement, had a mane which trailed behind it along the ground.

'Not long ago the white-tailed gazelle was common here,' explained George Schaller. 'Now they're confined to the eastern part of Mongolia. There are 300,000 of them, and they migrate in the spring to new pastures in huge numbers, rather like the wildebeest in Kenya.'

'Have you heard about the latest gazelle cull?' asked Peter.

George shook his head.

'During their annual migration, the Mongols cull the white-tailed gazelle. The meat used to be sold to the USSR in vast quantities. During the Second World War it was one of Mongolia's top contributions to the Soviet war effort. Last year, 18,000 were shot for much-needed foreign exchange, and the carcasses were all sent to Hungary. However, the Hungarians rejected them because they complained about the amount of lead in the meat. I don't know whether they were shot with Kalashnikovs, but the flesh was apparently riddled with bullets. Fortunately for the Mongolians, the Austrians are not fussy about lead in their schnitzels. They bought the lot.'

'Don't domestic animals compete with gazelles for grazing?'

'It's an empty quarter,' George explained. 'The area is full of lethal flies which domestic animals can't cope with. The Mongolians avoid the eastern steppes. It's virgin grassland, a paradise for the gazelle.'

'Not for much longer,' Peter cut in. 'There's talk of a new rail link with China and the discovery of oil.'

I was later to learn that the pressures of new development are not just to be found on the Mongolian grasslands. The very depths of the Gobi desert itself are under threat.

We reached the river Tola, and as we crossed the makeshift bridge the water swirled past us in full flood.

'It's been the heaviest rainfall in living memory,' said Peter. 'We've been coming here for over twenty-five years and I've never seen this river so high.'

Beyond the river, marmots popped out of the ground on either side of the track. We stopped for a lunch of pickled cucumber and mutton and Dasha showed us how to flush marmots out of their underground burrows. Kneeling on the ground to the rear of the animal's hole, she made a peculiar high-pitched whistling sound. Moments later, out popped a marmot (*Marmota bobak*). It sat up on its hind legs, looked around inquisitively, saw us, and scuttled back into its burrow.

'There's a hunting season for marmots,' Dasha explained as she stood up and dusted down her long, purple Mongolian cloak. 'They're very good eating and a change from mutton. The only restriction is that we can't shoot them with a bow and arrow.'

'Why's that?'

'Long ago, a famous archer called Tarbagan Bator was reincarnated as a marmot. So no Mongolian shoots a marmot with a bow and arrow in case they kill Tarbagan.'

'Do you believe that?' I asked Moonlight Dream.

'Oh, yes,' she replied with a laugh. 'We all do. Marmots can also tell us what the weather will be like.'

'How?'

'When they wake up from their winter sleep, they forecast the weather for the following spring and summer. If they wake up and the summer is going to be mild they push lots of earth out of their burrows. But if it's going to be a bad summer they only throw out a little earth. It's the same in the autumn. We can tell by looking at the amount of earth that they use to stop up their burrows whether the winter will be good or bad.'

'So what's the rest of the summer going to be like this year, Sarantuya?' asked Anna with a laugh.

'Wet, wet, wet,' said Moonlight Dream, 'and cold. You wait and see for yourself.'

We didn't have to wait for long. That night, after travelling 350 kilometres, we pitched our tents in what seemed to me to be a very exposed spot on the slope of a treeless hill. It rained, it hailed, it snowed. It was Mongolian mid-summer and minus three degrees centigrade at night.

Unfortunately, the cuddly-looking marmot is also a carrier of plague, which is still endemic in Mongolia. Indeed, in the thirteenth century, the Golden Horde could have unwittingly carried the Black Death into Europe by bringing with them fleas from infected marmots. If this theory is correct, then the heirs of Genghis Khan wreaked greater havoc in Europe by transporting the marmot's fleas than they did with fire and sword.

The following morning dawned cold and grey, with a chill wind which caused the tent canvas to flap noisily. I substituted the Russian khaki battle-dress top for my battered and patched sports jacket which had safaried through Africa and, feeling much more at home, crept out of the tent. Chain-smoker Mike Samsonov was wheezing his way through a disturbed sleep, and from Peter's direction rumbled long, contented snores. It was 5.30 a.m. Moonlight Dream and I had drawn the short straw and were the appointed cooks for the day.

The Russians' cooking equipment consisted of two cast-iron rings which were heated by pump-operated, petrol-powered, mini-flame-throwers. This equipment terrified me. Having once watched an African colonel try to light a fire with petrol and lose all his hair in the process, I have treated petrol with the greatest possible respect ever since. The colonel, using a gun instead of petrol, later progressed to become a short-lived Head of State of his country, but I will always remember him for his attempt to light a fire.

Moonlight was already up and busying herself in the makeshift kitchen tent.

'Man's job to light the fire,' she said with a giggle.

I gingerly attempted to pump the cooker which had been left full of petrol overnight. However, the pressure was already up and my erratic pumping sent petrol spraying over the rice which Moonlight Dream was carefully measuring into a bowl. Never one to get upset, the delightful Dream just giggled. I was alarmed. At that moment driver Vanya appeared. Having served with the army in Afghanistan, he knew all about these military petrol-powered cookers. Moments later, a long jet of flame was hitched up to a cooking ring. Moonlight Dream poured sweet condensed milk over some fresh rice and I vowed to keep well away from this lethal cooking apparatus. My father once claimed that even a cigarette lighter would not work for him; I and my family are well aware that I have inherited his non-mechanical gene.

After breakfast, our convoy was soon heading south along the rutted dirt track. All at once Anna asserted herself.

'Stop, Vanya! Stop!' she cried out. Vanya obediently applied the brakes. Without another word, Anna scuttled out of the back of the jeep and started to scurry, hamster-like, three times around an *obo*.

I had read about these *obos*, shrines to the guardian spirits of a pass or valley which lies ahead of a traveller. They are dotted round the high spots of Mongolia and fashioned from a framework of branches which are dragged up the steepest slopes to form a rock-filled landmark.

'Out, out,' said Peter. 'We must all do it. Anna insists and she's the boss!'

We walked solemnly around the pile of rocks, topped by a fluttering red rag, in which were stuck not only worthless Russian rouble bank notes but also rims of car wheels, shredded tyres and, amazingly, a steering-wheel. Whether the latter was a thanksgiving for an accident avoided or a prayer for an accident-free onward journey I could not discover. It was the Russians and Anna in particular who performed the ritual semi-seriously. Dasha and Moonlight Dream stayed in the truck and looked on, their faces inscrutable, their thoughts unknowable.

Anna placed some Mongolian bank notes behind one of the rocks. 'They will all be stolen,' Mike confided to me when we were out of earshot of Dasha and Moonlight Dream. Mike hadn't a high regard for the Mongolians. He considered them to be ungrateful for all the benefits the Russians had brought them.

Mike's opinions were reinforced when we later passed the former Russian military base of Arvai Hez. The buildings were stripped of essentials. Everything moveable had been looted.

'Ungrateful barbarians,' Mike whispered in my ear. 'They gave us twenty-four hours to get out and then stoned us as we left. If we hadn't come into their country they would be part of China by now. Swallowed up by that insatiable Dragon, just like their brothers in Inner Mongolia.'

What he said was, in part, true. The Mongolians in Inner Mongolia had been swamped by Chinese migrants, just like the Tibetans. Although the Mongolians had suffered considerably under Russian tutelage, at least their countryside was gloriously empty and free of Russian settlers.

'We are sandwiched between the Bear and the Dragon,' Vice-Minister Shiirevdamba had said to me. 'We have to live with it. It's a fact of life. If forced to make a choice, we will come down on the side of the Bear.' I realised that Shiirevdamba was Russian-educated and owed his position to the Russians. Nevertheless, I have heard similar sentiments echoed by many ordinary Mongolians, and have yet to meet a Dragon-lover.

Every *aimak*, or provincial headquarters, in Mongolia looks exactly the same, and Avaikhez was no exception. The solitary, tall chimney-stack of a sulphurous, coal-powered electricity generator, whether belching forth black smoke or not, advertises an *aimak* from a great distance. The generator is surrounded by mandatory concrete blocks of dilapidated flats, a provincial office of no architectural merit, a central square surrounded by rusting sign-boards proclaiming out-dated Communist slogans and what looks like a derelict and unused basketball pitch. Sometimes there is half a kilometre of concrete road, but at this time of acute petrol shortage and rationing there were no vehicles. The whole unsightly township is encircled by lines of settled *gers* with wooden stockades. We waited in Avaikhez for over three hours until bureaucracy was satisfied, a necessary requirement for receiving the permit to proceed into the next provincial territory.

While we waited, I watched bandy-legged Mongols rolling down the central street of Avaikhez. They had no doubt acquired their rolling gait from a lifetime in the saddle, but I wondered whether the toddlers with equally bandy legs were victims of premature riding lessons or of rickets.

After a further 300 kilometres of gradual descent through the seemingly endless steppes, we reached the River Tuyn Gol, which was in full flood. This river flows into Lake Orog Nur at the foot of the snow-capped Ikh Bogd mountains. The setting was enchanting, but as we pitched our tents there was no obvious sign as to how or where we were going to cross the raging torrent.

We woke next morning to the sight of two laden Mongolian lorries stuck in the Tuyn Gol, one of which had water flowing through the driver's cab window.

'Come on, John,' George said. 'Off with those trousers. You and I'll try to find a safe place to cross.'

The current was strong. The water was very cold. The disconsolate truck drivers were sitting on top of their cabs and shouting conflicting instructions.

'Don't listen to them,' said George. 'If they'd done what we're doing they wouldn't be where they are now.'

The bottom of the river was full of ledges and holes. One moment we would think that we had found a suitable route, the next we were floundering up to our armpits. Eventually we found what we thought was a suitable crossing-point.

'Come over here,' we called out to Vasily, the driver of the Gaz 66. Vasily set off. The Gaz 66 is no stranger to crossing fast-flowing rivers and Vasily was making good progress when he was abruptly distracted by a Mongol on the far bank who was waving his arms and urging him to follow a different route.

'Stay over there,' George bellowed.

'Take no notice of him,' I shouted.

Vasily became confused, decided to take a middle way between the two conflicting sets of instructions and moments later, the Gaz 66 stalled in a steaming mass of froth and bubbles. The water level was halfway up the side of the vehicle and it was carrying all our food.

Peter climbed out of the door of the cab and clambered on to the roof. The Mongols on the bank pointed at him and roared with laughter. Face was immediately and irretrievably lost.

Driver Vanya sprang into action. Instructing Eugenie, the other

Gaz driver, to follow him, they both successfully negotiated the 'safe' route to the far bank. Then, after an hour of ropes, push and shove, we managed to tow the stranded Gaz and our leader to the far bank.

Peter insisted on helping the Mongolian drivers on the wise premise that we did not know when we might need their helping hand. After another hour of push, pull and shove we managed to free up one of their stranded vehicles, but the other one was stuck too deeply in the river-bed. We were later to learn that it finally made it to the other bank two weeks later.

However, considerable damage had been done. Our food supplies had become thoroughly soaked and the next three hours was spent sun-drying buckwheat, semolina and a huge mound of congealed macaroni. Soggy wads of biscuits were meticulously separated and dried in the sun. Nothing was wasted. It couldn't be – once in the Gobi we would be a long way from fresh food supplies.

A plague of mice-like creatures called pika (*Ochotona oalasii*) swarmed everywhere. The earth seemed to move around our piles of drying food. Hawks circled near the vehicles and swooped on them out of a clear blue sky. When we finally set off we had seen flocks of Demoiselle cranes preparing for migration and *Aegypius monachus,* the largest vulture in the world.

That evening, as we pitched camp in a delightful valley near Bayan Tragan, there were many well-dressed travellers descending on the hamlet by foot, on horse or by motor-bike. An annual *naadam* festival was due to be held there the next day, and the three Mongolian 'manly sports' of archery, horse-racing and wrestling were on the agenda. These traditional gatherings of far-flung herdsmen take place all over Mongolia during the brief summer period. They are a throw-back to the great tribal gatherings, instituted by Genghis Khan and his successors, where disputes were settled, laws were passed, and successors to the Great Khan elected. One of these gatherings was called in 1241 to choose a successor to Ogodei, the son of Genghis Khan. The Mongolian Golden Horde had already swept past Budapest, leaving a trail of devastation in their wake, and were poised to ransack Vienna. Matthew Paris in his *Chronica Majora* describes how Europe felt:

In this same year (1240) a detestable nation of Satan – to wit, the countless army of the Tartars – broke loose from its mountain-environed home and, piercing the solid rocks (of the Caucasus), poured forth like devils from the Tartarus . . . Swarming like locusts over the face of the earth, they brought terrible devastation to the eastern parts (of Europe), laying it waste with fire and carnage. After having passed through the land of the Saracens, they have razed cities, cut down forests, overthrown fortresses, pulled up vines, destroyed gardens, killed townspeople and peasants. If perchance they have spared any suppliants, they have forced them . . . to fight in the foremost rank against their own neighbours . . .

For they are inhuman and beastly, rather monsters than men, thirsting for and drinking blood, tearing and devouring the flesh of dogs and men. They are dressed in ox-hides and armed with plates of iron. They are short and stout, thickset, strong, invincible, indefatigable, their backs unprotected (to stop them running away), their breasts covered with armour; they drink with delight the pure blood of their flocks. Their horses are big and strong, and eat branches and even trees; they have to mount with the help of three steps on account of the shortness of their thighs.

They are without human laws, know no comforts, are more ferocious than lions or bears, have boats made of ox-hides which ten or twelve of them own in common . . . They can cross the largest and swiftest rivers without let or hindrance, drinking turbid or muddy water when blood runs short. They are wonderful archers . . . They know no other language than their own, which no one else knows, for until now there has been no access to them . . . They roam with their flocks and their wives, who are taught to fight like men. And so they came with the swiftness of lightning to the confines of Christendom, ravaging and slaughtering, striking everyone with terror and incomparable horror . . .

However, the call back to the steppes was too powerful to resist, and the Horde scurried back to the great council or *quriltais* in central Mongolia, over 5,000 kilometres away. They were obliged by law to attend; but no one would have wanted to be absent on so momentous an occasion, for the descendants of Genghis Khan were already involved in the family feuds which would eventually lead to the break-up of the Mongol empire. In the West, popes and emperors, kings and princes were awaiting the end of the known world. They saw with relief and amazement that the Golden Horde had vanished as swiftly as they had appeared. The fortuitous death of Ogodei saved the rest of Europe from the total devastation which had overtaken Russia and other countries further east, even if the Horde unwittingly left behind them the scourge of the Black Death.

A modern *naadam* is only a faint echo of those great tribal gatherings of the past but is still an impressive sight, and women can participate in two of the 'manly' sports, horse-riding and archery. Many centuries ago women also participated in wrestling, and Marco Polo recorded a famous female wrestler who acquired great riches and fabled numbers of livestock by toppling her male challengers. More recently, there was a famed eighteen-year-old girl who became annoyed when a yak bull tried to mount a yak cow that she was milking. She grabbed the bull by the horns, wrestled him to the ground and pinned one horn firmly in the soil, thereby immobilising him.

At Bayan Tragan we filled up the vehicles with petrol bought with our ration coupons at what must be the remotest petrol pump in the world. There was just a *ger*, a shack and a pump. We waited for over an hour while the 'attendant' was called back from tending his flock by a helpmate, who brought him in on the back of a motorbike. This was the last place that we would be able to obtain petrol before we entered the Gobi. Once in the desert, it was 500 kilometres before the next supply point.

We stopped for lunch near three *gers* nestling in an enclave of a horseshoe-shaped hill. I walked over to one of them.

'The door's open,' I called out. 'There's no one about.'

'Go on in,' said Dasha. 'I expect that the owner has moved off for a few weeks to settle his flocks in another grazing area.'

On the little cast-iron stove in the centre of the circular tent stood a pot of fermented milk (*kumis*) and some rock-hard cheese. Pinned to the solid wooden pole which kept the tent erect was a picture of Genghis Khan.

'They've left a meal for you,' Dasha explained. 'It's the custom in these parts to leave doors unlocked so that passing strangers can help themselves to food and drink.'

While I gnawed at the cheese and sipped the sour *kumis* I reflected that in a land of huge distances and harsh weather conditions, this custom ensures that travellers do not go hungry.

'If you stole any of the owner's personal possessions you'd be in big trouble,' said Moonlight Dream, reading my unspoken thoughts. 'We Mongolians have eyes like hawks. We'd track you all the way back to Nairobi!'

Later that year, when back in Nairobi, I remembered her words. On my wall I had hung a photograph of a Mongolian *ger*, taken against the background of a thundery sky and a double rainbow. Outside the *ger*, the tiny figure of a man wearing a bright red cloak or *del* could just be seen. A Mongolian friend, on entering the room and seeing the picture, burst into loud laughter.

'What's the joke?' I asked, puzzled at his finding my picture so uproariously funny.

'Can't you see?' he said, shaking all over with laughter. 'The man outside the *ger* is peeing, and looking angrily over his shoulder at the photographer who has caught him in such an undignified situation.'

It took a magnifying glass and some intense study of the minute figure to confirm that my friend's natural eye was absolutely true.

The next day was to prove a special one. After stopping at Bayan Tsaagan to buy fresh supplies of mutton, we travelled on another 200 kilometres and at last reached the trans-Altai Gobi, the intermediate stage between the steppe and the true Gobi desert, which stretches for thousands of kilometres through Mongolia and China to the east and west, and to the south, into the depths of Xinjiang Province in Western China. With a whoop of delight Vanya slammed on the brakes.

'Onions! Gobi onions!' he cried out. He leapt from the jeep and started to pick the chive-like stalks of the wild onion that had just come into flower and had turned the grey, pebble-strewn desert a light purple. These chive-like onions gave a much-needed lift to the congealed macaroni. Vanya collected bundles of them, salting them in jars both for us and for the Russian winter. I was later to discover that the Chinese who travelled with me in Xinjiang looked down on the pungent desert onion, even when we had run out of vegetables. For some reason they concluded that picking and eating them was unclean.

'We're now on the fringe of the Gobi,' Peter said. 'The onion can't grow on the steppe. You'll see camels soon.'

We spotted them just before dusk, a long line of domestic Bactrians making their way towards a group of *gers* in the far distance. We were still a long way from the home of the domestic camels' wild relative. But we were getting closer.

After travelling a further 250 kilometres we reached our goal. Bayan Toroi, 'the place of poplars' (*Populus diversifolia*), an oasis on the fringe of the Gobi desert, positioned strategically between the great Altai and Edrengiyn Nuruu mountain ranges. This latter range forms the northern boundary of the Great Gobi Reserve, the home of the wild camel. It had taken us four days and we had travelled over a thousand kilometres on dirt tracks.

2

Hie to the Deserts Wild

Since men live not for a hundred years it is vain to scheme for a thousand

Chinese proverb

'Avermet! Avermet!'

The bull-like bellow was followed by the crash of a clenched fist on the flimsy wooden door of the store which had been turned into a house for camel-handler Debbie Atkins.

'A-ver-met!'

Inside the store, Debbie backed away and flattened herself against the wall of her bedroom. The crashes on the door continued and there was a loud splintering of wood. A draught of icy air rushed into the storeroom as the door was wrenched from its hinges. Framed in the doorway was a Mongol of extraordinary size. Nearly two metres high and of enormous bulk, he swayed uncertainly before charging into the room, naked but for a coloured loincloth. Debbie could see that he was drunk, and totally oblivious to the extreme cold (it was minus twenty-five degrees centigrade outside). As Debbie remarked on a different occasion when she stumbled over a prostrate body lying in deep snow, 'When the Mongols drink, they mix their vodka with anti-freeze.'

'Avermet,' roared the wrestler, looking uncertainly round the

28

room. As he advanced, Debbie edged around the wall. Suddenly he spotted her.

'Avermet?' he queried in a much quieter tone, steadying himself on the wall with his right arm. Debbie took her chance, ducking under the outstretched arm to run from the building. She stood for a moment, gasping in the icy air, before racing past the towering radio mast towards Avermet's *ger* on the other side of the compound.

'Let me in, Avermet,' she shouted, panting for breath. 'Let me in.'

The felt door cover of the *ger* was pulled aside and Avermet, the head of the Great Gobi National Park A, stared at her for a few minutes and then broke into laughter.

'He's my friend,' he cried, pointing to the vast bulk that was shambling across the compound towards them. 'Wrestling friend. Drinking friend.'

Debbie knew that a wrestling competition was to take place that day at Bayan Toroi. She hadn't appreciated that the supreme challenger for the Bayan Toroi championship would turn up in her hut drunk, almost naked and bellowing for his drinking companion.

After this incident she decided to move into her own *ger*. It was more convenient, cosier and nearer the thirteen wild Bactrian camels that were corralled nearby. It also enabled her to avoid Avermet's more eccentric friends.

When we reached Bayan Toroi in August 1993, we learnt that thirteen young wild Bactrians (five males and eight females) had been caught by Avermet and his team and had been fostered on domestic females in the locality. A potentially explosive situation was developing. By December, two of the wild males could come into rut and two or three of the females into season. As all these camels were grazing with separate domestic herds, the males would attempt to mate with any likely looking domestic female and the females would attract domestic males. The end result could be uncontrollable hybrid offspring. These hybrids, and even the male camels themselves, might be killed by their Mongol herdsmen if they became too difficult to manage. As there were no more than six other wild Bactrian camels in captivity anywhere in the world, these captive thirteen were of great significance, especially as the total world population was thought not to exceed a thousand. Unless something was done immediately to control their breeding within a properly managed programme, the outcome could be disastrous. I thought I knew just the person for the job.

Thirty-three-year-old Debbie Atkins, who worked with camel-breeder Jasper Evans on his ranch in Laikipia, northern Kenya, had more practical knowledge of camel-breeding and record-keeping than anyone I have known. Internationally respected and tough, she could, I felt certain, survive the extremes of a Mongolian winter. Also a remarkable shot, she was not averse to carrying a pistol in the pocket of her shorts in Kenya. Fortunately, the United Nations Development Programme in Mongolia found the necessary funding, and by early December, just over three months after our expedition had left Mongolia, Debbie had arrived in Bayan Toroi. She soon proved to an initially sceptical Avermet and his fellow Mongolians that she was as tough as their own womenfolk. She established and supervised a controlled breeding programme during the bitter winter months. She survived being pinioned, one cold winter's day, against the stone wall of the camels' corral and thrashed about the body by the long neck of a furious bull camel called Harolt, driven frantic by the urge to find a mate. Having escaped with nothing worse than a bruising she then had to prevent the excitable Harolt from making advances to his mate the wrong way round. Using ropes and willpower, Debbie, despite her recent mauling, eventually turned him front to back and achieved a successful mating. No small achievement given the peculiar construction of the camel's lower anatomy.

On another occasion, during a wild camel survey, Debbie told me that the driver of their truck lit a fire under the vehicle to stop the engine freezing up in the sub-zero temperatures. Petrol was stored on the back of the truck in a forty-four-gallon drum. When the tarpaulin covering the engine caught fire in the middle of the night, it was Debbie who had the presence of mind to throw sand over the flames as the Mongols took to their heels.

For her heating and cooking, Debbie relied on a tiny cast-iron fire fuelled by dried camel dung, which invariably went out shortly after she retired to her wooden bunk under her covering of nine blankets. She also learnt how to cope with relieving herself in conditions that turned water into ice within seconds.

She would frequently be lowered down a deep well to smash the thick ice so that water could be drawn up in a bucket for herself and the camels. One day, as a Mongolian was handing her a block of ice from the bottom of the well, it slipped from her fingers on to the head of her unfortunate helpmate and split open his scalp. But the extreme cold immediately staunched the flow of blood and stopped septicaemia from setting in. Had Debbie accidentally killed her assistant, she would not have been incarcerated like the poor inmates of Urga prison earlier this century. Their condition was graphically described by intrepid British adventuress Beatrix Bulstrode when she visited the prison in 1919.

Ever curious, Miss Bulstrode had stumbled across some evil-smelling wooden coffins as soon as she entered the prison doors. Smaller than the human frame, iron-bound and secured by two strong padlocks, both Chinese and Mongolian malefactors had been placed inside them. The unfortunate inmates were fed and watered through a hole sometimes big enough for a head to protrude and sometimes not depending on hat size: 'In one way only did they [the Chinese] score over their Mongolian fellow-sufferers. Their narrower Chinese skulls enabled them, painfully and with difficulty, to protrude their heads through the hole in the coffin side. The Mongol cranium is too wide to do so at all.'

Most of these wretched prisoners had long since gone mad, and even the stoical Beatrix had to hurry away from this terrible scene.

Debbie managed to bring a wild Bactrian camel's head out of China. She somehow managed to get it past officialdom at the airport, even though its skin was decaying and its brain putrefying. When it arrived in Kenya it was distinctly malodorous.

In similar vein, Miss Bulstrode was to discover that the Mongolians disposed of their dead by leaving them on the outskirts of Urga, the former name of Ulan Bator. The Mongols felt that as the spirit departs from the body at death, the putrefying cadaver was of no significance and might just as well be disposed of by domestic dogs, vultures or wild animals. The Russian explorer Przhevalsky, who has given his name to the wild horse (*Equus przewalskii*), arrived in Urga at the end of the nineteenth century and commented, 'No sooner is a fresh corpse thrown into the street than wild dogs tear it to pieces, and in a couple of hours nothing remains of the dead man.'

Miss Bulstrode set about retrieving a Mongol skull:

Ten days or so prior to our departure I had found on a hillside some distance from Urga a fine, and apparently, clean, specimen of Mongol skull, and tyro in the subject that I was, thought that to possess and take it home with me would be interesting from an anthropological point of view. Threading a bit of string through the eye socket, therefore, I tied the skull to my saddle and rode back with it. My friends, very kindly, instead of crushing my aspirations, suggested that to let it steep for a few days in a pail of disinfectant might be a wise and sanitary precaution. When, however, I wanted to pack it up, I found on pouring off the disinfectant, that the dogs and vultures had not performed their functions with the thoroughness that I had anticipated, and that the cranium was still half full of decomposed matter.

Her travelling companion, a Mr Gull, whom she described at one point as a 'peppery little man' but whom she later married, not unnaturally objected to all this, and it is little wonder that she records a pretty young Mongol girl who '. . . obviously mistook me for a man, and all the time she was off duty she rode alongside the tarantass (Russian-made travelling cart) making overtures to me for sweets . . . I felt quite sorry for my companion that all her attentions should be squandered upon myself.'

Cast in the same redoubtable mould, Debbie was a worthy successor to the formidable Miss Bulstrode. When she returned to Kenya, having successfully initiated a wild-camel breeding programme, she was no longer the bronzed, slim, boyish figure that had arrived in Mongolia three months earlier. In her words, 'Having eaten little else besides mutton for three months it was hardly surprising that I looked and smelt like a mutton dumpling.'

★ ★ ★

Bayan Toroi is surrounded by rustling poplars and grazing livestock. *Gers* and wooden huts sprawl around a spring, the life-blood of the oasis, and the tall chimney of the coal-powered, electricity generating plant which enables the community to survive the bitter winters.

Avermet, the chief warden of the reserve, greeted us on arrival. He was tall and bulky, with a round flat face which carried a wary 'I'm not quite sure that I like you' expression. We were later to learn he was a man of variable moods. His compound housed two *gers*, one for himself and one for guests and a number of ramshackle concrete buildings grouped around a radio mast. The job of chief warden in this remote oasis is not sought after. There had been seven incumbents in the previous ten years, and as Avermet had been there for over a year and a half he had already upped the average stay. Avermet offered George Schaller, Mike Samsonov and myself the guest *ger*, which was gaily painted and sufficiently roomy to take all our kit. An hour or two after our arrival we were all settled in it, eating mutton, drinking vodka and listening to Avermet's problems, the most important of which concerned the wild camel.

'The springs are drying up,' he said. 'All those dry years in the '80s have ensured that the underground water supplies are depleted.'

It emerged that these years of drought had resulted in seven out of the fifteen springs in the reserve drying up completely, but the underground reserves had not had time to benefit from the recent exceptional rains. That could take at least three years. Wolves, which were on the increase, had preyed on the camels, especially the young, who had been forced to congregate around the greatly reduced number of water points. As domestic livestock was banned from the reserve, the options open to the wolf for securing a good meal had been reduced.

'How many camels do you think remain in the reserve?' Schaller asked.

'No more than 350, and numbers are going down every year.'

'What happens to them if they cross the border into China?'

The southern border of the 70,000-square-kilometre reserve, an area equal to that of Belgium and the Netherlands, lies contiguous with that of China. The camels are able to wander freely into China, but there is no protection when they arrive there.

Avermet shrugged his shoulders and then drew his index finger slowly across his throat. Schaller frowned. 'We haven't a clue what's going on over there,' he said. 'I wish we could get hold of some reliable information.'

When the Russians undertook an aerial survey of the reserve in 1981, they estimated camel numbers to be over 600, possibly higher. Now, according to Avermet, numbers were in steep decline. This explained why he had caught the thirteen young ones. If they disappeared in the wild, it was essential that there was a pool of young captive stock somewhere in the world.

That evening, I went for a stroll around the oasis to try to find some Mongolian horses. There are seven million horses in Mongolia. This means that there are approximately three and a quarter horses for every man, woman and child – and the children aren't taught to ride from a Mongolian Pony Club Manual. From the age of one to three they are strapped to a board behind their mother. From three to five they are strapped to the saddle. From five onwards they're on their own. Unstrapped and unsupported, I keenly wanted to ride one of these sturdy little animals, some of whom I had seen earlier with their manes trailing along the ground.

These Mongolian horses are rightly famous. The Mongols conquered most of the known world mounted on their backs. Genghis Khan and his heirs developed a complex postal system, a vast chain of horse remount stations which extended throughout their empire. At each of these stations remounts were ready and waiting for a rider, carrying news or an imperial decree, to continue his onward journey in the shortest possible time. Each station was presided over by a station manager, and by the end of Kublai Khan's reign, China alone had more than 1,400 postal stations.

To avoid drifting off to sleep, riders were strapped into their saddles just like their unschooled children. When changing horses these messengers hardly rested and, having unstrapped themselves from their mount, they frequently jumped from one horse to the other without touching the ground in order not to waste valuable time. When pressed for food, they tapped the jugular vein of their steed and drank some of its blood for nourishment, in exactly the same way as Masai cattle owners do today. The end product was a remarkably efficient postal service, by thirteenth-century or any other century's standards.

With all this in mind, it was with some diffidence that I approached a Mongol who had dismounted to talk to some people busily engaged in cutting out circular strips of felt to cover a new *ger*. I later learnt that when a stranger passes people fluffing wool for felt-making, he should compliment them and make suitable remarks for the long life of the end product. If this is not done, the passer-by is liable to have his mouth stuffed with wool to teach him good manners.

The stocky, trilby-hatted owner of the horse was dressed in a bright blue *del* with a dazzling orange sash tied tightly around his waist. The cheeks of his deeply lined face were burnished the colour of ripe plums by the effects of wind and sun. I mimed my request for a ride. He looked at me quizzically. When he grasped my meaning his expression changed to concern. Encouraged by the felt-cutters I persisted with the mime. Eventually, the reluctant owner walked over to his horse and secured a leading rein to its bridle. He then nodded to me and indicated that I could mount.

I eased my way into the upright wooden saddle and we proceeded to walk in a tight circle to polite applause from the felt-cutters. This was not what I had hoped for. More signs and mime encouraged the owner to let me trot and then canter, but still he held on tightly to the leading rein. The felt-cutters began to urge their friend to allow me to go solo. Finally he gave way with much blowing on the open palm of his hand to indicate that his little horse went like the wind. He untied the leading rein, I squeezed the horse's sides and immediately the little chestnut threw out his front feet as though dealing a pack of cards. We were off. I neck-reined my way past the oncoming rush of poplars as we galloped into the Gobi, the high wooden arch of the saddle banging mercilessly into the small of my back. Being carted by a pony 14.2 hands high was a novel sensation. For thirty minutes I enjoyed a non-stop whirlwind ride that I thought for a moment might end up in China. The chestnut's mouth was as hard as iron and he resisted all my efforts to slow him down. With my legs trailing on the ground and pebbles and sand flying up on either side of us we must have made a hilarious spectacle for the felt-cutters. Then the little horse decided that he had had enough. Coming to an abrupt stop he turned his head, caught my eye and inquired, 'What next?' in his very best Mongolian. Home it had to be. This time, not wanting to risk knee-capping myself on a passing poplar, I persuaded him to trot back to his owner, who welcomed me with a great 'hollo' which all too clearly expressed relief.

The true spirit of the Mongolian horseman lives on. In the 1930s Owen Lattimore saw a horseman who

. . . was riding a wild, lashing unbreakable devil of a horse; but he (the Mongol) was a devil himself. Bracing his hands against the brute's neck to keep it from getting its head down (it wanted to pig-jump the way Mongol ponies do instead of bucking), he tore the nail clean out of one finger. He didn't flinch and kept on riding like a wild one . . . He drove one wild horse alongside us, but no one could catch it – it was unbridled and we had neither lasso nor the regulation lasso pole. So the Mongol galloped up beside it, leaned over, caught it by the mane, drew himself over from his own bareback horse, still at full gallop, and slid down along the shoulder of the caught horse, hanging by the mane with one hand and grabbing at its nostrils with the other, to choke it. Fine riding, and the pain of hanging on by one hand which had the whole nail ripped off one finger must have been pretty bad.

[Later] the Mongol boy sat drinking tea for about ten minutes, examining the raw end of his finger where the nail had been torn off . . . Then, unbreakable young man, he jumped up and said he'd got to be getting along.

* * *

The next day, our team set out on a short camel survey into the Gobi through the Edrengiyn Nuruu mountain range which forms the northern border of the reserve. The little brown Gobi bear (*Ursus arctos pruinosus*) sometimes wanders out of the desert to these mountains. There are thought to be no more than thirty-five left in the world and in the last thirty years the bear's range has been reduced by half. Driving through a gorge in the mountains, we spotted wild rhubarb, the root of which is the bear's favourite food. When we eventually entered the desert it was, thanks to the unprecedented rains, covered in bright green vegetation. Young saxsaul shrubs, a favourite food of the camel, proliferated, and many colourful plants were in flower. Nikolai Nikolayevich bear-hugged Peter Gunin when he discovered a large, white mushroom-like flower (*Pitilotrichum caneseens*). The recent rains, the heaviest in living memory, had encouraged its deeply buried seed to burst forth and flower for the first time since the 1930s.

We camped near a deep cleft in a rock near the Otgon Us oasis. George Schaller and I walked through rust-coloured foothills brilliantly highlighted by the setting sun. Later, George discovered the lower jawbone of a young camel, a ball of camel fur and a pile of dried wolf droppings – a find which confirmed Avermet's remarks. Near the oasis we spotted Persian gazelles (*Gazella subgutturosa*), the wild ass (*Equus hemionus*) and a pair of rare houbara bustards (*Chlamydotis undulata*).

That evening, sentimental Russian songs echoed around the hills which were now lit by a spectacular full moon. It was Anna's birthday, and my tuneless rendering of 'Clementine' was a poor entry in the top of the Gobi pops. George looked uncomfortable and refused to be coaxed into song.

'The Russians are herd animals,' he commented dryly as he wandered away towards his tent, pouring the untouched vodka in his tin mug into the sand.

On our return to Bayan Toroi the following day, we found that a surprise visitor in an American jeep had mysteriously materialised: Stephen Kohl, from the Office of International Affairs, Department of the Interior, US Fish and Wildlife Service, United States of America. A fluent Russian speaker and consummate tooth-picker, he had arrived, somehow, 'to check on how we were getting along'. I thought it highly likely that his eight-line business card could be substituted with an ID card bearing three capital letters. Uninvited and unannounced, his appearance at this oasis on the fringe of the desert raised a Slavonic eyebrow, and Mike Samsonov eyed him with interest. But Steve had no desire to venture with us into the desert.

'Nope, I'm a man of the frozen wastes,' he told me.

But his preoccupation with personal hygiene, which included flossing around the clock, suggested that his more normal habitat was bounded by office space and city limits. He departed as mysteriously as he had arrived, but not before Avermet had announced that one of the herds, with a wild camel attached to it, had arrived in Bayan Toroi.

'You will soon recognise the wild camel,' commented George sardonically to Steve Kohl. 'It will look like a greyhound surrounded by St Bernards.'

He was right; the wild camel was grey, had two tiny humps and was thin, sleek and built for speed. In contrast, the domestic camels appeared ponderous, were covered in shaggy brown hair and their humps stood erect like mountain peaks or flopped flaccidly over to one side of their bodies. As we approached the herd, the wild camel veered away and strode purposefully away on its own while the domestic camels huddled closer and closer together. That evening a second domestic herd arrived. It contained the wild male called Harolt who was later to give Debbie so much trouble. At first he was docile and allowed us to handle him. Then he abruptly took a dislike to George Schaller and lunged at him with bared yellow teeth. He followed this hostile gesture by blowing his regurgitated breakfast all over him. George didn't wait to see what would happen next. He took off at high speed with Harolt in hot pursuit. Avermet opined that Harolt was allergic to cameras. After this incident, we were left in little doubt as to how dangerous these males would be during the annual rut.

Two days later, having travelled nearly 300 kilometres in a steady downpour over a seemingly endless expanse of black and white pebbled desert, with a break for a camp in a lunar landscape, we reached the green and extremely beautiful oasis of Shara-Khulsny-Bulak. Surrounded by sheer, towering brick-red peaks, this oasis is the last known refuge of the Gobi bear.

As we walked past the beautiful wild yellow clematis in full flower, whose shaggy seed-pods the Mongols use for stuffing pillows, we came across pile after pile of bear droppings. Our excitement mounted as it became clear that a bear was walking along the track in front of us. It had been gorging itself on wolf-berries, and as the steam started to rise from the neatly deposited piles of undigested fruit we knew that we were very, very close to this rare animal.

Then Moonlight Dream tripped on a rock and fell into a clematis bush. She spluttered an apology. 'Sorry, so sorry,' she said with a giggle as she brushed away tufts of grey, feathery seed pods that covered her jet-black hair. Choigun, our Mongolian guide, pursed his lips in disgust at her clumsiness. George muttered something about 'lack of fieldcraft'. We walked on more quickly until confronted by an oversize pile of steaming droppings positioned neatly in the centre of the track.

'He is here,' whispered Choigun, squinting through narrowed eyes at the rocks on either side of us. 'I can smell him. Keep very still.'

But we had to content ourselves with the smell of steaming, juicy droppings. The little Gobi *ursus* had completely disappeared. The following year I learned that in this same oasis a team of Japanese television 'naturalists' had tried to snare a bear using the wolfberry as a bait. A snared bear escaped with the wire still attached to its foot. Fortunately for the bears, the TV team was thrown out of Mongolia.

After another 100 kilometres of flat, featureless desert we reached the ruined desert monastery of Lamyn Toroi, which had been destroyed in the Stalinist purges of the 1930s. An atmosphere of indescribable sadness hung over its crumbling remains. The ever-present wind buffeted mud-brick ruins that seemed to be haunted by lost souls, condemned to an eternity of sighing for a paradise lost. One could sense the terrible tragedy that had taken place in this remote desert outpost of Buddhism. We cautiously picked our way among the shattered tiles and ornate wall carvings that had lain undisturbed since a day of appalling slaughter and destruction. The Russians fell silent.

'Look,' said Moonlight Dream, stooping to pick up a beautifully worked section of shattered cornice. 'This is what they did to us. I feel it so strongly.'

We were walking together, away from the others. Tears were streaming down her plump cheeks and she was clenching and unclenching her fists.

'I don't want the Russians to see me crying.' She wiped both sides of her face on the sleeve of her jacket. 'Dasha doesn't care. She doesn't feel anything. But I care. I care very much. Many members of my family were killed when the Russians destroyed these monasteries.'

'Something very similar happened in England,' I said in a futile attempt to say something to comfort her. 'Beautiful monasteries were destroyed, their land and possessions were taken over by the state. It must have been a similar situation.'

'How long ago did that happen?'

'About 400 years ago.'

'Four hundred years ago!' She looked up at me, her tear-stained face full of emotion. 'You've forgotten all about it. It's history. This happened during the lifetime of my father. My family feels it as though it happened yesterday.'

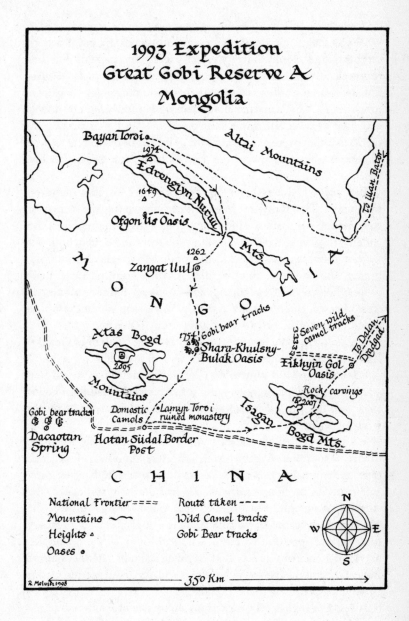

1993 Expedition
Great Gobi Reserve A
Mongolia

Bayan Toroi

Altai Mountains

To Ulan Bator

1974

Edrengiyn Nuruu

1649

Ofgon Us Oasis

M O N G O L I A

Mts

1262

Zangat Uul

Gobi bear tracks

Seven wild camel tracks

Xtas Bogd

1751

To Dalan Dzadgad

2695

Shara-Khulsny-Bulak Oasis

Eikhyin Gol Oasis

Mountains

Rock carvings

2007

Tsagan

Gobi bear tracks

Domestic Camels

Lamyn Toroi ruined monastery

Bogd Mts.

Dacaotan Spring

Hatan Sudal Border Post

C H I N A

National Frontier ====   Route taken ----
Mountains ~   Wild Camel tracks
Heights ᴧ   Gobi Bear tracks
Oases •

N
W E
S

R. Melvin 1998

350 Km

'I'm sorry.'

'We all feel it. Three of my uncles and two of my grandfather's brothers were monks. They were all killed.' She paused. 'Do you realise that in the early 1920s nearly a quarter of the male population of Mongolia were lamas? At that time there were over 800 monasteries. The Russians blew them up and pulled them down. They left us with Gandan, a showpiece in Ulan Bator, to fool the world that they were caring for Mongolian Buddhism.' She looked up. 'Come, let's walk over here. I don't want Peter to see that I'm upset.'

We walked slowly over to another part of the shattered monastery. The Russians were scavenging among the ruins for souvenirs. George was sitting propped up against the wheel of the jeep.

'The monasteries were our lifeblood,' Moonlight Dream continued. 'At one time they virtually ran the country. Of course, some of the monks were corrupt and dishonest. I know that people were cheated. But it was our system, a Mongolian system. It should have been reformed by Mongolians, not by Russians.'

'Didn't the people protest?' I asked. 'Did the children of Genghis Khan do nothing when the Russians were destroying their culture?'

'Of course we did something,' she said firmly. 'There was a civil war. Party members were hanged from trees. They had their hearts torn out and hung on banners just as they did in the time of Genghis Khan.'

I marvelled at the transformation. The normally jolly, giggling, carefree Moonlight Dream was shaking with emotion. We walked over to the remains of a mud wall and sat down side by side.

'Naturally, the Russians won. We had the bow and arrow, the weapon of Genghis Khan. They had Stalin's special troops, the NKVD. They came in with tanks and aeroplanes. Stalin himself directed the operation to put down the Mongols.' She looked up and gave me a grim smile. 'They say that Stalin had Mongol blood in his veins, which was why he took such a personal interest in our destruction.'

I wondered what deep-seated psychological problem had urged

Stalin to obliterate a large percentage of a population with whom he might have had blood-ties.

'What happened?'

'They shot over 50,000 Buddhist monks, including my relatives.'

I turned my eyes away from her face.

'I could show you the site of a mass graves not far from Ulan Bator,' she whispered, leaning over and clutching at my arm. 'Death squads were recruited and given a quota of people to shoot every week. Some say that by the time Choibalsan, Stalin's Mongolian stooge, died in 1952, over 100,000 people had been killed. That's one person in seven of the whole Mongolian population. Can you understand that?'

I understood only too well. Poor Mongolia. First the Mad Baron and then this.

'And they forced the herdsmen into collectives. And they . . .'

'Hey, John, Moonlight. Come on, we're going now.' Peter was calling us. It was time to move on.

'Don't tell Peter what I've told you,' said Moonlight Dream as we walked back towards the vehicles. She had recovered her composure and was smiling through her tears.

'Of course not. I won't talk to anyone.'

'I was a student of his at Moscow University. He was very kind to me. I don't want to upset him because I've been talking to you so openly.' She looked up and smiled. 'Most of my contemporaries don't think about it at all. Many of them don't even know what happened to the monasteries and the lamas. They don't want to know. They don't care. Why should they worry about it? It's history. All they want to do is make money.'

★   ★   ★

'Camels! Look! Over there.' Vanya pointed excitedly at a line of camels on the far horizon. The sombre ruins of Lamyn Toroi were ten kilometres behind us. This was a find.

'Are they wild?' I enquired as Vanya steered the jeep towards the herd.

George shook his head. 'They can't be,' he said. 'They would

43

have run away by now. The wind is blowing in their direction. If they were wild, they would have taken off before we spotted them.' We got out of the jeep and walked up to the herd of docile camels. 'This is the last thing we want to find,' George commented grimly. 'An uncastrated domestic male and fertile adult females in wild camel territory.'

'I expect that they come from the Mongolian border post,' said Peter. 'It's not far from here. It only gets visited once in three months so the border guards do what they like. It's against the regulations but it's impossible for Avermet to stop them from keeping domestic livestock. They wouldn't listen to him.'

I looked at the wooden nose pegs that had been inserted in the noses of the camels to provide a method of control. Peter Gunin answered my unspoken question.

Pointing at the peg in the nose of the bull camel he said, 'You can tell that these are Mongolian-owned camels because Mongolians insert the peg *under* the main cartilage and not above it, as Kazak herdsmen do. The flesh above the cartilage is more tender and makes the animal even easier to handle. However, the skin is weaker at this point and more liable to tear. If the camel shies away from its handler, then the nose-plug can rip out, causing the camel great distress. If you see a camel that has a bad tear above the nose cartilage and another hole pierced below it, then you can tell that the camel was originally bred by Kazaks and is now owned by Mongols.'

Four years later, when slithering down a slippery gorge with seventeen camels in the towering Arjin Shan mountains on the northern Tibetan border, I was to learn at first hand just how distressful a torn nose cartilage can be.

★ ★ ★

The commandant of the border post of Hatan Siidal was a portly officer with rimless glasses and a wide grin which revealed a fine set of gold teeth. He welcomed us effusively with mutton and vodka and seemed not to mind in the least that George and I were travelling with Russians.

'Last month,' he exclaimed excitedly, 'I saw thirty wild camels cross the border. They stayed for five days in the buffer zone. Then they disappeared.'

'Did they go into China?' asked George.

The commandant nodded.

'I expect they've ended up in a Chinese miner's noodle pot,' said George gloomily. 'Gansu province swarms with legal and illegal miners looking for gold and iron ore. A camel doesn't have a chance.'

Having promised Avermet that he would castrate the bull camel that we had found and keep the others under control, the commandant suddenly said, 'One of our camels went mad last month.'

'What happened?'

The commandant twirled his index finger round and round his head. His gold teeth flashed. ' It foamed at the mouth and then ran off into the desert.'

I had read that occasionally a camel can suddenly have a fit and take off, running on and on until it drops. Herdsmen are fearful of these bewitched animals which sometimes pass them at high speed, frothing at the mouth with a wild look in their eye. They consider them to be possessed by a malign spirit and make no attempt to stop them. The wretched animal gallops on and on, heedless of hours of daylight or darkness, not stopping to rest and ignoring any other camel, wild or domestic. After travelling for several days in this crazed fashion it slows and then drops down dead.

George combed his fingers through his hair. 'It sounds like rabies to me,' he said. 'It's another good reason why we don't want domestic camels wandering inside the reserve.'

The commandant told us that 250 soldiers were stationed on the international border between the Gobi A and B reserves. The frequency of the border posts and the high levels of manning reflect the Mongolian suspicion of the Chinese. To reinforce their fears, they only had to look at what happened to their cousins living under the Chinese in Inner Mongolia.

Inappropriately called the 'Mongolian Autonomous Region', the province has been inundated with settlers for many years. In

1954 it was estimated that the Chinese–Mongolian ratio was three to one, and Chinese settlers have been flooding in ever since. These settlers, often the poorest of the poor, have farmed the steppe land and driven the Mongolian semi-nomads on to the least productive grasslands where they have become settled ranchers.

Paradoxically, the Inner Mongolians have, since the death of Chairman Mao, been allowed to use their own written script, in contrast to Outer Mongolia where the Russians insisted that the Cyrillic alphabet be used. In Outer Mongolia, the Russians pursued a vigorous education and health programme that raised literacy standards from nine per cent at the turn of the century to over ninety per cent today. They also succeeded in vastly improving health standards, but, at the same time, they forced the Mongols into collectivisation and cruelly suppressed their religion. What has been retained in Mongolia in contrast to Chinese-ruled Inner Mongolia, is a small population that pursues a semi-nomadic way of life in a vast expanse of steppe land.

The pressures on land ensure that China will continue to turn hungry eyes northwards. An ever-increasing imbalance is building up between the vast empty plains and abundant, scarcely-tapped resources of Mongolia, and the busy, teeming millions of China.

⋆　⋆　⋆

The spectacular Tsagan Bogd range in the south-east corner of the reserve reaches heights of nearly 3,000 metres. The jet black rocks of these massive mountains are turned into spectacular contrasts of light and shade in a setting sun. The following day, as we were passing through a sheer-sided gorge, Peter suddenly ordered Vanya to stop. He then leapt out of the jeep with a great shout.

'George, John, Anna! Come and look at this,' he called out in great excitement. Peter had walked to one side of the gorge and was pointing at a huge slab of rock. It appeared to have recently fallen down from the side of the mountain.

'It's unbelievable!'

We looked at the rock and saw that there were two beautifully executed drawings carved on it of an ibex and a snow leopard.

'What a find! It's thousands of years old,' cried Peter.

'Why on earth did the artist climb up there to carve it?' I wondered, pointing at a rocky ledge many metres above the spot where we were standing.

George, who was more interested in wildlife than man, ancient or modern, shrugged his shoulders. 'It's a remarkably accurate drawing of a snow leopard,' he mused. 'And not a bad one of an ibex.'

Leaving the carved rock behind us, a very bumpy ride of another 100 kilometres brought us to the oasis of Eikhyin Gol, just outside the reserve. The former Russian scientific base there had been vandalised and some of their stores looted, but Eikhyin Gol was a pleasant place with a river which flowed into a dam where we could wash and swim. The oasis boasted a fine garden in which carrots, tomatoes and other vegetables grew. The Mongolians' natural aversion to vegetables had ensured that most of this abundant produce was rotting away.

That evening, the soft-spoken bespectacled Dzazvazal, the unfortunate official who was trying to persuade his countrymen to eat vegetables, admitted defeat and killed a sheep in our honour. He killed it by slitting open the stomach and squeezing the heart, in exactly the same manner as ordained by Genghis Khan in the *Yassa*, the ancient Mongolian law code. Though the operation sounds barbaric, it is in fact remarkably humane. In this case, the sheep gave one convulsion and then died. Dzazvazal butchered it with such expert speed that the poor animal had no time to grasp that it was being turned into mutton. I discovered that the secret is in selecting the exact spot to make the initial incision, a cavity where the skin is held taut between the soft belly and the arch of the ribs. The butchered beast was cooked in a metal pot that resembled a milk churn into which heated stones were placed. The lid was screwed down and the hot stones cooked the meat. Nothing was wasted and even the intestines were stuffed, Kikuyu fashion, with congealed blood, fat and meat and chopped into 'sausages'. We cheerfully washed these 'sausages' down with vodka and *kumis*.

After the meal, Dasha collected up the cleanly-picked mutton-bones from everybody's plate, cracked them open with a knife, and tipped them into a large saucepan full of luke-warm tea. She turned to me as she did so. 'You didn't pick all the meat off your bones,' she said, raising a finger and waggling it under my nose. 'That's very bad manners in Mongolia. We expect you to eat every scrap of meat and suck out all the juice from inside the bone.'

Mike Samsonov looked at her in disgust and shook his head. 'These Mongolians' he muttered under his breath.

'What are you doing?' I asked.

'Mutton-bone tea is the very best tea of all,' said Dasha as she sliced brick tea into the saucepan with a wicked-looking knife. When she had finished she threw in a handful of salt and placed the saucepan carefully on the fire. 'Just you wait until you taste it. It'll keep you warm and mend your stomach.'

'It'll do something completely different to your stomach,' Mike whispered in my ear. 'Don't touch it. It's disgusting.'

I drank it and understood why Debbie had said that after her three-month stay in Bayan Toroi she looked and smelt like a Mongolian pasty.

During the inevitable post-prandial sing-song, Moonlight Dream sang wistful songs to the memory of the Great Khan and a lost love.

'Not my husband,' she said with a smile. 'I love him and he loves me. He's not lost.'

'You hope,' said Mike. 'You don't know what he's getting up to while you're drinking mutton tea in the Gobi.' He laughed and, throwing back his head, launched into a powerful and sentimental rendering of a Russian love song.

Later that night, when I again tried to do 'Clementine' justice, George crept away to his tent with a pained expression on his face. Why do the British, unlike other nationalities, have songs that sound so trite and banal when performed under a star-studded desert night sky? Not even 'Danny Boy' can do such a backdrop justice. One or two Scottish songs nearly fit but they can't compete with the soulful tunes of the steppes and the mountains. On reflection, maybe it was my voice.

Over the next two days, George, Anna and I ventured deep into the Gobi to search for wild camels. We travelled into the heartland of the reserve, a barren, remote region where there were no vehicle tracks, no water holes and very little signs of the recent heavy rains. Apart from the low moan of the wind there was also total silence, undisturbed by the sound of a single living thing. To be enveloped by total silence in that arena of lost horizons is a humbling experience. However, I was well aware that in August the silence of the desert can be turned within minutes into a blistering explosion of flying dust and sand, an experience that I was later to undergo more than once in the even more harsh and remote deserts of north-west China.

After much fruitless searching we at last discovered the tracks of seven camels, all adult. We attempted to follow them on foot, but the animals were pursuing a migratory track between water points which could have continued for over fifty kilometres, and we were forced to abandon the search. George Schaller was very disappointed as he had expected to find wild camels in this area. All the indicators were pointing to a substantial reduction in their numbers. On our return to Eikhyin Gol, Zeshw, a reserve warden, told us that since 1986 the water-table level at Eikhyin Gol had dropped by thirty centimetres. Another bad statistic for long-term camel survival.

It was time to return to Ulan Bator. It took us five days. We left in a sand storm and arrived in a snow blizzard. On the first day we passed a second ruined desert monastery, Tsagan Dernsee Holoi, another forlorn place. Once again the ground nearby was littered with artefacts and the remains of ornate wall carvings. We then passed through a valley full of sand dunes which Peter Gunin said had formed only in the last twenty years – a stark reminder of Central Asian desertification and a changing climate. We skirted a lake, full of poisonous chemicals that had leached from a nearby industrial plant. A domestic camel lay dead on the shore, having drunk the toxic water.

We reached the *aimak* of Dalan Dzadgad, a stereotypical settlement of concrete flats, *gers* in stockades, a sports ground surrounded by out-moded political slogans and the mandatory tall chimney. A *naadam* was in full swing but my colleagues had planes to catch. Dalan Dzadgad was a depressing place. We could not even buy bread there.

On the fourth day after leaving Eikhyin Gol, we climbed up through the steppe lands, breathing deeply on the scent of wild flowers and navigating through a thick, swirling, highland mist. Then the track deteriorated into a quagmire and we walked behind our vehicles, in a steady drizzle, for many kilometres. We plodded along a rutted route similar to those encountered by eighteenth-century stagecoaches and, consequently, at the same speed. Before we reached Ulan Bator, the drizzle had turned first to a downpour and then to driving snow. We had covered over 4,500 kilometres and encountered sand storms, great heat, freezing temperatures, rain and snow. As John of Plano Carpini, a Franciscan friar who visited the grandson of Genghis Khan in 1245 on behalf of Pope Innocent IV, remarked:

> The weather there is astonishingly irregular . . . In the middle of summer when other places are normally enjoying great heat, there is fierce thunder and lightning which causes the death of many men, and at the same time there are very heavy falls of snow. There are also hurricanes of bitterly cold wind so violent that at times men can ride on horseback only with great effort.

On our last day, 30 August, the expedition members were invited to visit Hustain Nuruu, forty kilometres from Ulan Bator and the home of Przhevalsky's wild horse (*Equus przewalskii*). There was some consternation and indecision among the Russians in our party. The project to reintroduce the wild horse to the Mongolian steppe had been a Russian one before the collapse of the Soviet Union. It has now been totally internationalised, much to the dismay of Academician Sokolov of the Russian Academy of Sciences.

The wild horse was presumed to have become extinct in 1969, when the last one was apparently shot near Gobi Reserve B. My guide through the deserts of north-western China, Zhao Ziyung, later boasted to me that he had fired the fatal shot. Before this finality, and in striking contrast to the wild Bactrian camel, there were about 550 animals distributed in zoos around the world. At first it was hoped to reintroduce the horse into Gobi Reserve B, but Russian tests revealed a dangerously high level of radiation in that area. So an alternative but not totally satisfactory site was chosen, in an enclave in the green, rolling steppes at Hustain Nuruu, for the breeding and reintroduction into the wild of this stocky, sandy-coloured horse with zebra-like marking on its hind legs and a short, upright mane. The first twenty-one horses were brought to Mongolia from zoos around the world in 1992, and there are now well over fifty. Unfortunately for the Russians, a stallion presented to the project by the Moscow Zoo was found to be infertile. It subsequently died of a brain tumour. Whether or not this was a deliberate Russian attempt to sabotage the project, it swiftly brought a halt to further Russian involvement.

That evening, our team was invited to dinner with the Minister for Nature and the Environment, Dr Batjargal, in the Bogd Ula reserve near the site of some of the Mad Baron Ungern's nastier exploits. We dined in the imperial tent of no less a personage than the Great Khan Genghis himself, the main prop left over from a film set which had been acquired by the Mongolian government and erected in the Bogd Ula reserve as a bait for tourists. Smaller tents surrounded this imperial tent, and these had been converted into sleeping accommodation for visitors. The whole 'set' had been erected beside a river that flowed down from the surrounding hills. The tall, smoking chimneys of Ulan Bator's ageing power station complex and the chaotic rusting industrial debris that scarred the suburbs of the city were hidden by green undulating steppe that disappeared in thick forest – one of the rare occasions that trees could be seen in this part of Mongolia.

The inside of the imperial tent was hung with the skins of bears and snow leopards and gaily coloured Mongolian carpets were strewn over the floor. The gilded and glittering throne of the Great Khan was unoccupied, but we sat at intricately carved low tables to feast on elaborately cooked dishes of mutton washed down with vintage *kumis*.

All that was missing from this munificence was the large silver tree that stood in the magnificent pavilion of the Great Khan Mangu, the brother and predecessor of Kublai Khan. A Franciscan emissary from King Louis IX of France, Friar William of Rubruck, visited Mongolia in 1253 and stayed for about seven months. The pavilion, the Friar reported, was like a huge church with a middle nave between rows of pillars. Visitors entered through one of three doors on the southern side, and found themselves looking down the length of the great hall to the imperial dais at the far end. There sat the Great Khan in magnificent state on a spotted panther skin. To his right his son and brothers occupied pews lifted up to form a sort of balcony, and opposite them, on the Khan's left, were similar elevated seats for his wives and the palace women. Access to the Khan's throne platform was via two stairways, up which climbed the imperial butler carrying the drinking goblets. The centre-piece of this opulence was a magnificent silver tree that had been designed by a French jeweller who had been captured by the Mongols in Hungary:

Master William of Paris has made for him (the Great Khan) a large silver tree, at whose roots are four silver lions each having a pipe and all belching forth white mares' milk. Inside the trunk four pipes lead up to the top of the tree and the ends of the pipes are bent downwards and over each of them is a gilded serpent, the tail of which twines round the trunk of the tree. One of the pipes pours out wine, another *caracosmos*, that is the refined milk of mares, another *boal*, which is a honey drink, and another *terracina*, rice wine. Each of these had its silver basin ready to receive it at the foot of the tree between the four pipes. At the very top he made an angel holding a trumpet; underneath the tree he made a crypt in which a man can be secreted, and a pipe goes up to the angel through the middle of the heart of the tree . . . Outside the palace there is a chamber in which the drinks are stored, and servants stand there ready to pour them out when they hear the angel sounding the trumpet. The tree has branches, leaves and fruit of silver.

And so when the drinks are getting low the chief butler calls out to the angel to sound the trumpet. Then hearing this, the man who is hidden in the crypt blows the pipe going up to the angel with all his strength, and the angel, placing the trumpet to his mouth, sounds it very loudly. When the servants in the chamber hear this each one of them pours out his drink into its proper pipe, and the pipes pour them out from above and below into the basins prepared for this, and then the cup-bearers draw the drinks and carry them into the palace.

We were offered *cosmos* and, as the good Friar predicted, it made 'the inner man most joyful'. As a drink it is strongly recommended. Mildly effervescent, it is said to be a remedy for both rheumatism and tuberculosis. The dinner was, however, a much more sedate affair than those experienced by Friar William:

In summer they care only for *cosmos*. There is always *cosmos* near the house, before the entry door and beside it stands a guitar player with his guitar . . . and when the master begins to drink then one of the attendants cries with a loud voice, 'Ha!' and the guitarist strikes his guitar, the men in front of the master and the women in front of the mistress. When the master has drunken, then the attendant cries as before and the guitarist stops. Then everyone starts drinking, and sometimes they continue until they are disgustingly drunk.

When they want to challenge anyone to drink they seize him by the ears and pull them so as to distend the throat, then clap their hands and dance before him. In the same way, when they want to make a great feasting and jollity with somebody, one person takes a full cup and, supported by two others, one on the right and the other on his left, they come singing and dancing towards him. But as soon as he puts out his hand to take the cup they quickly withdraw it. This they repeat three or four times, until he has become so excited and so eager to drink that they give him the cup. And while he drinks they sing and clap the hands and stamp with their feet.

During the meal I asked the Minister how he felt about the destruction of the monasteries and the suppression of Buddhism.

'It must have been a terrible time for Mongolia,' I commented.

The Minister looked thoughtful. 'I'm not sure that I agree with you,' he said. 'The Chinese introduced Buddhism to Mongolia to stop our population increasing. They encouraged the growth of celibate lama communities so that it would be easier for them to control us. Fortunately for the Mongolians the Russians took charge, destroyed the monasteries and now we are breeding naturally again and the population is increasing.' He grinned. 'Of course, you must remember that I was educated in Moscow, so you should expect me to hold views like that.'

It did not seem the moment to remind him that under the Russians nearly 100,000 Mongolians had been killed.

'It is very difficult for Mongolians at the moment,' he said, waving his hand around his head. 'We are in complete mental turmoil.'

'How do you mean?'

'Not long ago we were taught that the Russians and communism were very good and that the Americans and capitalism were very bad. Now we are told completely the opposite. It is not easy for us.'

'Isn't religion important to the people?' I asked.

He laughed. 'Not to very many,' he replied. 'Today the Mongolian god is money. That's all we believe in now.'

As I was being driven back to my heavily fortified flat after this dinner with the affable Minister, a car in the erratic hands of a drunken driver careered towards us at full speed on the wrong side of the road. The Minister's chauffeur swerved on to the pavement just in time to avoid a head-on collision.

The Minister, who had remained totally calm throughout the incident, dismissed it with a laugh and said, 'Putting nomads into concrete flats results in that kind of behaviour. Most of our problems are caused by concrete and alcohol. Take my mother, for example. She has spent the best part of her life living in a *ger* on the open steppe. If she stays with me in my flat for more than a week she becomes dizzy and her nose starts to bleed.'

Twenty minutes later the lights on the car failed. Our driver negotiated darkened lanes, drove into a courtyard, unlocked and opened a garage door and then changed the vehicle for another one parked inside.

The next morning I discovered that all my travel documents were locked in the boot of the ministerial car. I took a taxi to the Ministry to tell the Minister my problem but discovered that he had already travelled out of town. My heart sank. The Russians were waiting to take me to the airport to catch the 10.30 a.m. Aeroflot flight to Moscow. There was only one flight a week and I had visions of heel-kicking in Ulan Bator.

Desperation had set in when suddenly I spotted the Minister's chauffeur, apparently moonlighting (or, more accurately, daylighting) at the wheel of a delivery van. I ran into the road, caught his attention and after a frantic five minutes trying to make him understand the problem, we set off for downtown Bator. All was well. Passport, ticket and roubles were still secure in the ministerial boot. I boarded the flight to Moscow with twenty minutes to spare. 'You will come back,' the Minister had said. 'My mother was a *shaman*, she looked into the future with great accuracy. I know that you will return.'

3

Where Men and Desert Meet

When the mind is enlarged the body is at ease
Chinese proverb

I took a deep breath and turned to look round at the impassive faces of the Chinese delegation. What were they thinking? Had they understood the paper? Were they asleep? One of them obviously did understand English. His paper on 'Economic Reform on the Nomadic Way of Life in the Xinjiang Province of China' had not set the conference alight, but it had certainly been delivered in passable English. I turned away. At the back of the hall, I saw a BBC microphone being pointed in my direction. I had to do it now.

'As you will have gathered,' I began lamely, 'the wild camel situation in Mongolia is extremely serious and a cause for great concern. Unfortunately, we have no knowledge of the current status of wild Bactrians across the border in China.'

I looked round the crowded conference hall and then turned again towards the three bespectacled, dark-suited Chinese who sat motionless with crossed arms three rows to my left.

'We therefore appeal to our Chinese colleagues to allow us to visit the four areas of Xinjiang Province where the wild Bactrian camel is still thought to survive. If we can do this, then we can ascertain . . .'

Afterwards, the three Chinese applauded politely. At least they weren't asleep, I thought as I sat down. But whether my coded appeal had been clearly understood I had not the slightest idea. After all, the Lop Nur area had been closed to foreigners since it became a nuclear testing area in 1950. Why should a foreign wild camel freak be allowed in in 1994?

My paper was the last to be delivered. The chairman of the conference on 'Biodiversity and Sustainable Development in Central Asia' stood up, summed up and bade us a safe journey home. The Chinese delegation filed out of the Children's Palace Conference Hall in Ulan Bator.

It was exactly a year to the day that the Mongolian Minister for Nature and the Environment had predicted that I would return to his country – but it wasn't the desert that had called me back from my desk at UNEP. It was warm, generous-hearted Nancy Nash, the Hong Kong-based wildlife conservationist, UNEP consultant and founder of the award-winning Buddhist Perception of Nature Project, who had engineered my invitation to address the conference on the wild camel. She walked over to me, exuding restless energy.

'Keep your fingers crossed. I was watching that Chinese Professor when you made your appeal. He may have looked inscrutable but he was taking it all in. I understand that he has a good reputation and is well thought of in Beijing.'

'But I'm asking for the moon, Nancy. The Professor would need to have a hot line to Deng himself to obtain permission for me to go into the Lop Nur area.'

Nancy, who combined her Buddhist beliefs with a healthy dose of realism, grasped my arm.

'Things are moving fast in China. Change is in the air. Who knows? Your appeal may have struck a chord which is reverberating in Beijing at this very moment. I have a feeling that your camel quest won't end here. Just look how you managed to get back to Mongolia, against all the odds and with no help from your masters in UNEP. Someone, somewhere is on your side.'

At ten o'clock that night there was a hesitant knock on my

hotel room door. Mindful of Debbie's experiences the previous December, I opened it cautiously. A young member of the Chinese delegation was standing nervously in the corridor.

'Professor Yuan would like to meet with you,' he said softly. 'Are you free to come to his room?'

I nodded and followed him up the flight of carpetless stairs to room 302 on the floor above. The Bayan Gol hotel was not the most prestigious hotel in the world, but it was the best in Mongolia. Engineer Cai knocked loudly on the Professor's door.

'Come in, come in,' a cheerful voice called out. The door was flung open and I was ushered into Professor Yuan Guoying's bedroom. A television set flickered in one corner of the fusty room, which had tightly locked windows partially covered with strips of frayed, crimson cloth. For some reason, the room reeked of coal dust. The sound on the TV was set at full volume. On the screen, Japan was invading Mongolia and bombs and shells were exploding everywhere. Professor Yuan, a short, rotund, vigorous-looking man in his mid-fifties, made no attempt to stop the noise of war. He was dressed in a sleeveless string vest and a vivid, pink towel was wrapped round his waist. Sharp, bright eyes twinkled behind rimless spectacles. I shook his outstretched hand.

'I liked your paper on the camel,' he began. 'Very interesting.'

'Thank you.'

'I have a great interest in the wild camel. Last year I saw one from the new oil road that is under construction in the Taklamakan desert. Unfortunately, it cuts right through their west-to-east migration routes.' He handed me a colour photograph which showed a camel disappearing rapidly over the top of a huge sand dune.

'You're very lucky,' I said. 'I haven't seen one yet.'

'Sit down, sit down,' said the Professor, propelling me towards his bed. He pulled out a tattered map of Xinjiang Province and spread it out on the bed beside me. Four circles had been drawn on the map. One of them encircled the Lop Nur nuclear testing area.

'We believe the camels are here, here and . . .' The Professor pointed at the four areas with a stubby finger. 'In the Taklamakan they are under great threat from oil development. But here and here and here,' he pointed to Lop Nur, the Arjin Shan mountains and the Mongolian border area, 'they still survive.'

'Have you any idea how many there are?'

'Maybe 800, maybe 1,000. I'm not sure. The last scientific research was carried out in the early 1980s.'

'By Professors Gu and Gao.'

Professor Yuan's face lit up. 'You know them?'

'I've seen their report,' I replied. 'UNEP has a copy.'

'I'm glad that you've read it. Their findings will be useful to us on our expedition.'

'*Our* expedition, Professor?'

Professor Yuan grinned boyishly. 'I would like to invite you to come to Xinjiang next year to join a team of scientists from my Institute to research the status of the wild Bactrian camel in China.'

I stared at him in disbelief. 'Have you the authority to issue this invitation?' I asked.

'Yes, of course,' he said abruptly, showing his annoyance at my tactless question. 'Otherwise, I would not be doing so.'

There was a loud explosion behind me. The Professor adjusted his glasses which had slipped to the bottom of his nose. 'I like old war films,' he said with a laugh, 'especially when the Japanese are being beaten.'

I glanced away from the television screen and returned to the present, resting my finger on Lop Nur, that mysterious lake that had eluded so many earlier explorers. I looked up at the Professor.

He read my thoughts. 'Yes, the invitation includes a visit to the Lop Nur area,' he said. 'It's called the Gashun Gobi, and the camels there are particularly interesting to us. It's the only area in the world where they have had no contact with domestic camels. They are genetically pure.'

Another explosion was overlaid with terrified screams and shouts. I ignored the compulsive call of the TV. If I had understood Professor Yuan correctly, he was extending not only an invitation to visit the three restriction-free areas where the wild Bactrian still roamed, but also to the forbidden fourth, Lop Nur.

'Is it safe to go in there?' I queried.

'Yes. Lao Zhao, who will be our guide, went in there last year with a Geiger counter. Radiation levels were well below danger levels. Anyway, all the nuclear tests are carried out underground these days, so don't worry. Have a beer.'

I declined, and the Professor turned his whole attention to the flickering screen. The meeting was at an end. I was too excited to think straight. It had worked, I had been given the invitation to go to China to follow up on our camel findings in Mongolia.

'Thanks, Professor, I can't tell you how grateful I am.'

'It's nothing. I liked your paper. I will send the invitation to UNEP. The expedition will take two months and we will set off in March or early April next year. That's the best time to go, because it's neither too hot nor too cold, even though it is the season of sand storms.' He paused for a moment. 'Will UNEP give you permission to go?'

I didn't hesitate. 'Yes, my contract finishes in March. There won't be a problem.'

I moved towards the door.

'We will provide the food, vehicles, petrol, equipment. We will organise everything.' He paused and smiled. 'You will find the money.'

'How much?'

'Thirty thousand dollars.'

I looked at his beaming face and twinkling eyes. Thirty thousand dollars was a lot of money. Far, far in excess of the amount my friends in UNEP's desertification department had scraped together for my 1993 expedition.

'I'll try my best, but I'll need a formal invitation in writing as soon as possible.'

'The invitation will be sent from the Xinjiang Environmental Protection Institute. I am the Vice-Director. It will come under my signature and will be sent through the National Environment Protection Agency in Beijing.'

NEPA was a partner of UNEP's and they had a representative in Nairobi. An invitation cleared by NEPA would help considerably to obtain UNEP funding and support.

I shook hands, left the Professor's room and raced down the stairs to the floor below, taking them three at a time. I knocked on Nancy's door. There was no reply. I knew where she would be and raced down three more flights of stairs.

In the hotel bar, Nancy Nash, wrapped in a blue Ladakhi cloak, fruit juice in hand, was perched on a stool talking animatedly to two conference delegates: Frank Roseby, a grizzled Australian sheep farmer who ran a research project in Xinjiang; and a strikingly beautiful environmental activist, Tracy Worcester, who had persuaded the BBC to send her to Ulan Bator to cover the conference. The atmosphere was sweaty and humid, and only half of the light bulbs appeared to function. The available drinks were fruit juice, beer or Genghis Khan vodka, but the barman had given up on the evening and was slumped over the counter, head on folded arms. Frank Roseby had presented a paper at the conference on 'Grazing Control in Unfenced Areas'. I was reminded of this as I noticed a couple, squeezed into a dimly-lit alcove, busily exploring parts of their bodies usually considered to be firmly fenced. A mountain of a man, his arms linked tightly round a tiny Mongolian girl, was attempting to shuffle backwards and forwards to the syncopated beat of Pink Floyd.

'I've got the invitation, Nancy.'

'I knew you'd get it,' she replied. 'Didn't I tell you that your camel quest wouldn't end here?'

Frank roused the somnolent barman and, over a fruit juice spiked with Genghis, I explained what had happened in room 302.

'A cause for celebration,' said Frank as my glass was recharged.

I looked round the bar. The Mongolian girl had given up on her dancing partner. Deprived of her support, he had slumped to the floor and lay spread-eagled across the tiny patch that served as a dancing area. Tracy's attention had been engaged by a thick-set man in a bright blue sweatshirt who appeared to be on the point of inviting her to marry him. Pink Floyd throbbed on and the rest of Saturday night melted away in a humid haze of vodka.

* * *

The previous December, Debbie had bought a pair of dog-skin boots in the notorious Ulan Bator Sunday market, and had vividly described the experience. The temperature had been minus twenty-five degrees centigrade and the market square was covered in thick ice. It was surrounded by a three-metre-high wall and the slippery surface had been littered with drunks and broken glass. Debbie had slithered round the square, landing on her bottom a number of times before buying the boots which later saved her toes from frostbite.

'It's not a pleasurable experience,' Debbie had said, 'but it's certainly an experience.'

Not wanting to forgo an experience of any sort, I found that I just had time to squeeze in a visit to the market before returning to Nairobi. Although Debbie had warned me about the scrum, I wasn't prepared to find 10,000-plus Mongolians, possibly a third of Ulan Bator's population, packed into the tiny square. One narrow hole-in-the-wall doubled as both entrance and exit, and to get in and out of the market during rush hour was a major undertaking. Unwittingly, I arrived at peak time. Having established with four black leather-jacketed Mongolian townies that I was attempting to move forwards and not backwards, I hooked on to two of them and allowed myself to be propelled through the wall. Once inside the market, the only available option was to rotate clockwise around the square with the human flow. A few fortunates had found space to spread cheap trinkets on the ground near the wall, but towards the centre of the square, vendors were forced to stand their ground while waving their goods above their heads. I was swept helplessly past knife-sellers, hat-sellers, boot-sellers, pot-sellers, sellers of gazelle skins, dog skins and even the skins of the highly endangered snow-leopard. The joys of the free market economy had clearly broken out all over. A man holding out a round, grey rock tried to pass it off as a dinosaur's egg. There were no market rules and not an official in sight. It was a pickpockets' paradise, but as the average Mongolian's standard of living is not high, there must have been meagre pickings in the pockets.

The human coil spiralled on. It was impossible to move in any direction other than that of the mob. When a circuit of the square was completed, the battle to escape began. But if that struggle against the surge of new arrivals was lost, then another circuit had to be made. I just managed to escape by locking arms with two old men wearing brightly coloured *dels* and 'pork pie' hats. Dressed in my old tweed jacket we must have made an extraordinary three-some, but respect for the 'old cloth', Mongolian and British, opened up a path before us. This market is definitely not a place for anyone prone to claustrophobia. As a permanent reminder of the experience I later discovered that the inside of my jacket pocket had been neatly slit with a sharp knife.

★ ★ ★

The following April, still wearing the same tweed jacket and with 19,000 dollars burning a hole in my trouser pocket, I was in the thick of another excited throng. Fortunately, we weren't heading in the same direction. They were pilgrims from Islamabad en route to Mecca and I was heading north, over the Hindu Kush to Urumqi, the capital of Xinjiang Province, where Professor Yuan was waiting for me. I'd managed to raise part of the Professor's monetary requirement and we had agreed in advance of my arrival that the expedition would have to be tailored accordingly.

My large old-fashioned Kenya canvas tent, sausage-shaped canvas kit-bag and khaki canvas hold-alls made me so overweight it was a joke. But the correct weight requirements did not bother Xinjiang Airways, which was to become my favourite airline. The tiresome requirement of one piece of hand luggage was also totally overlooked. In fact, my fellow Uighur passengers appeared to be unaware that the plane had a separate compartment for lug-gage. Every item of kit was 'hand luggage', and as a consequence aircraft seats were piled high with cardboard boxes, baskets wrapped in coloured cloth, carpets, bulging suitcases lashed with camel-hair rope, television sets, stereos and other glitzy electronic essentials of modern life. The distinctly Victorian look of my travelling kit, battered tweed jacket and green jungle hat stood out in contrast.

I supposed that it was on account of my rather eccentric appearance that I was given a seat at the front of the plane by the world-weary Chinese stewardess, whose expression showed quite clearly what she thought of my fellow passengers in general and the Uighur tribe in particular.

The man across the aisle had so much electronic gadgetry that he was forced to sit on the floor. Although there was a clearly signalled requirement to fasten seat-belts, no one appeared to take the slightest notice, least of all the stewardess. She was certainly not going to demonstrate how to fasten seat-belts when half the passengers were either sitting on top of their luggage or on the floor. And anyway, her nails needed attention.

'What do you do?' I asked the attractive girl who was seated beside me.

'I'm a Kazak model,' she replied with a bright smile. 'I'm on my way to Beijing. And you?'

'I'm looking for wild camels,' I said.

She gave another bright smile and turned to look out of the window. She must meet wild camel-spotters every day, I thought to myself. They must be as common in this part of the world as models from the Kazakhstan catwalk.

At this point, a member of the crew turned on pop music at something approaching full blast. As we took off, a Chinese female songstress moaned 'Love me baby' in a dreary monotone. It was a cloudless day. The snow-covered Himalayas glistened magnificently below us.

'K2, K2,' said the model excitedly as we flew past its towering peak.

As the mountains eventually gave way to the sand dunes of the Taklamakan I could hardly contain my excitement. The forbidding and forbidden deserts of Xinjiang that I had been given permission to enter sprawled endlessly in every direction. I recalled having read that the total landmass of these deserts was seven times the size of Sweden.

When our stewardess appeared with lunch boxes my companion asked for five. She then tipped her five-person lunch into a white plastic bag.

'Travelling in China very difficult,' she said with a laugh, noticing the amazed look on my face. 'Many delays, much waiting. This is my insurance policy against a future food shortage.'

The deserts finally gave way to the spectacular Tien Shan mountains, the backbone of Xinjiang, which almost bisect the province from east to west.

'You'll see Urumqi soon,' said the model, whose name I had now ascertained was Aisha. 'Not a good place. Very industrial. Too much smoke.'

The brilliant, clear sunlight which had high-lighted every snow-covered crevasse of the Tien Shan range abruptly turned to haze. As the plane started its descent I could make out, through the smog, the myriad of tall brick chimney stacks dotted haphazardly below us, trailing long fingers of black smoke.

'Much pollution in Urumqi,' exclaimed Aisha, at the same time patting her chest. 'People always have cough.'

The redoubtable Mildred Cable and Francesca French, travellers in Xinjiang in the early years of the century, had expressed these sentiments even more forcefully than my new-found Kazak friend.

The town has no beauty, no style, no dignity and no architectural interest. The climate is violent, exaggerated, and at no season pleasant. During the winter there are constant heavy snow-storms, but the snow must not be allowed to lie on the flat mud roofs, lest at the first thaw the water should leak into the houses. It is therefore shovelled wholesale into the streets, and trodden by the traffic to a hard, slippery surface, which makes walking extremely difficult for several months of the year. During the winter householders find it convenient to throw all sorts of rubbish into the street, where the constant falls of fresh snow cover up the garbage, but when the thaw sets in the mess is indescribable, and the town stinks. For one month of the spring, and one of the autumn, the mud-pits in the road are such that beasts are sometimes lost in them, and only the most athletic men can go on foot, as progress involves leaping from one stepping stone to another. The summer heat is even worse than the winter cold, and the dirty, dusty roadways are filled with jaded, unhealthy-looking people . . . For such reasons as these no one enjoys life in Urumchi [*sic*], no one leaves the town with regret, and it is full of people who are only there because they cannot get permission to leave and may not leave without permission.

Since the Communist government came to power, the roads have greatly improved and there is not as much rubbish in the streets. But the town is heavily polluted from the constant burning of low-grade coal, the people still look jaded, and the weather hasn't changed.

★ ★ ★

From time immemorial, Central Asia has been a theatre of war. Various people have fought over the immense areas which became known by the names of Dzungaria and Eastern Turkestan until united under the common name of Xinjiang ('new frontier'). In 1759 the area fell to China under Emperor Chien Lung. In 1867 the renowned conqueror Yakub Beg wrested the province from China and ruled Xinjiang from Kashgar. Nine years later China reconquered the province under the capable and energetic Tso Tsung-tang, and Yakub Beg committed suicide. Tso Tsung-tang's achievement was a great one. He had won by conquest over 1,250,000 square kilometres and his lines of communication were 2,500 kilometres long.

When China became a republic in 1911, Yang Tseng-sin, a mandarin of the old school, was appointed the Governor-General of Xinjiang and put down a number of rebellions in the province with energy and vigour.

During those early years of the century the last stage of 'the Great Game' between Russia and British-ruled India was being played out, and Xinjiang, strategically placed between Mongolia and the Himalayas, was an important buffer zone which, after the Russian revolution, the Russians might have conquered and incorporated into the USSR. The reason that they didn't was due to

Yang's vigilance, shrewdness and tact. He was murdered at a banquet in 1928 and his successor, Chin Shu-jen, a man of humble origins, provoked rebellion and war within Xinjiang by a mixture of misgovernment, greed and oppression. In five years he had crippled the province and left it desolated. He also broke all formal links with Beijing.

During this time the value of money fell swiftly, and the peasants were cruelly taxed and exploited by Chin's horde of ruffian soldiers, who created havoc. Discontent and lawlessness increased. Rebellion was in the air. The spark that set it off occurred in Hami, where a powerless Uighur king had reigned for three centuries. Chin abolished the monarchy and instituted an agricultural policy that confiscated the best farm lands from his followers. When a young tax-collector seduced an Uighur woman in Hami, rebellion broke out under the banner of Islam. Chin's hoodlum army suppressed the rebellion with a ferocious barbarity.

It was at this point that the leaders of the Uighurs and other Muslim minority groups appealed to a young Muslim Chinese General, Ma Chung-yin, to come to their aid. He collected about 500 men and, with incredible bravado, marched the great distance from Anhsi to Hami in the middle of a hot summer month through a waterless desert and with inadequate supplies. The conflicts raged throughout Xinjiang until, in January 1933, when the war was at its height, the Muslim Uighurs and the other tribal peoples who had joined them, attacked Urumqi, slaughtering every Chinese that they met on their way. Gates and doors were barricaded and, thanks to the soldierly qualities of some White Russian émigrés, the forces of Ma Chung-yin were repulsed. On 21 February they attacked again, and the next day savage fighting took place in the western suburbs of the city. No one was spared. Prisoners were tortured to death rather than shot, and 6,000 inhabitants of Urumqi were slaughtered. But the forces of Ma did not hold on to their conquest. Twenty-four hours later they were driven out of the city by reinforcements under the leadership of the White Russians. The Chinese later helped the Russians to oust Chin and, after this, Ma Chung-yin attacked Urumqi for a third time. Through the remainder of the 1930s and 1940s, instability, religious and racial tension, intrigue and terror was the sad plight of Urumqi and much of Xinjiang. Then, after the interlude of the Nationalist government, there was more savage fighting until the Communists came to power. Relative stability set in, even though the Cultural Revolution was carried through in Xinjiang with considerable severity.

With the break-up of the USSR and the rise in Islamic fundamentalism, Beijing has once again had to keep a wary eye on far-flung Xinjiang and intrigue in its capital, Urumqi.

The sights and smells of Urumqi airport were very different from those of Ulan Bator. Unsmiling officialdom stared unfeelingly as we struggled, like a defeated army, up a long flight of stairs with our boxes, cartons and canvas bags. There were no luggage trolleys and no assistance of any kind, and the stairs were designed to cause maximum inconvenience. When the top was eventually reached, the double-twist in the staircase ensured that the baggage that had been left behind was out of sight. This resulted in a madcap dash to the bottom to retrieve it before it disappeared, by which time the original consignment was lost to view. We were processed through China's back door by a seemingly endless army of young men and women, smartly-uniformed, steely-eyed look-alikes without a smile or a word of welcome. It was an hour-long struggle to enter China and, by the time the final scrutiny of visa, passport, luggage and camera was complete, I understood why the Kazak model had stowed away emergency rations.

'Why are you bringing 11,000 US dollars into China?'

The young girl with the white powdered face and bright red lips stared at me from under her peaked cap.

'I'm bringing it in to finance a scientific expedition.'

'Ah,' she nodded. 'Scientific. You are scientific?'

'Very,' I replied.

'How long are you scientific?'

'Six weeks.'

'Eleven thousand dollars for six weeks.'

'Yes,' I said unblinkingly. 'Many people. A team. Xinjiang Environmental Protection Institute.'

I showed her my letter of invitation. She showed it to her male colleague. He called his supervisor. They conferred, stared at me and conferred again. At last the girl raised her right arm. Crash went the official stamp of approval. I was in.

'Welcome, doctor, welcome.' Professor Yuan pumped my arm up and down enthusiastically. 'This is my son Xiao Yuan, and expedition member Mr Li.' I shook hands. They grabbed my luggage and propelled me towards a Chinese jeep.

'This way, doctor, please.'

'Not doctor. I'm not a doctor.'

Professor Yuan affected not to hear or understand.

'Ha, ha. Much luggage, doctor.'

Driver Song was seated at the wheel of the jeep dressed in a crisp white shirt and finely creased blue cotton trousers. He drew heavily on a cigarette and stared at my kit disdainfully as it was stowed in the back of the vehicle. Then he dusted the front passenger seat with a flowered, yellow cloth. I climbed in and we drove off into Beijing Road North.

Beijing Road North runs from the centre of Urumqi to the north of the city for over fifteen kilometres. A wide dual carriageway, poplar-lined, this thoroughfare is flanked by crumbling, rectangular concrete office blocks and row upon row of mud-brick, blue and white tile-covered shops and eating-houses. Much of this 1950s-style architecture is rapidly giving way to new high-rise development, fuelled, even in this remote corner of north-west China, by the changes wrought by the market economy. A chest-restricting mixture of coal-smoke and cheap petrol fumes casts a hazy pall over Beijing Road North and its environs. The sunlight is constantly filtered, the sky seldom blue and soot clogs every crack and crevice, covering old and new buildings alike with smears of black grime.

The Xinjiang Environmental Protection Institute, a purpose-built secretariat, flanks one side of a large courtyard just off Beijing Road North. Blocks of flats for Institute staff line the north and south sides of the courtyard, their dimensions varying according to the status of the occupant. Beyond a decaying brick wall to the east of the square lies the Scientific Academic Hotel that had been constructed to house visiting scientists and officials. Purpose-built to a standard design, it has three floors and three types of accommodation: VIP, with bathroom; semi-VIP, without bathroom; and basic, four iron beds to a room with metal bowl. Hot water for all categories runs from 9.00 p.m. to 11.00 p.m. – if the coal-fired boiler is working. Otherwise, hot water in thermos flasks is provided for either drinking tea or washing off the grime. Paper from communal lavatories must be placed in a wire basket, not flushed down the squat, and a notice proclaims that 'no water must be thrown into the corridor'. Each floor is controlled by three girls who try to ensure that these and other rules are strictly obeyed. I landed up in semi-VIP without bathroom because, as the Professor pointed out, 'The budget is tight. You only brought 11,000 dollars.'

That evening, Mr Zhao Ziyung, chain-smoking zoologist, ex wild-camel hunter, self-proclaimed exterminator of the last Przhevalsky wild horse, gold medal-winner as 'the ninth all-time explorer of China', and our expedition guide, came to my room with Professor Yuan.

Zhao, in his early sixties, had dyed black hair, knowing eyes, a lop-sided grin and a surprisingly soft handshake. He was wearing a gabardine raincoat and his flies were done up on the wrong buttons, causing his trousers to bunch at the top. The thick woollen sweater underneath the raincoat had holes in both elbows. He appeared to me to be a clever, likeable rascal, a survivor who had lived off his wits, dodging and twisting through the turbulence of the last three decades. Unfortunately, his father was dying, and after leading us through the Gashun Gobi he would have to return to Urumqi.

'Lao [old] Zhao is the only person in the whole of China who can take us through the Gashun Gobi. I wouldn't consider attempting it without Lao Zhao.'

Professor Yuan clearly had a great respect for Zhao, who was busy lighting up his second cigarette. I expressed my gratitude, Zhao gave a little bow, a half-smile and the two of them left the room.

The following morning the Professor, anxious to convert my dollars into local currency, took me to the Bank of China Central Branch, situated in the centre of the old city. But the old city, with its surrounding wall and massive wooden gates that had been repeatedly stormed by General Ma Chung-yin in the 1930s, had long since been demolished. Not a single building pre-dating the arrival of the Communists in the 1950s remained standing.

Outside the bank, a posse of acquisitive, wicked-looking Uighur money-changers looked hopefully at us as we entered the building at a trot. We climbed up a metallic silver staircase, squeezed into a narrow booth and waited patiently while an impassive girl, barely out of her teens, did her sums on a calculus. The calculus click-clacked, calculations were checked and rechecked, wafer-thin paper receipts were stamped. A supervisor stamped them again. Forty minutes later the girl, unsmiling and unimpressed, handed over packet upon packet of pristine bank notes through a narrow hole in the wall. Perspiration gathered on our brows as, mindful of the Uighur traders outside the bank, we stuffed bundle after bundle into our bulging pockets. We didn't have to tell each other to run. Sprinting back down the slippery staircase we pushed aside the heavy, finger-stained, quilt door cover and sped past the avaricious upturned faces of the money-changers.

Driver Song, cigarette in mouth, was waiting for us not far away, nonchalantly flicking at imaginary specks of dust on the bonnet of his car with a large yellow duster. He was wearing a different outfit, a natty, bright blue shirt and immaculately creased cream trousers. I hadn't quite fathomed Driver Song. He seemed much too pretty, precious and pleased with himself to be driving us across the world's most formidable desert. I felt safe in the hands of Zhao, but something about Song didn't give me the same sense of security. I clambered through the open door of the jeep, half expecting to feel the needle-sharp point of a Uighur knife in the small of my back.

'Too little money,' Professor Yuan commented when he had recovered his breath.

'Too little?'

He gave a long sigh. 'Too little for six weeks. We can only take one jeep, not two. Not enough money.'

I bit my lip. It had been difficult enough getting the $11,000 out of UNEP. The Professor had known how much I was bringing. I am afraid that at this point I didn't care whether we took an extra jeep. I didn't want to know.

'I'll call you at 7.00 p.m.' said Professor Yuan as he dropped me off at the hotel. 'Mr Xie Zhiqiang, Assistant Chief of the Environmental Protection Institute, is giving us a farewell dinner before we set off tomorrow.'

I took a bath Africa-style, in a red plastic bucket filled with water from the thermos. At 7.00 p.m. precisely the Professor knocked on my door.

Driver Song whisked us down to the centre of the city and dropped us outside a blue and white tiled building, festooned with a string of coloured lights and vertical yellow banners. We entered the restaurant through heavy red curtains and were ushered by a nervous, heavily made-up girl in a bright red cheong-sam to a room where a large circular table had been set for twelve. Mr Xie, a man of middle height and intelligent eyes, was there to greet us. Laughter lines etched into the corner of his eyes indicated a sense of humour. Lines round the corners of his mouth indicated much tougher aspects of his character.

'Was the old government *yamen* [office] near here?' I asked Mr Xie, using the Professor's son Xiao Yuan as an interpreter.

Mr Xie looked at me with a half-smile. 'Now, why do you want to know that?' he asked.

'I believe that a former Governor of Urumqi, General Yang Tseng-sin, had an unusual method of entertaining his guests in the old *yamen*,' I replied.

Mr Xie's eyes twinkled and he said something in Chinese to Professor Yuan. Turning back towards me he exclaimed with a laugh, 'Don't worry, we're not going to cut your head off during the meal.'

He was referring to the notorious occasion in 1916 when General Yang had invited to a banquet all those whom he suspected of plotting to overthrow him. When they were full of drink, he left the hall for a moment and returned followed by a soldier. While the band played on outside, he ordered the soldier to behead them one by one. Twelve years later the Chinese proverb, 'He who murders at a feast, shall have his own blood shed at a feast', was fulfilled. In 1928, the General was shot dead by his Minister of Foreign Affairs, Fan Yao-nan, while proposing a toast to a Soviet official at a banquet held after the Russian Language School's graduation ceremony.

'I'm sure you're not,' I replied mischievously. 'I just thought that one had to be careful when dining out in Urumqi.'

'In old China, yes, in new China, no,' said Mr Xie, bringing the conversation to an abrupt conclusion. 'The old government *yamen* was next door,' he added quietly.

The meal proceeded as Chinese banquets tend to, with numerous toasts in *maotai*, a powerful spirit that makes an excellent substitute for methylated spirits, while course after varied course was placed on the table. Steaming dishes of soup, mutton, beef, chicken, duck, fish, prawns and vegetables of every description followed each other in quick succession. A long, white fleshy object, delicately sliced into the shape of a flower which looked and tasted like a bicycle inner tube intrigued me.

'What is this?' I inquired of Xiao Yuan as I proudly held it up neatly in my chopsticks.

'A bull's penis,' he whispered. 'A great delicacy.'

Quick-witted Mr Xie caught my eye and told Xiao Yuan to tell me that it would build me up before we entered the Gashun Gobi.

When I thought this gargantuan meal had finally come to an end, a burner linked to a gas cylinder was placed on the table. A bubbling dish was placed on top of it, and the guest of honour was invited to make the first move. Xiao Yuan murmured that I was highly honoured. It was dog.

Muttering a huge apology to all the varied and beloved bitches called Sally that I had kept over the years, I fished in the bowl with my chopsticks and pulled out a tiny hind leg. How it stayed inside me until I returned to the hotel I do not know. I willed it away most of the night.

* * *

The next day we left Urumqi in a steady downpour. Our second vehicle, which looked to my unmechanical eye distinctly dodgy, was a wooden-sided truck with two bald tyres clearly hired at cut-price in the name of cost-cutting. Besides carrying all our food, water, petrol, tents and other kit, it also carried Mr Li. I was told that Mr Li was accompanying us in his capacity as a senior botanist. He was of medium height, with a long, angular face and narrow clever eyes which glinted behind thick spectacle lenses. He had a good knowledge of German having studied in the former East Germany. Goodness knows what subject he studied there. I doubt if it was botany, because I subsequently discovered that his knowledge of desert plants and vegetation was minimal. The Professor frequently deferred to him and I sensed that he had seniority in the Party structure. Maybe he had been sent along to keep an eye on us. Once when I handed him a miniature icon that a Russian had given me to keep me safe in the Gobi, he threw it angrily on the ground. 'You shouldn't believe in such rubbish,' he said, in a manner which suggested that he was used to keeping deviants on track. The driver of the truck, an inveterate hawker and spitter, was a solid, square-shaped, horny-handed toiler of few words called Xiao Kegang. I later discovered that he was also a remarkable chess player, who frequently outwitted the intelligent Mr Li.

As we left the city, the unrelenting rain turned the mud on either side of the road to thick black sludge. Mud-brick Uighur slums, enveloped in a thick haze of industrial smog, were surrounded by acres of sodden litter. Some of these slum houses had been demolished and rusty, broken window frames and doors were piled up for sale by the side of the road. Strips of plastic sheeting used by farmers to protect their seedlings from late frost festooned the way-side poplar trees.

We stopped for lunch at a truck drivers' café which nestled snugly beside three or four competitors in a long, rectangular single-storey construction covered with party slogans and white lavatory tiles. Driver Song, who was clearly as fastidious about his food as he was about the cleanliness of his jeep, chose the meal. His finicky nature didn't extend to his table manners, and he swept his discarded bones and unwanted food off the table and on to the floor in true Chinese style. However, when I unwittingly blew my nose into a red and white spotted handkerchief and returned it to my pocket he curled up his nose in disgust.

The Turfan depression lies in a hollow, the lowest part of which is claimed to be the deepest dry depression in the world. It was from this depression, 380 kilometres from Urumqi, that we intended to drive south through salt marshes into the utterly barren wilderness of the Gashun Gobi to search for the last genetically pure herds of wild camels. North of the Turfan depression, the snow-capped peaks of Bogd Ola (Mount of God) tower to heights of over 7,600 metres and mark the highest part of the Tien Shan mountains. In the centre of these uncompromising surroundings, Turfan city and its surrounding villages lie on a fertile island in a wilderness of sand, its edges lapped by grit and gravel and harassed by sand storms of incredible ferocity. This division between arid desert and fruitful land is as defined as that between shore and ocean.

The fertility is due to a remarkable irrigation technique known as the *karez* system. Long lines of earthworks stretch across the wastes of Turfan as though thrown up by giant moles. The mounds are hollow in the centre, and this opening leads down to an underground passage. Far below is a water-channel which conducts the melted mountain snows to the torrid fields which are waiting to be irrigated. The nearer to the mountains, the deeper is the *karez*, and at its start the water may be fifteen metres below the surface. At its final opening it flows almost at ground level and is as cool as when it left the hills. We passed a *karez* undergoing repair. Four men were working under a mound, excavating spoil which a donkey was hauling out on a pulley system. The expense of caring for the *karez* system is heavy, but Turfan produces such a phenomenal crop of fruit, grapes, raisins, grain and cotton that the time and expense appear to be justified.

The Gashun Gobi, stretching to the south and east of the Kuruk Tagh mountains south of Turfan, is one of the most hostile and forbidding regions on Earth. Freezing cold in winter and overwhelmingly hot in summer, in the spring and autumn it is blasted by sand storms which have been known to strip the paint from a vehicle. An aerial view of this desert would show a burning arid waste of dunes and multi-coloured rocky outcrops, interspersed with monotonous rolling expanses of gravel and crossed by occasional ridges of high mountains whose foothills dwindle to low rocky mounds. The whole of this stone desert is shadeless and exposed to scorching heat under a merciless sun. At night it is quite the opposite, and as darkness falls, the scorching heat gives way to a sudden chill which rises from the ground and strikes with a cold impact, leaving a warm upper stratum of air. Soon, this layer, too, is permeated by the penetrating chill.

In some areas of the Gashun Gobi that can still sustain life, an assortment of small animals such as gerbils, jerboas and insects emerge from their hiding places as soon as night falls. All through the hours of heat, they sleep in a tunnelled world underground, the openings to which are frequently to be found on the sheltered side of many a tiny sand-mound, blown up round the foot of a tuft of low bush or scrub. During the night, these creatures move ceaselessly, silently and invisibly over the sand. After sunrise, the sand is left patterned with all kinds of tracks left by these rodents, and various insects which scuttle underground as the sun rises. But this occurs in increasingly fewer areas, because as the winds become stronger, the Gobi becomes drier and even the smallest life-forms are forced to retreat.

Many people have entered this desert never to return. The more recent include Professor Penjiamu from the Xinjiang Research Academy, who vanished without trace on 17 June 1980, and five miners on an illegal quest for crystal, who disappeared with their vehicle in July 1990. In June 1996, a Chinese 'explorer' following our tracks to the ancient city of Lou Lan died of dehydration.

We soon discovered that the Gashun Gobi makes the Mongolian Gobi seem tame by comparison. There are no tracks through this

vast desert and, in some places, no vegetation or animal life what-
soever. It encompasses the famous wandering lake of Lop Nur
which has now been rendered totally dry due to up-river dams on
the river Tarim some 800 kilometres to the west. The Tarim car-
ries the melted snows from the Pamirs and other Central Asian
mountain ranges and brings life to parts of the barren deserts of
Xinjiang.

Lop Nur will always be associated with the great Swedish
explorer Sven Hedin. For 1,600 years the lake had lain in two separate depressions to the north-east of Charkhlick (Ruoqiang), and
had been revealed to the outside world by the Russian explorer
Colonel Nikolai Mikhailovich Przhevalsky in 1876. He discovered
that the Tarim river, instead of flowing due east, turned off to the
south-east to form, in the southern part of the desert, a double
lake, situated one geographical degree south of the place marked
from ancient times on Chinese maps as Lop Nur.

Przhevalsky's discovery created an extraordinary sensation in the
geographical world. When the first telegram containing his story
was flashed around the world, the geographer Dr E. Behm wrote,
'So at last the darkness which surrounded Lop Nur is put to flight,
and we shall soon see the lake on the maps as it really is. But who
could have guessed that there was a high mountain range [the
Arjin Shan] to the south of it? Our ideas of the Gobi desert are
about to be revolutionised.'

But it was Hedin who was responsible for the ultimate revolution
in ideas. In 1900 he walked to Tomenpu, a junction point on the
Konche Daria, a tributary of the Tarim, and discovered that an
ancient river-bed led off it to the east. Using camels as pack animals,
he followed this dry river-bed, which the Uighurs called the Kuruk
Daria or 'dry river', for over 500 kilometres, until he suddenly
came across the abandoned ancient city of Lou Lan, which had formerly been an important staging point on the middle Silk Road.
He returned to Lou Lan in 1901 and carried out a survey to the
south of the old city, where he discovered a huge dried-up lake site.
He concluded from these discoveries that, in about AD 330, there
had been a revolution in the course of the Tarim and subsequently

in the position of Lop Nur. After having flowed to the east for many centuries and formed its terminal lake in the northern part of the desert, the lower Tarim, or the part of it called the Kuruk Daria, had left its old bed and broken a new course for itself through the desert to the south-east where, in the southern part of the Gashun Gobi, it formed two new lakes. It was these lakes that Przhevalsky had discovered. At the same time, the old river course and lake dried up, and the town of Lou Lan was abandoned by its inhabitants and consigned to oblivion.

Marco Polo, who crossed the Desert of Lop to the south of the lake in 1274, had no idea either that the lake existed or that it moved from north to south. He was using the southern Silk Road, as the middle Silk Road through Lou Lan had long since been abandoned. And what is stranger, neither in ancient nor modern times did the Chinese realise that the lake that had been known 2,000 years earlier under the name of the Pu-chang Sea, alternated over a period of time from one lake bed to another.

Hedin concluded that the lake swung like the pendulum of a clock approximately every 1,600 years as each tributary in turn became silted up by the winds, desert sands and decomposing animal and vegetable remains. As the filling-up process was going on in the south, the arid desert regions to the north were being eaten away by the extraordinarily violent east-north-easterly storms, and while the level of the ground in the northern parts of the Gashun Gobi was falling, the bottom of the southern lake rose and became higher and higher.

The ultimate effect of this alternation between north and south is that the river and lake must eventually return to their old, previously dry beds. In 1901 Hedin predicted: 'In the light of the knowledge we now possess of the levels that exist in the Lop desert, it is not too daring to affirm that the river *must* some day go back to the Kuruk Daria . . . It is only a question of time when the country round about the lower Tarim will become so full of alluvium that the river will be forced to return to its northern bed.'

It is seldom given to a man that an improbable theory that he formulates is proven in his lifetime, but in 1921, the same year that

Baron Ungern-Sternberg was ravaging Mongolia, the Kuruk Daria suddenly filled with water. The Kuruk Daria which flowed to the then Lop Nur silted up and Hedin's pendulum swung, just as he had predicted it would. He was naturally overwhelmed, and in 1934 at the age of sixty-five he returned to Xinjiang and canoed down the now rapidly flowing Kuruk Daria river. He sailed into the newly formed Lop Nur, caught fish there, shot wild boar on its shores and predicted that the area would be the new grain basket of Central Asia. He even foresaw the revival of Lou Lan as a great Central Asian trading centre, fed by a road and, possibly, a railway:

> When the river and lake moved south about AD 330, the Silk Road had been cut, Lou Lan abandoned and forgotten. Now the water had come back into its old beds and new prospects of historic significance were unrolled before our eyes. Drought, the silence of death and oblivion had enveloped this region for sixteen centuries, but now it had suddenly come to life again, and it was reserved for our expedition to fasten together the links in the chain. Behind lay the 2,000 years in which Lop Nur had been known to the Chinese, and before – we grew dizzy at the thought of the countless shadowy years to come in which new arteries of communication – motor roads, railways, strategic roads – would be created in the heart of Asia, and new posts and towns would grow up in the desert region which for 1,600 years had been so poor that it could not provide a home even for scorpions and lizards. Only the wild camels had now and then wandered into it from their salt springs in the Kuruk Tagh – but now, when the water returned and men were approaching, these wandering ships of the desert would see with consternation the frontiers of their ancient sanctuary curtailed and withdrawn.

What Sven Hedin could not predict was the development of the nuclear bomb. Nor could he have foreseen that the Chinese would select the Kuruk Tagh mountain range and the Lop Nur area as their nuclear testing site. Nor could he have known that, because of this, the river Tarim would be dammed many kilometres away upstream for irrigation projects, out of the range of the testing area.

In 1976 the Kuruk Daria dried up once again after its brief awakening from its 1,600-year-old sleep. There was no rebirth of Lou Lan ancient city, though. Both the new and the old Lop Nur have disappeared, and the prophecy of a green hinterland has come to naught.

Following in the footsteps of Sven Hedin, our expedition found Lop Nur surrounded once again by 'drought and the silence of death'. The fish had long since disappeared and the wild boar had fled. The Kuruk Daria river was totally dry and the poplar trees that had flourished along its banks for the brief space of fifty years were withered and dead. It was a total reversion to Hedin's memory of the river as he first saw it at the turn of the century:

> I recalled in memory the aspect of the river-bed, broad, deep and winding, but dried up, with the dead timber on the banks. There stood the trees like tombstones in a cemetery, grey, split, dead for 1,600 years, and as brittle as though made of clay. No life, not a drop of water in that bed, where a mighty river once ran and the desert wind murmured in the summits of leafy poplars.

Paradoxically, the only beneficiary of this geographical upheaval is that mysterious 'wandering ship of the desert', the wild Bactrian camel. For had the desert bloomed, the camel would have been driven away from the area and hunted out of existence.

There is no fresh water in the Gashun Gobi, only salt springs. No humans, not even the hardy nomad, can survive in this utterly barren area of over 1,750 square kilometres. The only inhabitant of this huge space is the wild Bactrian camel. Far removed from contact with domestic Bactrians and fully adapted to drinking salt water, the camels migrate from water point to water point, some of which are over 100 kilometres apart.

It was dusk when we arrived at the village of Tikar, situated on the very edge of the fertile area of the Turfan depression. The setting sun, a bright red ball suspended behind a dust haze, gave the village an insubstantial and ghostly appearance. Horse-drawn carts clip-clopped down metalled streets. The large, mud houses looked prosperous and well-maintained. Many sported tall, newly-constructed, wooden, double-entrance doors. The source of this obvious prosperity, the grape, grew everywhere. In the hazy light the fresh green leaves of the vines could be seen thriving in small irrigated plots all around the village. Through open doors they could be spotted growing in the courtyards of houses, providing welcome shade for their owners as well as a source of income. An exquisite, delicate perfume from the flowering vines hung in the dusty, evening air. The contrast with the dead uniformity of the grey, shoddy blocks of flats in Urumqi and the polluted environment along the main road that we had recently followed could not have been sharper.

Every kind of vine flourishes in Turfan, but the most prolific produce is a small, sweet, seedless variety of grape. It is also the best fruit for export, and Turfan raisins are eaten throughout the whole of north and central China. These celebrated vines are cultivated with short trunks and very long branches which stretch outward in all directions around the houses, supported by upright posts.

Near each house in Tikar was a spacious building, the walls of which were made with sun-dried bricks laid so as to form a lattice-work which allows the wind to blow through. These are known as *chung-chi*, or grape-drying halls, and are only in use for a few weeks in each year. During that short time they are full of branched poles, hung over with thousands of bunches of the seedless grapes. The passage of the sun-heated air through the lattice work is all that is necessary to dry the fruit. If the bunches were exposed to the direct action of the sun, both the colour and flavour would be spoilt. The dreaded scorching wind which sweeps across the depression is exactly right for the drying process, and a week or ten days completes it.

During the long summer months, Tikar and the surrounding area form one of the hottest places on Earth, when the temperature can reach fifty-five degrees centigrade in the shade. Between

May and August many of the inhabitants retire underground, even though their houses have long verandas and spacious, airy rooms. In most of their interior courtyards, there is an opening which leads by a flight of steps to a deep dug-out or underground apartment. Here are comfortable rooms and a *kang,* the raised bed or sitting area constructed from mud which can be heated from underneath by charcoal, wood or dried animal dung during the freezing winter months. Many people eat and sleep underground in the very hot weather and only emerge at sunset. These underground chambers are not healthy as there is little or no ventilation, and the sudden chill of a dug-out on a perspiring body can result in fever.

The Uighur people have inhabited northern Xinjiang for centuries, and during the time of Genghis Khan the area was known as Uighurstan. They are not nomadic and have settled the area as farmers, traders and merchants. They outnumber the Chinese in Xinjiang and the province has officially recognised this by granting parity of their language with Chinese, and calling the province the Uighur Autonomous Region. The Uighurs do not, however, have parity of political power. In the village of Aksupe, which we were to visit much later, a young Chinese village head was elected from among five candidates, all Chinese, who had been put forward by the provincial government. He, poor man, could not speak Uighur and felt very isolated.

In the days of Sven Hedin, the people had enjoyed greater local autonomy and were overseen by Uighur village heads, called *Begs.* Today, the provincial and central governments keep a wary eye on the Uighurs lest the recently independent states to the west, such as Kazakhstan, which have broken away from the former Soviet Union, give the Uighur people similar separatist ideas. Islamic fundamentalism is another powerful underground force for potential discord which is carefully monitored by the vigilant authorities.

Tikar, which translates as 'last prayer', is the last human settlement reached before the Gashun Gobi. In the 1960s, many of its present Uighur inhabitants had been moved 500 kilometres from Sringar when it was taken over as the nuclear test site. Zhao had friends in Tikar, and it was possible that descendants of the guides recruited in Sringar by Sven Hedin were among them. The Tikar people had in the past shot wild camels, and I was keen to discover whether they had abandoned their traditional winter sport.

Lao Zhao took us to the house of his friend, Torde Ahun. A portly man of about sixty, wearing a black and white skull cap and a traditional Uighur cloak, he led us courteously into his palatial house. We all squatted on his large *kang*, which was covered with colourful locally-woven rugs.

'When I first came here they could only afford grass mats,' said Zhao with a throaty laugh. 'Just look at them now, they're all very rich.'

Giggling, fresh-faced, round-eyed girls of all heights and ages, wearing headscarves, long shifts and thick sagging stockings, peered at us from behind an open door. They were pretty, almost European in appearance and would have passed unnoticed anywhere in Central Europe. Egging each other on, the more daring among them sidled into dark recesses in the room, their drooping stockings indicating a huge untapped market for suspenders. They stared at us (and especially me) as we tucked into chicken, mutton, rice, nan bread and tomatoes. We chopsticked our way through as much of this as we could until, finally replete, we sprawled out on the *kang* to sleep.

Next morning, to everybody's delight, we discovered that Torde Ahun's grandfather was Ordek, Sven Hedin's famous guide. It was Ordek who, in March 1900, had been sent off with a horse into the desert by Hedin to retrieve their only spade, which he had left behind. A sandstorm sprang up and Ordek lost his way. As he stumbled about in the vast wilderness to the west of the dried-up lake of Lop Nur, he came across a clay tower, and the ruins of a number of houses containing some beautifully carved wooden boards which lay half-buried in the sand. Ordek had made the momentous discovery of the ancient city of Lou Lan, which had been abandoned for over 1,600 years. He somehow managed to catch up with Hedin's caravan. Hedin immediately realised the significance of Ordek's discovery and the value of Ordek himself, for he later commented cryptically, 'He did not give up until he had found the spade.'

We were later introduced to Torde's relative Sadiq, a nephew of one of Hedin's boatmen on the 1934 expedition. Sadiq, a quiet, earnest Muslim whose ambition was to make the pilgrimage to Mecca, was quite overwhelmed when I managed to show him a photocopy of a sketch made by Hedin of his uncle. The end result was much mutual back-slapping, hilarity and numerous group photographs.

Sadiq, however, had another claim to fame. He had been fined 20,000 Yuan ($2,000) in 1994 for shooting a wild camel in the Gashun Gobi. It emerged later that our guide Zhao was treated as a local hero in Tikar because he had caught two young wild camels in the Gashun Gobi in 1972 and brought them out alive – an incredibly difficult thing to do. One of them, a male, is still alive in Beijing Zoo. What else, I wondered, had this man done?

This interlude with the Uighurs of Tikar had delayed our departure, and it was nearly midday before we finally left the village. As soon as we did so the scenery changed dramatically. We entered a vast, empty bowl of grey dust which rapidly turned into a sterile area desolate beyond belief; an area in which no mammal, bird, insect or isolated pocket of vegetation survived. I then realised the significance to the Uighur people of the remarkable *karez* irrigation system, for without it, life was unsustainable in the Turfan depression.

But although the dust bowl through which we passed was devoid of permanent life, trucks and tractors still ploughed a track through it from north to south. Eighty kilometres to the south of Tikar, twelve iron-ore mines were working and vehicles returned to Turfan laden with iron-ore. But once we had passed the mines, we were completely on our own in those totally dead surroundings. We headed for the Kuruk Tagh mountains, the northern boundary of the habitat of the wild camel and, in more recent times, the Chinese nuclear testing area.

After driving 226 kilometres we came to Wanwan Quan oasis, surrounded by mountains which glowed rust-red in the evening light. This was the Katara Tagh or Red Mountain range. We were at last back in a land of the living and, near the oasis salt spring, we saw seven goitered gazelles and picked up wild camel droppings. Lao Zhao led us into a nearby valley, where we stopped and pitched camp on a stony ridge in the middle of a dry river-bed. No sooner had we done so than, to our amazement, two men appeared out of nowhere pushing a hand-cart. Apparently they had been asked to guard some illegal mining equipment deep in the Kuruk Tagh mountains. For forty days they had sat there, terrified by wolves and the lost spirits of the dead that (as they believe) haunt the Gobi until, verging on starvation, they had decided to walk back to the iron-ore mines in the hope that they would pick up a lift to Turfan. One of the men had a graveyard cough which I attempted to dose with precious whisky. As they pushed their rickety hand-cart slowly away from our camp, I wondered how they could possibly survive the crossing of the terrible landscape that lay ahead of them.

The evening was cold and the night was colder. The temperature dropped to minus four degrees centigrade, and I shivered in my lightweight Kenyan sleeping-bag until, unable to sleep, I wandered out of my tent. The sky was clear and the dry desert air had become a beautiful backdrop for countless glittering stars stretching from one horizon to another. The Milky Way was not the whitish haze seen in western skies, but looked like a phosphorescent shower of myriad spots of light. Desert travellers become great star-gazers and, when dust is not obscuring the view, can look out over an uninterrupted line of cloudless, horizontal skies. When the moon rises, the desert takes on its most captivating appearance, the austere outlines of rock and mountain are softened and the harshest formations become invested with a subtle charm. A full moon can turn a barren wilderness into a world of dreams. I fervently hoped that this magic scene was not heightened in its subtle intensity by the glow of excessive radiation.

4

Yonder is the Gate of Hell

With coarse food to eat, water to drink, and the bended arm as a pillow, happiness may still exist

Chinese proverb

'Boots, Lao Zhao. That's what I don't understand. Why did he leave his boots?'

Zhao shrugged and gave a half-smile. We were standing in a hunters' hide, hollowed out of a sand dune and cleverly angled so that it covered the western approaches to the Karwa Bulak salt spring. A number of well-defined camel tracks trailed away in a westerly direction to inhospitable stone desert and clusters of jagged hills sprinkled with multi-coloured pebbles glinting in the afternoon sunshine.

Zhao had just unearthed a pair of lace-up boots, torch batteries and a whip, as well as the lower jaw-bones of two adult wild camels. The hunter's stay had all too clearly been a profitable one.

'Maybe his feet became so hot that he had to take his boots off,' said Xiao Yuan with a laugh.

'What do you mean?' I asked. 'I thought the Uighurs hunted during the winter.'

Xiao Yuan pointed to a pile of burnt-out charcoal. 'They do, but first the hunter digs a hole in the sand, fills it with charcoal, sets the charcoal alight, covers it with sheet metal and then lies down, gun in hand, waiting until a camel wanders out of the desert to drink.'

'There's not much chance of a miss,' I commented. 'The camel's a sitting target.'

'Sure, even I could shoot it,' said Xiao Yuan, somewhat too enthusiastically.

I recalled the barren country that we'd driven through over the last four days – the dry, sheer-sided, rust-coloured slopes of the Kuruk Tagh mountains, riven with gullies, that we'd explored one by one in a fruitless search for wild camel. I again had the sobering thought that this area, the westernmost boundary of the wild camels' habitat, was only thirty kilometres north-west of the Chinese underground nuclear test site, where wits and cynics had advised us to look out for the three-humped camel. I relived a vision of the seemingly endless expanse of pebble-strewn desert that we'd crossed as we headed south-west, and the wild, isolated mountain range that had been criss-crossed with camel tracks. I remembered the excitement that we had all experienced when we found a hollowed outline in the sand covered with fresh droppings, indicating where a camel had recently rested, and the subsequent fruitless six hours spent tracking that wandering, lone bull camel. I thought back to one camp pitched in a dry, waterless gully, and to another on a pebble-strewn, rust-coloured slope exposed to a cold, westerly wind. During all those daylight hours, travelling on foot or by jeep, we had not seen a single water-point, fresh or salt. And now, having finally reached this slushy, salt-encrusted oasis surrounded by tufts of dry *fragmitis* grass and ageing tamarisk bushes, we found this cruel evidence of hunting.

I turned away from Lao Zhao's all too obvious endorsement of the camel hunter's skills. The tracks of a donkey cart were clearly defined in the sand and I followed them down to the edge of the spring, where Professor Yuan was ferreting about in a tamarisk bush looking for evidence of wild camels. I stood for a moment, suppressing emotions of sadness and despair that my Chinese colleagues seemed incapable of understanding.

My reverie was abruptly terminated. Something hostile was

crawling up my leg. I looked down and saw a multitude of menacing ticks advancing towards me across the salt-encrusted sand from every direction. As I backed away the ticks changed course, following the vibrations set up by my feet.

I ran back to the sand dune. Lao Zhao roared with laughter and pointed meaningfully at his groin. Hastily dropping my trousers I picked off two fat invaders, hooked heads poised, just before they had a chance to bury their mandibles in a warm, moist part of my body. They were large, much larger than any tick that I'd ever seen. In comparison to the little pepper tick of the African plains, they were enormous.

'That's why we wear these,' said Xiao Yuan, rolling up a trouser leg to reveal a pair of woolly long-johns. 'Tick protection as well as cold prevention.'

Lao Zhao held up a lighted cigarette and cheerfully indicated that he would happily perform a de-ticking operation with a glowing fag-end should I require it.

'Lao Zhao says that it's a good thing that ticks only like salt water and that they can't survive in the rest of the Gobi. Otherwise, we'd all be smoking fifty cigarettes a day.'

So the poor wretched camel has to endure ticks as well, I thought grimly. After a possible 100-kilometre trek to find water it eventually arrives at an unappetising salt spring. More often than not it will then have to break through a hard, salty crust before it can slurp up unpalatable slush. While doing this it has to withstand an invasion by bloodthirsty ticks whose life-cycle depends on the camel's arrival. If the animal's luck has really run out, it will be shot by an equally bloodthirsty Uighur hunter lying on a hot bed of charcoal. Some life. The Mongolian Gobi with its freshwater springs and freedom from hunters was a paradise in comparison.

We drove on past a low line of spectacular hills, glowing black and deep orange in the fading light. The ground all around them was littered with small pebbles of a similar colour. Stones in the Gobi can be found in a host of colours: rose pink, lime green, peach, lilac, dark red and a deep jet-black which, burnished by sun, wind and sand, seems to have been polished with a shoe brush.

One of the most startling tints on many of the hills is rust, and there are high jagged peaks of a green shade that seem, from a distance, to be overgrown with lichen. Other hills are covered with chips of white, as though a miraculous snow storm had dusted them with powdered snow. Under a bright blue sky, these strange formations of rock and stone give the impression of a gigantic coloured rock garden.

That evening we camped on an exposed and windy ridge. As the wind howled around our sagging, heavy-duty white canvas kitchen tent in an atmosphere thick with cigarette smoke, I taught some of the team pontoon. The gambling instinct of the Chinese, long suppressed under Communism, blossomed in these unlikely surroundings and the boiled sweets staked changed hands at an alarming rate. In one corner of the tent, studiously ignoring the gamblers' shouts of triumph or despair, the Professor sat humming to himself, swaying rhythmically backwards and forwards. In another corner, Lao Zhao, upturned cigarette delicately balanced between his thumb and index finger, sat slumped in the sand watching the scene through half-closed eyes. Nothing would persuade either of them to join in the revelry. I reflected that they were old enough to have been at the forefront of the Cultural Revolution.

The wind freshened.

'They said on the radio that a sand storm is coming our way,' said Xiao Yuan, scooping up his winnings.

'When will it reach the Gashun Gobi?' I asked.

'They can't say,' replied Xiao Yuan. 'It could miss us altogether or we could land up in the thick of it.'

The smoky atmosphere had become oppressive. Driver Song, who was playing in white knitted gloves, was chain-smoking in time with Lao Zhao. My head felt thick with smoke and I made my excuses and left the gamblers to play on. It was a dark night and the stars were hidden by cloud and dust. My tent door flapped wildly. When I saw the level of grit and sand covering my sleeping-bag and belongings, I chided myself for stupidly leaving it unfastened.

The next morning it was clear from the expression on the Professor's face that a disaster had occurred. He was squatting beside the rear wheel on the right-hand side of our truck.

'What's wrong, Professor?'

Professor Yuan stood up. 'Come and look,' he said. 'Some leaves of the truck's spring are broken.'

It was true. Three of the leaves of the spring above the right-hand rear wheel had snapped.

'If the remaining leaves break, then the truck will collapse,' the Professor continued. 'If that happens, then we're in trouble.'

Big trouble indeed. We were less than halfway into the Gashun Gobi, and already over 150 kilometres from any human settlement.

The Chinese clustered together and chatted heatedly among themselves. Voices were raised. Objectors were silenced. There was a short outburst of shouting.

The meeting had clearly been inconclusive. The Professor walked over to me and said, 'We want you to decide. We have discussed the situation among ourselves but cannot reach a decision. Driver Song wants to go back, Driver Xiao Kegang wants to go forward.'

'What do you think we should do, Professor?' I asked.

The Professor frowned. 'I think that we should ask you to make the decision.'

It was quite a decision to make. I knew roughly the distance we had to cover to get back to Tikar. But I had no idea of how much trackless waste lay ahead, nor the condition of the country.

'Are we nearly halfway yet?' I asked.

'No, and we won't be for another two days,' he replied. 'The desert gets worse. We have almost one thousand kilometres to cover before we reach the road to the Dun Huang oasis.'

'Is it possible to repair the spring?'

The Professor called out to the truck driver, Mr Xiao, who walked over to us carrying heavy-duty wire and an iron bar.

'We can try to repair the spring with this,' the Professor said.

I took a deep breath. Having come all this way, how could I turn back?

'Let's repair the truck and go on,' I said.

'It's a big risk. The truck is carrying all our food, water and petrol. If it can't move, nor can we.'

'You could send the jeep off on its own to get help.'

'Mr Song is not reliable.'

I looked at him. 'You asked for a decision,' I said.

For over two hours, driver Xiao hammered at the end of an iron bar in an attempt to force it into a support position between the broken and sound leaves of the spring. He then painstakingly wired everything together. When he was at last satisfied, he turned to the Professor and nodded.

'We go,' the Professor said. We packed up our remaining kit and scrambled into the vehicles.

We set off into the very heart of the Gashun Gobi, an area too remote for potential hunters and judged to be over 250 kilometres from any human settlement. It was near here that the five crystal hunters had disappeared with their vehicle in July 1990. As we entered a vast plain littered with jet-black pebbles and surrounded by mountains tinged with blue, Driver Song pointed to something shining unusually brightly about half a kilometre to our left. We reached the spot and, within minutes, were clustered excitedly around the remains of a space capsule. Painted lime green, just under two metres tall and constructed of incredibly hard metal, it was grooved vertically on the outside.

'Look, there's more over there!' shouted Xiao Yuan.

We soon discovered that the desert was littered with metallic fragments from space. But Lao Zhao had spotted something else, a fifteen-foot section of round heavy-metal piping.

'Just what I need to replace the chimney of my fireplace in Urumqi,' said Lao Zhao, handing it to the driver to tie on the top of our provision truck. In addition, two metres of twisted metal was also lashed to the side of the truck in case we were forced to use it as a 'spare' spring. I unscrewed a piece of metal from the capsule as a souvenir. Unfortunately, it eventually ended up in Ashford Borough Council's rubbish tip after a friend of mine thought he had seen it glowing in the dark.

The remains of this rocketry had been scattered around a wilderness of unimaginable bleakness. Nothing we had seen in the Mongolian Gobi or previously in the Gashun Gobi could remotely compare to it. A kingdom of death surrounded us; not a beast, not a track, not even the skull of some old wild camel which had dragged itself here to die in solitude. Occasionally we saw a dried-up tussock in a gully. Jet-black shale littered the surrounding hills. The shale was loose and sharp and we slithered and slipped and tore our hands and clothing in an attempt to climb some of the highest peaks. The wind freshened, forcing us to cling with one hand to sharp rock as we gripped binoculars or spotter-scopes with the other. Far, far below, a forgotten disordered world, tinged with a wash of pale blue colour, sprawled around us like a gigantic maze. There were no vehicle tracks to show that others had penetrated this area. Here and there a broken shard of space debris glittered in the sun, a sun that seemed to be constantly positioned directly above us. There was no shade. In one place we found old camel droppings scattered on the ground, dry, hard, and bleached a dirty grey by the burning desert sun.

'They are more than four years old,' said Lao Zhao grimly.

What had driven these wild camels to enter Hell itself? There was no water for many kilometres. Fortunately for us, the gates of Hell had opened on a quiet day. When the fearsome, howling desert winds stoked up the furnaces and hurled the sand, shale and shingle through these gullies and round these hillocks to create a seemingly unending inferno, then nothing, not even the mysterious, ghostly wild camel could survive.

We returned to our vehicles and drove another eighty kilometres until we reached a salt spring, where we pitched camp. Lao Zhao was keen for us to visit a smaller spring about fifteen kilometres to the east, where he felt certain that we would at last catch up with our elusive quarry. So the Professor, Xiao Yuan and I set off with Lao Zhao on an evening reconnaissance in the jeep. However, the spring was totally dry. Apart from a camel's distinctive tracks which indicated a fruitless search for water, there was no sign of any recent camel activity. A migrating swallow, probably blown off course or caught up in a sand storm, lay encrusted in the dry salt. Only a tamarisk bush, its light purple flower fronds struggling to blossom, gave any hint of life in this windswept arena of desolation. Lao Zhao was becoming increasingly anxious about his lack of success, and insisted on leading us on a search for another salt spring which he had visited in 1985. We became lost, ended up on an endless expanse of cracked mud flats, got lost again and eventually found our way back to our camp long after dark. Lao Zhao ruefully concluded that the whole area was getting drier and drier due to the draining of Lop Nur. The spring that we were unable to find showed up quite clearly on our 1991 satellite map. Four years later it had vanished.

During our hopeless search I saw my first *yardang*. These ancient sediment remains, which once formed the bases of lakes or depressions, have been eroded by winds and storms over countless millennia. This wind action has left tall, free-standing columns and pillars of layered sediment, moulded into weird and wonderful shapes, some resembling watch-towers or temples, others looking like giants' tables and others, as in this case, forming a huge overhang which, tilting like the tower of Pisa, seemed destined to topple on to the cracked mud beneath it.

That night, the long-predicted sandstorm finally came upon us. As the strength of the wind increased, the Chinese reluctantly forsook the time-consuming procedure of making their own noodles and resorted to our emergency dried rations. We livened these up with boiling water and slurped them down with diced, peppered donkey meat. After a pull at the *maotai* bottle we left the warmth of our kitchen tent and ran out into the howling gale to check on ropes, pegs and wildly flapping canvas. Later, huddled in my tent, it seemed that the full blast of the force-seven gale which was sweeping over hundreds of kilometres of desert was expending all its energy on those few metres of canvas. The initial wild flapping was merely the overture to a grand chorus and when, in spite of precautionary piles of rocks and stones, the cords on one side of the tent suddenly freed themselves from their moorings, the tent was instantly transformed from relative order to utter chaos.

Loose ends of canvas smacked at everything and dust flew every-where. My Chinese colleagues were of course experiencing similar problems. No one could leave their battered stronghold to help the other. It was each to his own in the swirling mass of grit and sand. Having ensured that knife and torch were in reach, I covered my head with a large cloth in a puny attempt to keep dust out of eyes, ears, nose and mouth, pulled the sleeping-bag tightly around me, curled up my knees and waited for the worst. The full frontal attack kept going all through that very cold night, but the wind eased off at daybreak and, in the hazy early morning light, I saw that the Professor's tent had disappeared and he was curled up in the cab of the truck. Lao Zhao was lying inert under a chaotic mess of torn and wildly flapping tenting. We emerged one by one, unrecognisably grey with dust, spitting, hawking and coughing. All except for Lao Zhao, who snored on under a waving litter of shredded sheeting and twisted metal.

We were fortunate. The storm had lasted just under forty-eight hours and had been the *sarik-buran,* a yellow sandstorm, and not the dreaded black sort which can be an even more terrifying experi-ence, as this description by the German archaeologist Albert von Le Coq shows:

Quite suddenly the sky grows dark, the sun becomes a dark-red ball of fire seen through the fast-thickening veil of dust, a muffled howl is followed by a piercing whistle, and a moment after, the storm bursts with appalling violence upon the cara-van. Enormous masses of sand, mixed with pebbles, are forcibly lifted up, whirled round and dashed down on man and beast; the darkness increases and strange, clashing noises mingle with the roar and howl of the storm, caused by the violent contact of great stones as they are whirled up through the air. The whole happening is like Hell let loose, and the Chinese tell of the scream of the spirit eagle so confusing men, that they rush madly into the desert wilds and there meet a terrible death far from frequented paths.

Any traveller overwhelmed by such a storm must, in spite

of heat, entirely envelop himself in felts to escape injury from the stones dashing round him with such mad force; man and horse must lie down and endure the rage of the hurricane, which often lasts for hours together. And woe to the rider who does not keep a firm hold on his horse's bridle, for the beasts, too, lose their reason from terror of the sandstorm and rush off to a lingering death in the desert solitudes . . .

Next morning the wind died down. On the horizon, a slender spiral of sand rose, circled, glided along the ground and then vanished into the sky. Then, all at once, the desert floor became alive with these 'dust devils', sending sand and stone spiralling upwards. These whirling columns of sand gave the impression of an invisible being wrapping a layer of dust around its unseen form. Some chose to whirl to the left and others to the right. In Central Asia, as in Africa, many people still consider dust devils to be the home of lost souls, eternally restless spirits who agitate the desert in a desperate search for rest and peace of mind.

'That one is the male and that one is the female,' said Xiao Yuan with a laugh, pointing to two dust devils that appeared to be dancing with each other, spinning round and round in opposite directions. 'We call them *kwei*, and you can always distinguish which is which by the way they fold their dust cloak around them, right to left or left to right.' The 'couple' moved towards us but fortunately turned aside before they were too close.

We struck camp and drove on. I discovered that the road from Hell is paved with red shale. It lasts for sixty kilometres until it meets the middle Silk Road, long since obliterated and unused since Lop Nur swung on its pendulum 1,600 years ago.

Although the silk industry gave its name to the Silk Road, information concerning it leaked out very slowly. 'Silk-weaving Ceres' was the name by which China was spoken of in Rome, but the art of silk production remained unknown until a Chinese princess travelling to the kingdom of Khotan, to the south-west of Lop Nur, hid some eggs of the silkworm in the fold of her headdress and hatched them in Khotan, where the mulberry grows prolifically. The source of China's silk was then revealed, and Khotan became a centre of the Central Asian silk industry. The middle Silk Road, leading to the north of Lop Nur and Lou Lan, developed into a busy thoroughfare. Silk was highly prized by merchants and aristocrats because it was a fabric in which lice could not cling, burrow or lay eggs. Wool, cotton, felt or velvet were potential maternity wards for lice. I wondered whether silk long-johns would have foiled those monstrous ticks.

We eventually reached the south-western shoreline of Lop Nur. The lake bed spread before us to the horizon, covered in wave upon wave of *shor*, a saliferous mud, which when it dries out becomes as hard as brick and rises in ridges and crests to an average height of a metre. A four-wheel-drive can quickly plough to a halt in the malodorous quicksand of mud and sink beneath its surface. The crests and ridges which form the *shor* are composed of salt crust and clay. They resemble a deeply ploughed field which has been frozen over by winter frosts. It would be another year before we were to discover for ourselves the dire risks involved in attempting to cross it.

In December 1930, when two members of Sven Hedin's team – the Swede, Nils Horner, and his Chinese assistant, Mr Chen – reached the spot where we now stood, they had a great incentive to walk on. They knew that the far end of the vast sea of *shor* was lapped by the fresh waters of the newly formed Lop Nur, and that beyond the farthest shore lay that mysterious city of Lou Lan. They had travelled for fourteen days without finding fresh water and the incentive to strike out was compelling:

On December 8th 1930 . . . we left what had once been a promontory of the lake coast and made our way out over the dry, hard, bumpy salt crust of old Great Lop Nur. Although the ground was hard, dry and firm under our feet, we nevertheless felt as though we were putting out to sea. We now followed the west-north-westerly course which should take us to Lou Lan, the ruined city, although we had to reckon on finding a barrier in our way – the water of the new lake. But the new lake was just what we were looking and longing for. Everything was still as hopelessly dry as anything possibly could be – salt as hard as stone. As at sea, we had only the compass to steer by; there were no longer any landmarks.

We, too, could strike out on foot across this wasteland with only our compass to steer by, but we knew that we would never find the fresh water that Horner had looked and longed for. Sixty-five years later, Lop Nur was dry.

We left the shores of Lop Nur and immediately entered the vast plateau of Da Ping Tai, a featureless wasteland covered in black pebbles, which led to another sea of *shor* where miners had attempted to extract salt in the early 1990s. We camped that night by a salt spring which had mercifully escaped the miners' attention. We spotted a pair of yellow wagtails (*Motacilla flava*) darting over the encrusted white salt, and later that evening Lao Zhao had to be restrained from stalking a flock of Pallas' sand grouse (*Syrrhaptes paradoxus*).

The night was very cold, minus seven degrees centigrade, according to the Professor. The water in the salt spring froze and so did the bristles of my shaving-brush. I shivered and shook all night in my sleeping-bag. My groin was the only hot spot, a tick having decided to pitch camp there.

The next morning, after thawing out our stiffened limbs, we moved on towards the Aqike valley, described by Academician Sokolov in 1958 as the heart of wild camel country. A small range of mountains running east to west shields this valley from Lop Nur to the north, and to the south the Kum Tagh, a formidable 500-kilometre barrier of sand dunes, prevents the wild camels of the Gashun Gobi from meeting up with their cousins in the Desert of Lop. It is the strategic position of these sand mountains that ensures that the Gashun Gobi camels remain genetically pure.

We camped by Shang Shi Chan (Sweet Water Spring), which was the first fresh water that we had come across in eleven days of travelling. Two thousand years ago this spring was a premier watering-point on the middle Silk Road, and could water up to a thousand men and their camels and horses. Today it serves as a watering-point for men engaged in activities that spell doom for the wild camel: hunting and illegal gold-mining. We found yet another dead wild camel near the spring, and the inevitable hunters' hide. Sweet Water Spring was too far away to attract the Tikar hunters. They would never have ventured this far south in their donkey-drawn carts. The hunters must have come from the oasis of Dun Huang to the east. This was a new and worrying development.

The wind was again approaching gale force when we reached a water-hole where Lao Zhao had shot a wild camel some years ago. He showed us his hide with a worrying degree of enthusiasm. There were occasions when I wondered whether the old poacher was the committed gamekeeper that he pretended to be. A few grey, bullet-hard droppings pointed to camel activity, but it was not recent. Fifty kilometres further on, we reached another water-point, Chang Baishan (Long White Mountains). By now a full gale was blowing. We hastily pitched camp and saw to our alarm that two more leaves of the spring above the right-hand rear wheel of the truck had snapped. Only one remained intact. More alarmingly, two leaves on the left-hand rear wheel of the truck had now split in two. Driver Xiao made temporary repairs with metal from the space rocket, but we all knew that with defective springs on either side of the vehicle it could easily collapse.

The wind bombarded the tents with sand and grit all night. Next day, visibility was down to less than a hundred metres. We struggled in the driving sand through a dough-like surface of grey, salty sludge to a second saline spring. This was also dry. By this time, the jeep's engine was boiling over every twenty minutes and we had to stop and face the engine to the wind to cool it down. Over the last few days, as we had travelled further and further away from civilisation, Driver Song had developed an increasingly mutinous attitude problem. Like the engine, he was permanently on the verge of boiling over. During the escalating stops to cool the engine, he made it quite clear through displays of flamboyant petulance just what he thought of the expedition, his fellow travellers, the Gobi and, not least, the wild camel. It was very tiresome.

Lao Zhao grew despondent. 'The camels have fled,' he said morosely, drawing deeply on his upturned cigarette. He was conscious that, as the expedition guide, he was rapidly losing face.

The next day the Professor and I left the truck at our camp and took the jeep with its surly, sulky driver into the Aqike valley. Illegal miners, encouraged by the relaxation of rules forbidding such activities, had clearly been scrambling over hills to the north of the valley in an attempt to strike gold. Two illegal mines had been set up and near one of these, a deep pit had been dug to collect water brought in by truck. Last year a wild camel had fallen into the pit and drowned.

We reached sticking point. The Kum Tagh sand dunes shimmered menacingly in front of us behind a twenty-kilometre sea of forbidding *shor*. The Professor and I were keen to attempt the crossing but not with our supply truck so far away and a truculent driver at the wheel. We retraced our tracks and returned to camp, determined that one day we would return and cross the *shor*. Next morning we struck camp early and headed slowly due east for the oasis of Dun Huang. We still had nearly 300 kilometres to cover over trackless Gobi, and the truck's springs were never far from our thoughts. After easing ourselves slowly over another vast plateau strewn with black and white pebbles, we came to another sand dune barrier which runs from north to south to form the easternmost boundary of the wild camel. We had now crossed their habitat from north-west to south-east. We had observed how they were under constant pressure from hunters and miners, but had uncovered little evidence of fresh camel activity. More worryingly, we hadn't seen a single live beast.

In the early 1930s, these north–south sand dunes formed an impenetrable barrier for Sven Hedin when he and his team attempted to travel in two Ford motor cars to Lop Nur from the east, and he was forced to abandon the attempt. We were more fortunate. Lao Zhao knew the exact position of the only gap in the 150-kilometre line of dunes. After breaching this gap and travelling for another hour we reached the aptly-named Devil City. Myriad *yardangs*, which resemble a vast array of buildings large and small, were set out in lines alongside a perfectly formed grid of 'streets'. Driver Song hastily adjusted his devil deterrent, the bright red duster which flew from his jeep's aerial.

We drove on for a further three hours over more utterly barren Gobi.

'Hey, what are you doing?' I cried out as I saw Lao Zhao suddenly scrabbling in the back of the jeep for his shotgun.

Lao Zhao shouted something to Driver Song, who began to slow down.

'There. Look over there,' said Xiao Yuan, grabbing my sleeve. I followed the line of his outstretched arm and saw two goitered gazelles standing on a tussock of grass and sand about seventy-five metres away.

'No. Lao Zhao,' I cried out as he started to clamber out of the jeep, gun in hand.

'Lao Zhao says that it doesn't matter. We are out of the camels' area now,' said Xiao Yuan.

'I don't care if we're out of Xinjiang Province,' I shouted. 'The goitered gazelle is a Grade B protected species and we're supposed to be conservationists. Stop him, Professor.'

The Professor intervened. Lao Zhao lowered his gun and climbed back into the jeep. Excellent guide though he was, I wondered whether he would ever change from being a compulsive hunter and a potential liability. Two years later, the same scenario repeated itself over another gazelle near the Arjin Shan mountains. This time, Zhao pulled the trigger and I hit the roof. This incident resulted in the Professor convening a Communist-style 'self-examination', during which the old rascal confessed publicly to his wrong-doing. But I don't imagine that his conversion to conservation lasted long.

We came to a river, the Shule He. The Shule He, whose source is an underground freshwater spring, sustains life in the oasis of Dun Huang and its surrounding settlements before petering out into the desert. The sight of clear, fresh, running water was so astonishing after our crossing of the barren wasteland that we tore off all our clothing and splashed about like excited children on an outing to the seaside. All except for Driver Song, who fastidiously washed his face, his socks and his jeep.

'We have reached Houken,' said the Professor, pointing to some ruined mud houses surrounded by dead poplars about a kilometre from the river. 'There used to be a few herdsmen living here but it's been abandoned. No one lives here now.'

But the Professor was wrong. As we left the jeep to explore the ruins of Houken, two wild-eyed, mangy dogs bounded up to us.

'Hi. Hi. Hi,' a voice called out and a mountain of a man, clad in a threadbare blue serge 'Mao' suit, emerged from a tumbledown house and strode over towards us. His flat, round face was burnt black by exposure to wind and sun and his swarthy complexion was accentuated by a generous topping of snow-white hair. Realising that I was a round-eyed foreigner he stared incredulously at me for a moment and then gripped my arm with powerful fingers. Shaking with emotion, he embarked on his story in passionate tones.

'I am fifty-three years old,' he said, stubbing his forefinger in my chest. 'I have been here since I was twenty-five.' His immeasurably sad eyes rested on mine. 'Can you imagine that? For twenty-eight years I have lived here with neither wife nor family.'

'Why have you chosen to remain here?' I asked innocently, using Xiao Yuan as an interpreter. 'It must be very lonely for you. Why don't you bring your wife here?'

'Chosen! Chosen! I have no choice,' he replied gripping my arm more tightly. 'I committed a crime,' he said with a throaty laugh. 'My crime was that my father was a landlord in Dun Huang. For that, they spat me out of the mouth of China.'

I turned to Xiao Yuan. 'Has he really been forced to live in exile without his family on the fringe of the desert for all those years?'

Xiao Yuan confirmed that this was the case.

'I had done nothing wrong. Nothing wrong at all,' bellowed the old man. 'I was a good Communist. I gave my support to the party. I . . .'

The Professor lost interest and walked away. Mr Li set off to look for the much sought-after liquorice plant (*Glycyrrhiza glabra*), which he had been told grew nearby. Lao Zhao leant on the jeep, looking at the old man, an amused smile on his face. Driver Song stared into the wing mirror and started to remove an unwanted whisker from his chin.

'I was my father's only son,' the exile continued, 'and had done nothing to upset the authorities. They took my father away and then forced me to live out here.' His eyes moistened. 'I never saw my father again. At first, I was not entirely on my own; others whose fathers had been prominent in Dun Huang were sent out with me. But they have all died. I am the only one left, together with my sheep, my goats and the blessed fresh water of the Shule He river.'

He stared at me intently, willing me to understand.

'For years I saw no one for months on end,' he concluded with a grim laugh. 'I became one of the forgotten ones.' His stare intensified. 'Can you imagine that, foreigner? But things are improving. I am now allowed to visit Dun Huang once every two months to visit the few remaining members of my family who remember me.'

Still holding tightly on to my arm, he propelled me towards his little one-room mud house. Xiao Yuan followed reluctantly as we entered the little hovel, which contained a wooden bed, a chair, a stool, a radio and a cast-iron cooker. Chickens and sheep wandered in and out as we sat facing each other.

He poured me a cup of tea from the battered, blackened kettle which was steaming gently on top of the cooker. As I sipped my tea from a chipped rice bowl, he once again took hold of my arm, as though to reassure himself that I was not a devil from the desert, a product of his disordered mind or an apparition from a deceitful dream. Having assured himself that I was real, he begged me with tears in his eyes to allow him to cook us a meal, but by now Xiao Yuan was clearly bored with his emotional outburst and had no sympathy for his story. After all, he had admitted that he was the son of a landlord. He was lucky that he hadn't been shot.

'My father wants to move on,' said Xiao Yuan impatiently. 'He wants to reach Yungmenguan before dark.'

The old man shrugged his shoulders and relaxed his grip on my arm. 'I can see that you don't have the time to talk to someone like me,' he said poignantly. 'Try to come again. I'm always here.'

I sensed the terrible loneliness of this solitary exile as we piled into our vehicles. Had he but known it, I would have willingly sat up half the night talking to him and hearing out his story, but it wasn't possible. I stared back at him, this fall-out from the Cultural Revolution, as he stood, hands on hips, silhouetted against the setting sun. How many more lonely, old people who have been spat out of China's mouth were dotted around the fringes of this fearful desert, I wondered.

In striking contrast to the tragic atmosphere that hung over the ruined village, a beautiful lake had formed in the flat, desert land-scape nearby. Fed by the Shule He, it glittered in the rays of the fast-setting sun. Zhao's trigger finger must have itched as we spot-ted duck bobbing about on its rippling surface. The lake was fringed on one side with the previous year's growth of *fragmitis*, a hardy desert grass that can be cut when green and fed to domestic animals. When it is dry and hard, the grass can be chopped, mixed with mud and used as a building material. It can also be woven into baskets and mats, made into awnings or turned into makeshift hal-ters and bridles for horses or bullocks. When constructing desert roads, it is frequently used to 'thatch' sand dunes, to form a barrier against drifting sand blown up by the wind. Five hundred kilome-tres of new road that leads to oil wells in the Taklamakan desert is flanked on either side with 'hand-thatched' dunes. However, *frag-mitis* grass grows quickly and its stalk rapidly hardens, so that even the wild camel has difficulty in digesting it.

The dry, feathered flowers of *fragmitis*, coloured bright gold by the light of the sun, swayed gently in the breeze and provided a magical backdrop for what occurred next. Set in the middle of a prominent ridge overlooking the lake, a solitary, mud-built gate, gleaming brick-red, reared up majestically in front of us. We had reached the 2,000-year-old Han dynasty Jade Gate. We drove up to this entrance to old China, the ancient gateway to the long-abandoned middle Silk Road. It had taken us twelve days to make our historic north–south crossing of the Gashun Gobi.

In AD 399, during the reign of the Eastern Chin Emperor An Ti, the priest Fa-hsien, together with more than ten disciples, had set out through the Jade Gate for India. His chronicle graphically describes the country that we had just crossed: 'Beyond the Jade Gate is a desert belt, the home of malevolent spirits who stir up hot winds. No one has survived. There is no bird in the sky and no beast on the ground. There is nothing to close off the limitless prospect. He who seeks a landmark finds only the bleaching bones of men and animals to mark the way.'

We had been to the heart of the homeland of the malevolent spirits, where no animal except the wild camel exists. We had discovered bleached bones and been blasted by winds both hot and cold. But we had survived.

In fading light we off-loaded our equipment in the courtyard of caretaker Cao Hai, a stooped, bespectacled, scholarly man who lived in a modest concrete house beside the Gate. It couldn't have been a popular posting and I wondered whether he too had committed a cultural indiscretion resulting in banishment. He lived with a plump, wide-eyed teenage son who stood gawping unhelpfully at our struggles to put up our tents in the dark and in an increasingly hostile wind. Later that evening Cao Hai, his son, and the only other inhabitant of Yungmenguan, a sunburnt, woolly-headed herdsman who could have been another involuntary exile, entertained us with mutton and *maotai*.

'I would like to give you something,' said Mr Cao when the last morsel of mutton had been gnawed from the bone. He walked over to a corner of the dimly-lit room and knelt down beside his wooden bed. Pulling a battered cardboard box from underneath, he rummaged inside it for a moment and then walked back to me, clutching something in his hand.

He gave a little bow and handed me a 2,000-year-old arrowhead. 'For you,' he said, 'to remind you of your crossing of the Gashun Gobi. I believe that you are the first recorded foreigner to have completed the journey from north to south.' His son grinned mawkishly but I remembered what Sven Hedin had written when he tried to penetrate with vehicles beyond the sand dunes to the east of Devil City in 1934: 'A *terra incognita* extended on every side. No European had ever set foot there. To westward the only route ever travelled was our own – sixty-six miles to the sand barrier which the Ghashun-gobi [*sic*] had raised in our way. The sand had beaten us . . .'

It was humbling to feel that the boy's father might be right. As Hedin had also written, '*deseriderium terrae incognitae* had decoyed me into reckless adventures'.

Later that evening, the curator told us how both policemen and government officials from Dun Huang travelled into the desert to shoot wild camels for 'sport'. How only the week before, a jeep full of trigger-happy policemen had passed through the Jade Gate.

I turned to the Professor. 'What can we do?'

The Professor had his answer ready. 'We need to establish a protection area for the camel, with strict controls against illegal mining and hunting.'

Mr Cao nodded solemnly in agreement. His son giggled and clapped his hands in time with his father's bobbing head.

'Will the local authorities agree?'

'Yes, if we can attract international support.' Professor Yuan paused for a moment and smiled. 'That's your job,' he said.

Next morning, while relieving myself in the shadow of the old city wall, I noticed a tiny green object lying among the black pebbles spread out before me. Mr Cao confirmed that it was a bead, as old as the arrowhead, that had once formed part of a girl's necklace. I felt that it was an omen. We visited the impressive remains of the mud wall that demarcated the westernmost boundary of Han China. It predates the Great Wall by many centuries and the dry desert wind has preserved it for many kilometres, together with its watchtowers and stacks of petrified firewood that would have been used as beacons to warn of hostile attacks from across the desert.

Shortly afterwards, we left for Dun Huang with only one sound leaf on either side of the truck's rear axle. It ploughed along in front

of us, mingling black smoke from its exhaust with clouds of powdered sand. I confidently expected its demise at any moment and
instinctively rubbed the little Russian icon which I always carried
in the breast pocket of my shirt. After eighty-five kilometres, telephone poles popped up dramatically one after the other along the
line of the horizon that stretched in front of us. As each pole
appeared we let out a great cheer, for we knew that they ran alongside a newly constructed tarmacadamed road to Dun Huang. As
the truck lurched out of the pebble-strewn sand of the Gashun
Gobi and mounted the smooth surface of the motor road, there
was a loud crack. The remaining leaves of both springs snapped.
Like a dancer doing the ultimate in splits, the vehicle collapsed in
a heap on the side of the road.

5

In the Shade of
the Oasis

People must adapt their thinking to the changed conditions
Chairman Mao

Driver Song sat in his jeep dressed in freshly washed clothes, stared at his smooth face reflected in the driving mirror, frowned and delicately plucked a few grey hairs from his temple. He had successfully persuaded himself that he had prematurely aged as a result of our privations in the desert. When he had finished plucking his head, he started to scratch at a real or imagined itch with the little fingernail of his left hand that he had carefully allowed to grow out like a bird's talon. From time to time, he paused to flick a speck of dust from his sharply creased trousers or to give his shiny black leather shoes a flick with a duster. This self-satisfied preening had been triggered by his success in extracting a higher daily rate of pay from the Professor. The carefully timed demand, preceded by threats of strike action, was justified by excessive wear and tear both to his delicate nature and his jeep. As there was no replacement driver and vehicle available in Dun Huang, the Professor's hand was forced.

In contrast, Driver Xiao, who appeared quite content with his service conditions, engaged himself in an ostentatious display of clearing dust and desert sand from his throat. 'Botanist' Li joined in, and even the overweening Driver Song hawked and spat delicately through the open door of the jeep. Professor Yuan bustled busily about in the warm sunshine, humming loudly and pausing to jump up and down in spontaneous spasms of happiness and delight. Spring was in the air and a gentle breeze wafted delicate scents of peach and apricot blossom through the dour concrete yard of our one-star hotel. We had managed to buy two new springs, our truck was repaired and, for the most part, the team appeared to be content.

Dun Huang is a bustling, thriving town, distant in spirit and attitude from the harshness of the desert which relentlessly encroaches on its suburbs. Outside the recently reconstructed modern centre, and away from the smoke-laden patchwork of haphazard industrial development, the oasis stretches from north to south for twenty kilometres. Substantial mud-brick farmsteads stand in the centre of communal farmland, surrounded by thick mud walls.

During the Han dynasty (206 BC to AD 220), the name Dun Huang ('Blazing Beacon') alluded to its watchtower and fire beacon which were used to signal an attack by invaders from out of the desert to the west. Later, the name was changed to Shachow, 'City of Sands', but when that town was destroyed, the new town that was rebuilt on the same site reverted to the former name of Dun Huang. The desert town figures prominently in Chinese history and has had a chequered and colourful career. In AD 787 it fell to the Tibetans, who remained there until the middle of the following century. From 919 it was for more than a hundred years virtually independent, but recognised the Chinese court. In 1035 it fell to the Tanguts, in 1227 to the Mongols and in 1524 to the Mongol Khan of Turfan. In 1725 the Manchus established a military post there, and thirty-five years later it was reoccupied by the Chinese. The place attracted this military activity because it was situated where the old Silk Road between China and the West crossed the road that led from India through Lhasa to Mongolia and Siberia.

That evening we walked to the crowded marketplace to have a meal in a Chinese Muslim restaurant. A full moon bathed the market square in a pall of suffused light that was brightened by the tiny coloured electric light-bulbs strung out over the bustling stalls. Having been suppressed for decades, everyday petty commerce had returned to Dun Huang with a vengeance. The market teemed with traders and hawkers, young and old, male and female. Their wares were mostly cheap factory-produced household articles, or garishly-coloured dresses, blouses, suits and jeans. Youths crowded excitedly around full-size, green-baize, private-enterprise snooker tables mounted on massive and ornately carved wooden legs. The volatile spectators erupted into loud cheers when a player made a good shot or laughed uproariously when an easy pot was missed. Smartly dressed hostesses called out to passers-by in an attempt to persuade them to sample exotic teas. In the butchery, the skinned and bloody carcasses of pigs and sheep swung gently in the wind. Apples, melons, raisins and dates dominated the fruit stalls and bright red tomatoes embedded in a mass of greenery were spread out on tables in front of tiny blue-suited voluble old women whose creased and crumpled faces were burnt brown by the sun. Male and female tailors and leather-workers of all ages, shapes and sizes squatted, hunched over their antiquated, clattering treadle machines. I handed one old crone my battered tweed jacket and she expertly covered the frayed ends with soft brown leather.

A wizened old man in a faded Mao suit slowly rotated a smoke-blackened metal tube over an open fire. At frequent intervals there was a minor explosion, at which he opened the container and emptied freshly popped, fluffy white corn on to a sheet of newspaper spread in front of him. He looked up impassively as two girls dressed in racy modern style stooped to pick up two paper bags filled to overflowing with freshly popped corn. They were dressed identically in yellow neck scarves and delicate, turquoise green silk blouses tucked into tight-fitting navy blue skirts. Their heavily powdered, deathly-white faces were offset by carefully applied deep red lipstick, finely pencilled black eyebrows and heavily lacquered false eyelashes. They must have been twins, only a fetching dimple distinguishing one from the other. A green jade comb was stuck into the backs of carefully groomed hair that had been coiled round and round, beehive fashion, on the top of their heads. They chattered to each other like excited starlings as they walked away, their black plastic high-heeled shoes click-clacking merrily on the grey market flagstones. A group of old women, crouched on tiny green-painted wooden stools, turned their heads away. Their blue-serge-suited husbands, huddled in the shadows behind them, stared impassively at the two girls. Were they casting their minds back to their youth, when they had been at the forefront of a revolution that had caused so much terror and destruction in the backward province of Xinjiang? Were they staring after the two girls in longing, frustration and despair, or was it something else? What are old people's feelings when confronted, as they are today, with everything that they had been taught not only to abhor and despise, but to destroy? I thought of the lonely old outcast at Houken, forced to live on the fringe of the desert, while his home town changed beyond recognition. The snooker players, the stall-holders, the popcorn seller and the two twins were an outward expression of a society that had been suppressed for forty years. What were these old men and women thinking? Their expressionless faces gave no clue.

In the grimy, smoke-filled interior at the back of our café, a whistling, shirtless, sweating cook swung, pulled and stretched thick strips of noodle dough which, when kneaded to his satisfaction, were scooped up by a grubby urchin who sliced them into small pieces with an awesome chopper and then threw them into water boiling in a capacious iron cauldron. Pop music blared from a ghetto-blaster which dangled from a precarious electric cable, enervating not only the patrons of the café but two fat, sleepy carp which struggled half-heartedly to survive in a shiny enamel tub of dirty water. We had chosen the liveliest of a somnolent trio for our supper.

Driver Song and Mr Li began a heated argument on the quality of the steaming bowls of noodles. Nearby, a pretty Uighur girl raised her tightly-scarfed head and smiled shyly up at us. The chain-smoking, gap-toothed Muslim café owner exchanged cheerful banter with the Professor who, now that the truck had been successfully repaired and a painful suppurating thumb had healed, was in excellent spirits. Mr Zhao, dressed in a surprisingly smart raincoat topped with a waterproof cap, puffed unceasingly on an upturned cigarette. He still felt keenly his inability to have provided us with a wild camel sighting. Our taciturn truck driver stared glumly at Driver Song, who having successfully concluded the argument with Mr Li, abruptly turned his attentions to the Uighur girl. Mr Li alerted his digestive juices with a monstrous hawk and spit as the fish curry arrived on the table together with a plate of piled-up, crispy batter bread, dripping with grease. The team rapidly emptied their bowls in a noisy, feverish attempt to fill their tummies as quickly as possible. I was a non-starter in the race to finish first. We washed away the fish, vegetables and noodles with a 'special' Beijing beer as a love-sick youth wailed from the ghetto-blaster.

Later, we strolled back to our hotel, past chess players, holding their game on the pavement by the light from paraffin lamps and surrounded by groups of well-informed male spectators who periodically shouted advice or encouragement. Horse-drawn taxis covered in brightly coloured awning, the horses festooned with brass bells and gaudy harnesses, clattered and jangled up and down the road competing with bicycle-powered 'garis' for custom. Market stalls sprawled haphazardly down each side of the street, interspersed with fortune-tellers, remote-controlled pistol ranges, dumpling stalls and bubbling pots of noodles. In the background, the all-night building shift was hard at work, their concrete-mixers churning away amidst a maze of twisted, bamboo scaffolding.

Dun Huang was alive and pulsating in the balmy evening air. The oasis-dwellers appeared to be relaxed and happy. The contrast with that barren, desolate, uninhabited, lifeless 1,500 kilometres of desert that we had just crossed could not have been sharper.

★   ★   ★

'Are you a Christian?'

'I believe in a God,' I responded to Professor Yuan's pointed question.

'Not too strongly I hope, or it won't work.'

We had returned to our hotel and the Professor was busy tearing up the multi-stained, threadbare, blue carpet from the floor of our room.

'I tried it once with a strong Buddhist and it didn't work with him.'

I watched in amazement as he ripped the carpet off the concrete. Satisfied with his work, he stood up. 'It never works on a carpet,' he said. 'On the ground or on concrete, but not on a carpet.' He walked over to the bathroom. I heard the sound of running water.

'This should do,' he said, as he placed a coloured metal bowl on the bare floor. 'Remember, you mustn't fill the bowl more than three-quarters full and it must be metal. Plastic will not work. Now, please help me with the table.'

Having cleared everything away from the top of a large wooden table that stood between our iron beds at the end of the room, we placed it carefully upside-down on top of the metal bowl. The Professor bent down, made one or two adjustments, nodded his head and said, 'Good.' Then he bustled out of the bedroom, returning moments later with his son and Driver Xiao.

'Now then,' he explained, 'follow me very carefully. Stand at each corner of the table and place the third finger of your right hand on the top of the upturned leg. It must be the correct finger.' The four of us did so. 'Now empty your mind, please, and stare at the fingernail that is touching the table leg.' We emptied our minds and stared. 'Don't push the table, just touch it very lightly. If it starts to move, walk with it.'

After a few moments, the table wobbled and then appeared to float slightly upwards. All at once, it started to rotate clockwise, slowly at first and then with increasing speed.

'Walk with it, don't lose finger contact,' the Professor called out.

The speed increased until suddenly we were all running to keep up with the revolving table. Inevitably, contact was broken. When we lifted the table off the metal bowl, the water was still whirling around inside. There was a wet patch on the table top that matched the size of the bowl.

Mongolia, August 1993: stuck in the Tuyn Gol. Peter Gunin sinks with the Gaz 66.

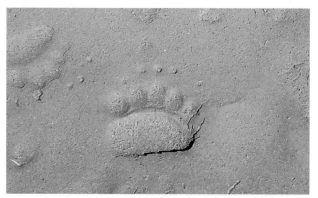

A footprint of the Gobi bear in the oasis of Shara-Khulsny-Bulak. There are thought to be no more than thirty-five left in the world.

The ancient rock carving of an ibex and a snow leopard which we found in the Tsagan Bogd mountains.

Tikar, March 1995: Sadiq, a nephew of one of Sven Hedin's boatmen on the 1933 expedition, holding a picture of his uncle.

A Tikar resident passes judgement on our decision to enter the Gashun Gobi.

In the Gashun Gobi. The Kuruk Tagh (Dry Mountains) stretch away to the west.

Two hundred miles from the nearest person, in any direction. The heart of the Gashun Gobi.

Space litter: Lao Zhao with a piece of high-tech debris.

A hunter's hide in the Gashun Gobi, concealing the lower jaw bones of two wild camels, three gazelle legs, discarded boots, a whip and some torch batteries.

An illegal miners' water-storage pit, in which a wild camel died in 1992.

Looking out over the fearful Desert of Lop. The Kum Tagh sand dunes stretch away into the distance, four hundred miles from east to west.

The highlight of the expedition makes for a unique picture: a female wild Bactrian camel with her seven-hour-old calf.

Wilfred Owen country: the result of damming the river Tarim for irrigation.

March 1996: a Uighur elder offers advice before our second venture into the Gashun Gobi.

Driver Li's pigeon, which went with us all the way.

Camel-spotting. Xiao Yuan (left), Professor Yuan (centre), and Xiao Zhao.

The author at Tu-ying – an outpost of the ancient city of Lou Lan.

Homing beacon: base camp for the expedition to Lou Lan. Professor Yuan put a light-bulb on top of the mast to guide us home.

Lou Lan: a door lintel still intact after 1,600 years of desert storms.

The watchtower of Lou Lan, still keeping sentry, and one of only two landmarks in the featureless desert.

Stuck on the *shor* – the morning after a miserable night towards the end of the 1996 expedition.

April 1997: crossing the Arjin Shan mountains. Jasper Evans sees snow for the first time since the Second World War.

One of our camels gets stuck in an ice crevasse.

Camping in the Arjin Shan at minus ten degrees.

In the foothills of the Arjin Shan – rough going for camels.

The beasts of burden: three of our domestic Bactrians on the 1997 expedition.

Chief herdsman Ahun overlooking the dried-up lake of Lop Nur.

Our domestic camels venture into the winter grazing area of the wild Bactrian.

The wild camel migration route, showing clearly how they migrate in single file.

The skull of a fourteen-year-old female. She most likely died of natural causes.

Jasper grinds up camel maize for our morning porridge after our camels had disappeared.

Back at last to the Hongliugou valley. We had been in the desert for nearly six weeks.

Base camp in the Hongliugou, south of where the driver said he'd seen a 'wild man'.

Our guide, Lao Zhao, the poacher-turned-gamekeeper who is alleged to have shot the last Przhevalsky horse in 1969.

'Chinese magic,' said the Professor with a laugh. 'You have very good power. Come, let's try it with the two of us.'

We did and it worked even more quickly than before. The table revolved at a breathtaking speed and we both collapsed on our beds, laughing and panting, when we were eventually forced to break contact.

But it hadn't seemed magical. It had felt perfectly natural. As though the Professor and I were a conduit for a force of energy which, when it combined with wood, metal and water, forced the table to rotate. I've since performed the Professor's Chinese magic in Kenya and England. But it doesn't always work, and it didn't work with Mr Li and Driver Song.

'That's because they have negative thoughts,' the Professor said.

★　★　★

Lao Zhao ran an index finger along his throat. It was all too apparent what he was indicating. Abbot Wang should have been executed and, quite clearly, Lao Zhao would have been more than happy to carry out the execution personally.

'Stein was a thief,' the Professor said. 'The biggest foreign thief who ever came to China. He stole our Buddhist heritage and bribed that traitor Wang to help him to do it.'

Lao Zhao nodded vigorously in agreement.

We were gathered outside the famous Caves of a Thousand Buddhas fifteen kilometres south of Dun Huang. It was a rest day before we resumed our journey into the desert.

On the face of it they were right, and I couldn't argue with them or attempt to defend Stein. It seemed odd that the irreligious Professor should be defending Buddhism and relics from 'old' China, but I suspected that he was actually defending his country's self-esteem. After all, Buddhism had been the state religion of China for most of the time since the middle of the fifth century AD, and may possibly have first reached China seven hundred years earlier when many Chinese Buddhist monks journeyed to India on pious pilgrimages to the sacred sites connected with the life and works of the founder of their religion.

The Caves of a Thousand Buddhas comprise hundreds of grot-toes, carved in a hillside and filled with Buddhist statues and paintings which had been sculpted, painted or financed by religious travellers, monks and scholars over the centuries. Because Dun Huang was an important cross-roads, many travellers rested there and, over the centuries, numerous abbeys and monasteries were founded. In places where wood is scarce and the climate is harsh, a cave is an obvious repository for religious works of art. The most remarkable of these pilgrims was the seventh-century traveller and renowned Chinese scholar, Hsuan-tsang, universally known as the 'Master of the Law'. Concerned that some passages in the Holy Books that he had studied were irreconcilable, Hsuan-tsang con-ceived the bold plan of gaining accurate knowledge by undertaking a pilgrimage to India to bring back with him a library of sacred Buddhist books.

After numerous adventures and considerable hardship he even-tually reached India, where he was rewarded by an ample opportunity to study Buddhism and was able to collect a large number of books which were eventually to lay the authoritative foundation of Buddhism in China. Fifteen years later he journeyed back to China, this time crossing the treacherous Desert of Lop.

Hsuan-tsang later retired to a monastic life, where he could study undisturbed and translate into Chinese some of the 657 Buddhist books which he had brought back from India, and also make use of the 157 relics that he had collected.

But the fate of the manuscripts, scrolls and paintings that he had deposited in the grottoes of Ch'ien Fo-tung, the Caves of a Thousand Buddhas, remained a closely-guarded secret until May 1907 and the arrival on the scene of the archaeologist, Sir Marc Aurel Stein. Stein, a native Hungarian and naturalised Englishman, entered a chamber in one of the caves that had remained sealed for over a thousand years. Inside, he was to make the most momentous discovery in the whole of Central Asian archaeology.

The priest-in-charge of the Caves was Abbot Wang Tao-shih. In March 1907, when Stein made his first visit to the Caves, Abbot Wang was away on a begging tour, but the archaeologist was able to inspect a manuscript that had been retrieved from behind a sealed chamber. Greatly excited by what he had seen, Stein returned in May and, with the help of his wily secretary Chiang-ssu-yeh, began to put pressure on Wang to open the chamber. Persuasion, diplomacy, the evocation of the name of Hsuan-tsang, who fortuitously turned out to be Abbot Wang's patron saint, and above all the jangle of money-bags, finally won Wang round. His secretive and underhand measures revealed that here were manuscripts in Uighur, Sogdian, Runic Turkish, Sanskrit and Tibetan, and texts in the most ancient of known languages of Central Asia such as Khotanese, Saka, and Toacharish. There were superbly embroidered pictures and fine block-printed pictures from ninth-century China. The total number of manuscripts and rolls of printed matter amounted to no less than nine thousand. There were also specimens of silk which showed the high standard of silk-weaving long before the Han dynasty. Wang was by now accepting 'judiciously administered doses of silver' and, although he was at first reluctant to release the precious Chinese scrolls, Stein managed to obtain fifty of these together with many other precious texts and paintings.

Stein congratulated himself on the results of his skilful bribery, but his '. . . time for feeling true relief came when all the twenty-four cases, heavy with manuscript treasures rescued from the strange place of hiding, and the five more filled with paintings and other art relics from the same cave, had been deposited safely in the British Museum.'

During the next twenty years the Chinese and the Japanese were able to obtain more of the Dun Huang manuscripts, although many of these were pilfered and ended up being sold in local markets. In 1920, White Russians desecrated the Caves, making fires in some of them and carving graffiti on the walls. We can only speculate on what the Red Guards would have done to the manuscripts had they still remained in the Caves in the 1960s and 1970s. Mercifully, the paintings and sculptures were untouched during the Cultural Revolution. Under the aegis of UNESCO, the Caves today are well cared for and protected. The paths worn smooth by countless pilgrims over the centuries are now trodden by the inquisitive, irreligious visitor.

There were vivid depictions of the Buddha's early life painted on the walls – the miracles of his childhood, the scenes of his youthful pleasures and the tragic encounters which called him to higher things. The paintings and sculptures are for the most part miraculously preserved by the dryness of the climate and the care and attention over the centuries of a long line of pious monks. The murals on the walls and ceilings of the Caves portray scenes of religious processions and of Paradise, with contrasting scenes of evil teeming with demons and monsters. Other paintings symbolise the various forces of nature which render man helpless; sandstorms and natural disasters set against towering mountain backdrops under malevolent, dark, cloud-filled skies. Where there is no landscape or other pictorial scene, the space is filled with the thousand Buddha decorations, row upon row of minutely stencilled Buddhas which have given the Caves their name. In one vast cave there is a huge figure of the Buddha on which, it is said, Abbot Wang lavished some of the largesse that was given to him by Aurel Stein.

My Chinese team colleagues were not impressed. Lao Zhao was clearly bored. Driver Song sniggered over the lifesize figures of Buddha and his companions and Mr Li did not bother to walk round the Caves at all. They had been taught at an early age to reject such artistic, religious symbolism as completely worthless. Their regard for these ancient works of art was no higher than that of a person who surveys a wall papered with posters. All they cared about was that Wang was a traitor, Stein an arch thief and that China's honour had been impugned.

'But surely Stein and the other turn-of-the-century archaeologists saved many priceless works of art,' I asserted. 'The twentieth century hasn't exactly been peaceful in Xinjiang, Professor. Look at the destruction caused by the rebellion of General Ma, the Cultural Revolution, the Muslim abomination of painted works of art, the apathy and ignorance of farmers, and the insensitive irrigation projects, not to mention earthquakes. Weren't these foreigners preserving your works of art for future generations?'

I normally tried to avoid discussing anything controversial. As far as politics are concerned, when in China I do not hold an opinion on anything. When China was playing war games over Taiwan, my only concern was for the camel. But having expressed his antipathy to Stein so vehemently, I wanted the Professor to explain himself.

The Professor looked at me disdainfully. I was mouthing a time-worn argument.

'Whose generation? What generation? A Western generation? It's all a cover-up,' he said. 'You Westerners say that you stole from us to preserve these relics for the future. But just think how many priceless antiquities were destroyed when you British bombed Berlin in the Second World War and the museum received seven direct hits? What kind of preservation is that? And anyway, who are you to preserve our culture? If we wish to destroy our property, then we have an absolute right to destroy it. No, the so-called archaeologists who came here at that time were thieves. Terrible thieves. And Stein was the biggest thief of them all.'

Lao Zhao nodded vigorously in the background and yet again drew his finger across his throat and muttered, 'Wang.'

'What about Sven Hedin?'

The Professor paused to consider for a moment. 'Hedin was different. He put the desert on the map. He filled in the blank spaces.' He smiled. 'But even Hedin did a little stealing. He was a petty thief. We forgive Hedin.'

'What is Mr Li saying?' I asked. He had rejoined us and had been talking heatedly to Xiao Yuan.

'He says that these caves are bad and that the painted figures and pictures give people bad ideas. They should all be destroyed.'

'But doesn't history have something to teach us? I think that these works of art, created under hardship by deeply religious people, have a great deal to teach us all.'

Mr Li gave me a withering look.

'He thinks that both history and religion are a very bad influence on people,' Xiao Yuan interpreted. 'They are both irrelevant. They prevent people from thinking about the most important thing in life, the future.'

We wandered away from the Caves through a dignified archway of desert poplar trees (*Populus diversifolia*), the ancient oasis tree that thrives near the Caves of a Thousand Buddhas.

'You see this tree,' said the Professor, abruptly changing the subject and plucking a leaf from a gnarled branch under which Stein could well have rested. 'It has a peculiarity in that it bears one narrow, willow-shaped leaf on its new growth and another which is serrated and broad on its mature growth. It is the first tree to change colour and shed its leaves in autumn, and because of this we call it *wutung*, a word associated with sadness and sorrow.'

We walked on and came upon another desert poplar that was covered all over in black, hairless caterpillars that were rapidly denuding it of its fresh, green leaves.

The Professor turned to me with a wry smile and his eyes twinkled behind his thick-lensed spectacles. 'There,' said the Professor, 'that's exactly what Stein did to Xinjiang. He stripped her of her beauty.'

On the afternoon of our rest day, we headed a few kilometres south of Dun Huang to the Lake of the Crescent Moon, surrounded by clumps of desert poplar, which nestles among the Kum Tagh sand dunes – that long line of dunes which stretch to the east from Dun Huang to the south of Lop Nur and then far away to the innermost depths of the Desert of Lop to the ancient city of Miran. These formidable sand dunes tower over the lush, green, fertile oasis of Dun Huang and can reach heights of between 100 and 175 metres. The outlines of their ridges and slopes are constantly changing under the ferocity of the seasonal winds. The clean-cut edges of sand give off a striking contrast of light and shade. The projected angles of the dunes that bask in sunshine reflect an intense brilliance, while the surfaces that lie in shade remain black and sombre. The sands of the Dun Huang dunes are composed of the tiniest fragments of multi-coloured quartz – blue, green, red, purple, grey and white – and this blend of colours gives an iridescent sheen to the sand-hills which, in turn, respond to every change of light. The contours of the dunes also alter from season to season as the surface changes under the influence of the lightest breeze, and every wind lifts the tops of the ridges in a spray of sand which is deposited on nearby dunes. It seems incredible that such a mighty rampart is composed entirely of shifting sand.

However, as the climate becomes steadily drier, these striking dunes pose a continual threat to the existence of Dun Huang, and some Chinese scientists assert that unless preventative action is taken, the oasis will be buried under sand in the space of fifty years.

Within this immense sterile wilderness, which not even the wild camel can penetrate, there lies a beautiful crescent-shaped lake. For thousands of years it has been fed by a spring which the action of the winds prevents, in some mysterious way, from being infilled with sand. This sand-girt lake is referred to in many ancient Chinese books as one of the beauty spots of Central Asia, and an envoy sent to Khotan from the Imperial court in AD 938 spoke of its charm and of the towering dunes.

On the south side of the lake a modern pagoda and a pseudo-temple have replaced an ancient Buddhist lamasery which was destroyed during the Cultural Revolution. The former temple was known as the 'back door of Paradise', a haven of peace and tranquillity, where pilgrims came to seek out a retreat in which to meditate, and the sick the sacred spring water to heal their infirmities. Today, the pagoda and temple, although well constructed, stand untouched by any spiritual atmosphere and have a feeling of emptiness and neglect. There is no priest with acolytes lovingly tending a Buddhist shrine, as the shrine that was destroyed has not been replaced. Our party, who were totally unmoved by the charm of this magic setting, walked noisily through the buildings singing songs extolling the glories of Communism. The beautiful, clear blue, crescent-shaped water surrounded by a crescent of lush grass remained, but the guardian spirits of the place had long since fled. A target for archery and a rifle range had been set up nearby and, as if it were raising a massive protest to this sacrilege, the lake had contracted by nearly a third in the past fifty years.

Visitors to the lake in the early years of this century spoke of the strange phenomenon they referred to as the 'singing sands'. This alluded to the deep rumbling noise that erupted from inside vibrant sections of the sand dunes when they moved across their surface. When Marco Polo passed near the Kum Tagh he reported on the desert sand-hills that emitted a sound like distant thunder. Tales from travellers in the deserts of Arabia described similar noises when certain sand-hills were battered by prevailing winds. Arab desert-dwellers, too, were familiar with a sound which reminded them of the bellow of an angry bull camel.

Xiao Yuan, Driver Song and myself clambered up through the shifting sands of a dune near the Crescent Moon Lake. It was hard work, one step forward resulting in two slithery steps back, but when we eventually reached the peak of the dune it was worth the effort. The lime-green poplars of the oasis sprawled away to the north. In striking contrast to this hazy sea of green, huge pyramids of sand stretched unendingly to the south, east and west, their cleanly-cut edges appearing as sharp as a razor. We climbed down from our look-out point and up to the summit of another dune. Then we ran at high speed back down through the burning sands to the rest of our team who were waiting for us by the lake. In spite of all this hectic activity the sands declined to sing for us, and the caretaker later confirmed that they don't 'sing' any more. I wondered whether they abandoned their rumbling songs when the spirits fled from the ruins of the lakeside temple in the wake of the Red Guard.

* * *

Next morning, the beautiful, crisp, spring light could not transform the polluted, concrete sprawl of Liu Yuan into anything other than an ugly, run-down railway town. We had driven there from Dun Huang to say goodbye to Lao Zhao who, having successfully guided us across the Gashun Gobi, was now returning home to visit his ailing father. We would miss him. He had proved to be an invaluable guide and stabilising influence during the Gashun Gobi crossing. It was no fault of his that we had failed to come across a single wild camel. We were all somewhat apprehensive that we were about to launch ourselves into the 'fearful' Desert of Lop without his assistance.

As we breakfasted from dirty, chipped bowls on cold batter bread and watery, noodle soup, a stiff wind blew scraps of paper and plastic across the central square in front of us. Driver Song had chosen this 'greasy chopstick' café after much indecision. It was not an inspired choice. The café, its floor littered with the debris of earlier meals, was crowded with noisy soldiery, civil servants and, most unusually, an Uighur beggar, whose presence in front of a foreigner was too much for one fat, perspiring official. This gentleman was seated in a cubicle and firmly wedged between two equally corpulent, unbuttoned army officers whose belts were slack. He was heavily into demolishing a double portion of noodles and his stomach strained to escape his beltless, ill-fitting trousers. Seeing the beggar approach us, he waved his free hand in the air and slapped it down on the table in front of him. As he did so, the restraining button on his trousers broke free.

'Get out! Get out!' he shouted at the beggar, at the same time clutching the top of his trousers which had parted to reveal a pair of striking red underpants. 'Begging is not allowed. It is against the law.' His protest, diminished by his state of dress, was totally ignored by the Uighur, who continued to advance towards us.

'Red cloth keeps away the devil,' Lao Zhao said. 'He must have a problem down there.'

The beggar held out a grimy hand and the Professor handed him my half-finished bowl of soup which he swallowed in one gulp. Without a glance at the bureaucrat who was concentrating on the more important matter of making ends meet, the Uighur returned the empty bowl and shuffled out of the café, banging the door behind him. The official scowled at us ferociously as he eased himself out of the cubicle. Still clutching his trousers he waddled into the dark smoke-filled kitchen in search of first-aid. The soldiers stared at us with menace and muttered to each other as we moved towards the door.

We left Mr Zhao to catch the slow train to Urumqi and then began a long search in the dilapidated back streets of Liu Yuan for vinegar, an essential noodle condiment for Chinese in Xinjiang and the one provision that we had forgotten to buy in Dun Huang. We managed, after many false starts, to fill our plastic containers with the black, sticky liquid, and then our two vehicles headed west towards the Desert of Lop, described by Hsuan-tsang as:

. . . an enormous desert of drifting sands that accumulate or disperse at the caprice of the whirlwinds. The desert stretches in all directions as far as the eye can see, and none know how to find their way. For the only guide there are the bones of men and animals left behind by other caravans. Nowhere is there water or pasturage. Often the desert winds burn like fire, and then men and animals fall swooning on the ground. Sometimes come sounds like singing and whistling, sometimes like cries of anguish; and those who hear them grow dizzy and incapable of deciding which way to go. Travellers often lose their lives there.

6

The Fearful Desert
of Lop

Where shadows pass gigantic on the sand
James Elroy Flecker

'Look out, John. Duck!'

I was sitting in the front of the jeep, dozing.

Opening my eyes I turned round to Xiao Yuan. 'What do you . . .?'

I soon knew what he meant. There was a loud crash as something metallic hit the door of the jeep. I ducked as another missile hit the window by my side. The window cracked but didn't splinter. Driver Song accelerated. We were in the centre of a washed-out culvert. He spun the wheel, and set the jeep at a rocky incline in a desperate attempt to get us up on to the track.

A blunt instrument was hurled at the back of the jeep. Suddenly, on either side of the culvert, groups of men leapt up – screaming, shouting, faces contorted under brightly coloured head-scarves. One of them slashed at the jeep's tyre with a razor-sharp kitchen chopper. I ducked again as an axe handle struck the windscreen with a resounding thud.

Song was over the top now. He accelerated and drove at speed along the remains of what once had been a road. The Professor was shouting to his son who was rummaging in the back of the jeep for our shotgun. Driver Song drove off the track and parked on top of a mound of gravelly sand.

'They're not following us. They're after our truck,' Xiao Yuan said as he handed his father the shotgun. 'They're trying to steal our supplies.'

Our truck was lumbering behind us along the road that I'd recently christened 'the road of a thousand wash-outs'. Built by the Chinese nationalists, it had been abandoned in the late 1960s. The culverts which we encountered roughly every fifty metres had been systematically washed away by the torrents of water that streamed down the gullies of the Arjin Shan mountains when the snows melted in July.

We jumped out of the jeep. The bandits, who numbered about twenty, were definitely no longer concerned with us. They had regrouped to lay siege to our truck as it slowed to reconnoitre the wash-out. The Professor ran towards them, shotgun raised. He stopped, took aim, fired high above their heads and then fired again.

In spite of their numerical superiority they hesitated when the first shot was fired. When the second shot rang out, they gave way to our firepower and ran off in the direction of the mountains, their pale blue, pink, purple, green and yellow head-scarves disappearing and reappearing as they zig-zagged over the broken landscape. One of them stopped to give a defiant shout.

'Who were they?' I asked when our team's excited chatter had died down. 'What are they doing here?'

'I don't know,' Professor Yuan said as he replaced the shotgun in its case. He was excited and beads of perspiration dripped from his face. 'They could have been illegal miners or plant-hunters.'

'Plant-hunters?'

'Yes, there are certain protected medicinal herbs that are only found in this desert. They can get a lot of money for them in Dun Huang.'

'But why attack us?'

'No vehicle ever travels on this road. A new one has been constructed through the mountains. We are over 180 kilometres from

Dun Huang. They could kill us, steal our equipment, and our abandoned vehicles wouldn't be found for days, possibly months. Before Liberation, many bandits, usually Kazaks, used to live in the Arjin Shan and frequently attacked travellers. I didn't think that an attack like this could possibly happen any more. But the new market economy has brought back many bad habits to China.'

I hadn't reckoned on the camel quest leading to encounters with axe-wielding Kazaks. As we resumed our journey along this abominable washed-out road it wasn't just camels that I kept an eye open for.

About seventy kilometres of desert separates the Arjin Shan mountains from the Kum Tagh sand dunes, and the old Nationalist road, which bisects the desert, eventually disintegrates completely in a large flood-riverbed. This riverbed enters a sheer-sided valley and then spirals up into the rugged mountains. It was dry, but flood-water levels showed that in July and August it turns into a raging torrent as winter snows melt on the towering peaks. Although there was no longer a road, the road-builders had carved patriotic slogans into slabs of rock: 'Prepare a good harvest; get ready for war' and 'Our cause will triumph over evildoers'. After ascending a further ten kilometres of tortuous, dry, boulder- and tree-strewn riverbed, we reached the Lapeiquan freshwater spring, where another rock-sign proclaimed, 'The water here gives you a bellyache.' But it didn't. We drank our fill, topped up our water containers, bathed in the freezing, crystal clear spring and washed some of our filthy clothing. It was a beautiful spot and the Professor decided to camp in the foothills near Lapeiquan for three days. We could then make daily sorties into the desert on foot or by jeep in our unending search for the wild camel. At this point, we had been crossing the desert of Lop for five days and the bandits were the only other human beings that we'd seen.

That evening, just before the sun set, Xiao Yuan and I decided to climb the nearest mountain behind our tents. At first it was an uphill walk, but as we climbed higher the treacherous black shale started to slip under our feet. Footholds had to be carefully tested before another step upwards could be made. Xiao Yuan was above me and from time to time would unwittingly send a shower of sharp shale crashing down around me. Before too long we were halfway up. My heart was pounding and, as I paused to get my breath back, the magnificent sunset highlighted exposed sections of the mountains round about us with a fiery, red glow of menacing beauty. Our camp grew smaller. I could just make out the Professor standing on a rock, head upturned, anxiously watching our progress. Both Xiao Yuan and I were strangely overcome with a grim determination to get to the top. I climbed more slowly as the side of the mountain became smoother. I am not an experienced climber and foot support became increasingly difficult to find, while it grew harder to see the way forward in the rapidly failing light. Xiao Yuan had reached a small ledge and called back to say that he was attempting the final climb to the top. It looked very difficult and dangerous to me. For the first time I experienced a twinge of fear in the pit of my stomach, and decided to shed my pride.

'I think we had better go back,' I called out. 'It's getting too dark to see.'

Xiao Yuan laughed the laugh of a 27-year-old. 'It's okay,' he called. 'Follow me.'

When I reached the ledge I knew that I would be crazy to attempt the final climb. The shale had given way to smooth rock. A small, sensible voice deep down inside sent a warning signal to my brain. Fortunately, I got the message.

'I'm going back down, Xiao Yuan,' I called out when I had recovered my breath.

A wind had sprung up. There was no reply. I called out again, but he'd rounded a slab of rock. My words were blown away. I quickly discovered that descent was much more difficult than the upward climb. The shale was treacherous. Clinging on desperately when my feet started to slide from underneath me, I slashed my hands and trousers on jagged rock. The chill, damp sweat which broke out on my forehead was not caused by exertion. The wind was much too cold for that. After an interminable time and a number of near escapes I eventually reached the foothills and safety. It was dark when I finally made it back to our camp, but the moon was up and shining brightly when, to my relief, Xiao Yuan, who had had to descend by a totally different and more arduous route, strode home thirty minutes later. Of course, we should never have attempted the climb, and we had put ourselves needlessly at risk. But one does these things.

Next morning, I was awakened by Xiao Yuan tugging at my tent flap.

'Wild camels,' he whispered. 'Come quickly, there's a herd near our camp.'

I flung on my clothes and joined him outside. He pointed away from the mountains towering behind us and into the desert. I looked through my field-glasses. They were camels all right. I could see them quite clearly, an adult herd of about eight. Grabbing my camera, I walked quickly with Xiao Yuan in the direction of the grazing herd. We tested the wind. It was blowing from the mountain in the direction of the camels. Using every piece of available cover, we made a wide easterly detour, turned so that the wind was blowing across us, and stalked closer to the camels.

'Keep right down,' I whispered to Xiao Yuan. 'We're close now. If they see us, they'll scatter.' We edged closer. I cursed under my breath as I carelessly dislodged a boulder which clattered down the side of a gully. The camels took no notice. Bent nearly double we moved closer still. I looked at the camels through the field-glasses. They were chewing the cud, like contented Hereford cattle. Surely they must have got wind of us by now? I stood up. Something was wrong.

'Hey, Xiao Yuan. These aren't wild camels at all. Look most of them have got nose-pegs.'

I handed him the glasses. The camels had seen us now and had raised their heads to stare, but they made no attempt to run off. I knew for certain that they were domestic camels, possibly a lost herd.

We walked up to them. 'Kazak,' I said using the nose-peg knowledge acquired in Mongolia. 'Look at their humps, they are much too big for wild camels and some of them are floppy. We should have known.'

We laughed, although the joke was on us. I knew that domestic camels will not join a wild herd, but a thwarted bull in rut will run 100 kilometres to find a female, wild or domestic. Stray domestic camels in this wild camel habitat were an unwanted concern.

Later that day, on a foot survey covering thirty-five kilometres, we saw two herds of the Tibetan wild ass (*Equus hemionus kyang*), a desert fox, and picked up the horns of the wild *argali* sheep; but there was no positive evidence of a single wild camel. Not a footprint or a tuft of hair. We had climbed mountains which gave us stunning views of the shimmering landscape, scanned the pebble-strewn desert endlessly with field-glasses, but without the slightest success. I was beginning to wonder if the wild Bactrian camel still existed. We had travelled over 2,000 kilometres and hadn't seen a single one.

Two days later, after further fruitless foot patrols, we took to the jeep. If we couldn't find the camel on our feet we would have to continue to search by vehicle. We headed towards the Kum Tagh sand barrier, seventy kilometres due north of our camp. The going over this boulder-strewn desert, riven with gullies and dried-up water courses, was slow and gut-shaking. To make matters worse, Driver Song's vehicle frequently boiled over and he had reverted to the sulks. I had to control myself from boiling over as well. Nerves were taut as we bumped endlessly up and down at under fifteen kilometres an hour. After about five hours we reached the dunes in a howling sand-laden wind. Visibility was falling rapidly. Huge slabs of rock and sand towered over us – breathtakingly beautiful, but full of hidden menace. It was quite possible that we were the first people ever to have set foot in this part of the Kum Tagh.

It was then that I said that I wanted to walk and the Professor berated me for my stupidity. But I'd had enough of the jeep. My back ached. My mouth was full of sand. My head had been banged countless times on the badly sited roll-bar which supported the jeep's canvas top and I'd also had more than enough of Song's sulks. No, it was time to walk, and walk I would. Stalking ahead, impervious to the mutterings behind me and the rapidly declining visibility in front, I entered the maze of dunes.

'Where are you going?' the Professor called out, his voice barely audible in the howling wind. 'This is senseless.'

I stuck my arm out horizontally and continued to stride ahead. What spurred me on I will never know. I just kept on walking. Three kilometres and two massive sand dunes later, I suddenly spotted a wild female Bactrian camel, standing alert and staring at me, with a sack-like object at her feet. I froze in utter amazement. Why isn't she running away, I thought. She must be sick and has come to this barren spot to die. The 'sack' moved slightly and I realised what we had just found. Who sent the spark that manipulated the compass bearing in my head I will never understand. All I do know is that the odds on finding a needle in a haystack are a great deal lower than finding a camel with a new-born calf in the Kum Tagh.

The mother was nervous. In normal circumstances she would have fled long before we came upon her, having heard the clatter of our jeep's engine or smelt us on the wind. But she stood her ground. Her body hair was moulting. Great patches of grey skin were exposed along her side. Tufts of wool hung down from her long neck. But she seemed to be in good condition. Her small, pointed upright humps were firm and full of fat.

All at once, the young calf struggled to its feet and attempted to suckle. I could see one of its humps quite clearly, mounded on its back like a little, grey mole-hill. The other, which was much smaller and barely visible, seemed to have slipped down one side of its spine. By this time, the Professor, 'Botanist' Li and Xiao Yuan had spread themselves around the two camels in a semi-circle. At first, the young calf couldn't find the teat. It nudged and nuzzled its mother under her neck and then sank to the ground in exhaustion, wholly oblivious of its wide-eyed audience. It rose to its feet once again and with more frustrated nudging explored its mother's nether region. At last it found what it was searching for, latched on to a teat and drank. The Professor was beside himself with excitement and trying to edge as close to the camels as possible. Li, seemingly oblivious of the extreme delicacy of the situation, strode unfeelingly towards the mother and her calf. I frantically motioned them to stay where they were. We were all quite close enough for our cameras.

My camera! You idiot! I shook my head in despair. My video camera was in the jeep. In my hurry to get out and walk I had left it behind. I turned and started to run, following our tracks back to the jeep. I had to get my video. It was an unrepeatable opportunity to capture unique footage. Three kilometres is a long way in a driving desert wind. My feet felt like lead. My heart pounded as I cursed my stupidity. At last, panting and puffing, I reached the jeep. Driver Song gave me a disdainful look and said something in Chinese. His feet were propped up on the dashboard and he was, unbelievably, polishing his shoes with a duster. Song and I had not been getting on too well that day, but there was no time for niceties. I said nothing about our discovery, grabbed the sturdy leather Mongolian hunting case in which my camera was packed and slammed the jeep door shut. Exasperated with myself beyond measure for leaving it behind, I half ran, half walked, back through the driving wind. I fell, and then, for a ghastly moment, sensed that I'd taken a wrong turning and was lost. I could no longer see our footprints, which must have been covered by the driving sand. Lost in the Kum Tagh. What an end! Then I recognised a landmark, the straight-sided dune. As I rounded the dune I saw to my utter relief that the camel and its calf were still there. Mercifully, the other members of the team had held their ground and had not disturbed it. If she had taken off and left her offspring behind, it would most certainly have died.

I fumbled with the plastic bags I'd tied around the camera to protect it from dust, conscious that at any moment the camel could suddenly take off. Now for the battery. It was flat. As with other aspects of life, I am an amateur when it comes to photography. I yearned for my old clockwork Movikon 8mm cine camera which unfailingly worked whatever the situation. When will video cameras shed their dependence on short-life batteries? Fortunately I had brought a spare. Keep still. Hold your breath and shoot. The camera rolled.

The calf was still attempting to suckle, but its mother had had enough. She was agitated and on the point of flight. She nuzzled the little calf and then, slowly, very slowly, began to walk away from us, the calf staggering tremulously along behind.

I had captured the shot of a lifetime, but only just.

That evening, after a celebratory supper, the Professor brought out assorted bangers and fire-crackers and the impressive backdrop of the towering peaks of the Arjin Shan mountains echoed and re-echoed to his pyrotechnics. Still in party mood, he later sang lustily and lengthily to the waning moon and then hopped about, chanting stirring revolutionary choruses. We all shared his delight, but after this raucous display I felt certain that we would see no more wild camels in the Desert of Lop.

But I was wrong. During the course of further arduous foot surveys over the next two days we saw another forty-seven, including two lone bulls, and four more Tibetan asses. Our luck had changed at last.

The next morning the clear skies of the past few days vanished and I woke to flapping canvas and a gale-force wind. I switched on the radio and tuned to the BBC World Service.

'It has just been reported that the Chinese have conducted an underground nuclear test at the Lop Nur nuclear test site in Xinjiang . . .'

I digested the implications of this news item. We were under 250 kilometres from the nuclear test site. Maybe that was why the weather had changed so abruptly. Fortunately, we had already decided to strike camp and head south-west through the Arjin Shan to the valley of Hongliugou, which runs out into a more westerly section of the Desert of Lop. With the possibility of nuclear dust being blown about, I was more than ready to get moving.

We followed the dry riverbed past Lapeiquan and climbed to 4,000 metres, where the strong winds brought driving snow in spite of it being the middle of May. It was a long, spine-crushing, head-banging drive of 250 kilometres, made doubly difficult by the fact that Driver Song had run out of cigarettes and had resorted to smoking brick-tea wrapped in filthy newspaper. His nerves were taut and so were ours by the time we eventually reached the abandoned nationalist fort at Bashkagun, at the head of the Hongliugou valley. We had crossed a seemingly endless, deeply rutted, sandy mountain plateau, passed spectacular *yardangs* resembling cottage bread loaves, grotesque faces and a serrated city wall. However, when we finally reached Bashkagun, the normally taciturn Driver Xiao Kegang, who had been driving the truck ahead of us, jumped out of his cab beside himself with excitement. He couldn't stop talking and the words tumbled out to the accompaniment of exaggerated, animated gestures.

'We had just passed the salt spring down there,' said Xiao Yuan, who had been sitting with him in the front of the truck, 'when suddenly a wild bull camel ran out of the reeds. It raced along beside the truck and then fled into the valley.'

In spite of the nuclear testing, our luck was holding, although I was sorry I'd missed the sighting.

The old fort was filthy. Abandoned in the late 1940s, generations of soldiers and herdsmen had stripped it for firewood, covered the walls with obscene graffiti and left an indescribable amount of ancient litter. It seemed imprudent to pitch camp in a howling gale. So we cleared up, as best we could, some of the litter in a building with half a roof and bedded down surrounded by yellowing newspaper, discarded broken bottles, and much worse.

At 4.00 a.m. we were all abruptly woken as a vehicle drove into the courtyard outside. A jeep door was slammed shut. There was a great deal of shouting.

'Keep very quiet,' said the Professor, reaching for his gun. 'They could be bandits.'

I unsheathed my knife and waited. There was a succession of loud bangs on our dilapidated metal door. Professor Yuan, dressed only in woolly long-johns, cocked the gun and wrenched open the door. A swarthy man, with flowing jet-black hair and dressed in army fatigues, stood four-square in the doorway. But he was no soldier. He was simply a Kazak herdsman who had come with his father in an ancient jeep to look for their flocks which were grazing nearby. They soon settled into our disgusting quarters and the early morning hours passed by in animated chatter with the Professor and 'Botanist' Li, much to the annoyance of Driver Song, who made it quite clear that he would be driving no further unless he got some sleep.

The next morning Song indicated, with theatrical aplomb, that he had a stomach-ache. By this time he had become both a pain and a cross that we all had to bear, but as he was as anxious to abandon our makeshift go-down as we were, he was persuaded to get behind the wheel. We drove down the Hongliugou valley for thirty kilometres, through a spectacular cleft in an overhanging rock that had been crafted by frustrated flood-water over the centuries. The riverbed petered out into a vast flood-plain. The Kum Tagh, blotted out by dust and sand, lay to the north. Our plan was to leave the jeep and walk back into the Desert of Lop, following the foothills of the Arjin Shan, to continue our camel quest.

According to our satellite map, two more dry flood-plains lay in front of us to the east. We reasoned that camels could be moving through them and up into the valleys, but the satellite camera must have been on a tilt when it took the picture. It was a much further walk than we or the map anticipated, and by the time we had covered twenty kilometres we had still not come to the first flood-plain. The wind was now blowing much more fiercely across the totally featureless desert. We plodded on. 'Botanist' Li pulled up a lone plant, pronounced it to be very rare and promptly threw it away. Professor Yuan was determined to reach the dry river, and after a further two kilometres we did. The riverbed was ten kilometres further west than the map indicated and, by this time, the sky had turned an ominous yellow; a major sand storm was developing. We had to rely on a compass and our footprints to guide us back along the twenty-one kilometres to our waiting jeep. But our footprints were rapidly being obliterated by the driving sand and visibility was down to ten metres. If we missed our direction by even a degree, we were in trouble.

Our luck continued to hold. In spite of the howling wind and stinging sand blowing directly into our faces from the west, we managed to keep sight of our tracks. Four hours and twenty minutes later we staggered back to the jeep where Driver Song, complete with bellyache and smoke-filled cab, seemed relieved, for a change, to see us.

★　★　★

Regiment 36 lies 180 kilometres west of the Hongliugou valley. There are 189 Regiments in Xinjiang. Some are settlements for ex-soldiers, compulsory or otherwise. Others are former correction camps for victims of the Cultural Revolution. Yet others, more ominously, are not located on the official maps at all, so one can't be certain what goes on there. But one can guess. This *tuan*, or regiment, was originally an army agricultural colony, like all of them strategically positioned to quell discontent. In the 1960s it was converted to a camp where dissidents were 're-educated through labour'. It is situated five kilometres west of the ancient city of Miran, a strategically important city during the Han dynasty and later during the five-century supremacy of the Shanshan and Khotan kingdoms and a subsequent period of Tibetan rule. Przhevalsky had first encountered the mud ruins of Miran on his 1876 expedition financed by the Russian Ministry of War, when he was nominally in search of a route to Lhasa. It was this expedition that reached the south-western lake bed of Lop Nur and ended age-old speculation as to its existence. Thirty years later, Stein conducted a most thorough research of the site and six camels carried away his discoveries – or loot, depending on your viewpoint (a camel can carry over 150 kilos). Sadly, by the time we reached Miran, the howling sand storm made it practically impossible to wander round the Buddhist *stupas* and ancient Tibetan fort for any length of time. Our approach to Miran had been particularly hazardous as the swirling sand frequently obliterated the track. Only a long line of telegraph poles prevented us from losing our way.

In Regiment 36 we were made welcome by the rotund, ever-smiling Mama Feng and her dutiful, giggly daughter, in their caravanserai comprising eight crumbling, mud-built, one-roomed huts, a kitchen and a dining-room surrounding a muddy courtyard. The dining-room boasted the inevitable TV. Deprived of his staple diet of entertainment for many days, the Professor was soon firmly ensconced in front of the box, flicking contentedly from channel to channel. The accommodation was five-star compared to no-star Bashkagun (a tin bowl, a tin bed, a hot thermos and a thick over-rug), but no sooner had I digested an enormous and tummy-warming plate of noodles, mutton and veg, watched by a beaming Mama Feng, than the police arrived.

'Why are you staying here instead of in the official hotel?' I was asked by an unsmiling, hatless, open-belted, open-necked officer who had marched into Mama Feng's kitchen with a fawning young recruit in tow.

The answer that I liked it here, liked the good lady and her daughter, and found her food delicious cut no ice.

'Foreigners are obliged to stay . . .'

So I was forced to leave my companions and was eventually deposited in a cheerless room in a soulless concrete block, supervised by a dour dame who unfeelingly resented being roused at midnight. The loo was reached after a walk across two courtyards and through two iron gates. This was, I suppose, in theory an improvement on Mama Feng's accommodation, where there was no loo at all. However, the indescribable condition of the official hotel toilet, where previous occupants appeared to have missed the hole with unerring frequency, made me long for the open fields that surrounded Mama Feng's hostelry.

'Don't make love to a person in this room who is not your wife,' the notice on the wall of my bedroom proclaimed. In the room next door, a baby yelled all night.

At seven o'clock the next morning, loudspeakers strategically positioned along every street blared forth the local and national news. At seven-thirty, fifteen minutes of martial music, presumably the official accompaniment to noodle swallowing, was followed by strident exhortations to put in a hard day's work, eliminate reactionary tendencies and further the people's revolution. At eight o'clock the population were all working hard on their irrigated farms.

I don't think that I am cut out for life in Regiment 36.

One hundred kilometres to the west of Regiment 36, the old city of Ruoqiang (Charkhlick, on the old maps) seemed down-trodden and depressed, as though its ancient, pulsating Uighur heart had been ripped out and replaced by a lifeless socialist-style substitute. The market-place was a slab of concrete covered in debris and broken glass, surrounded by empty decaying stalls. A mustard-yellow post office with peeling paint, a large, half-occupied hotel and a few other indeterminate buildings dominated the empty, joyless streets that radiated away from them. As a cross-roads to Korla to the north, Tibet to the south, Kashgar to the west and Miran and the Desert of Lop to the east, it should have been as full of bustle and life as it was when Przhevalsky, Hedin, Stein and other explorers visited it at the turn of the century. But it was life-less, and the wind, the tail-end of our sand storm, which howled through its dispirited streets and shredded the emerging, tender leaves of its poplars, was an appropriate backdrop for this grey, dusty, soulless town.

From the depressed oasis of Ruoqiang, our 1,500-kilometre route by road back to Urumqi led us north in a howling gale along a road paved with yellow bricks, broken now and pot-holed, but a testimony to the thousands of Regiment labourers involved in its construction. At some places along the way, sand dunes of both the Gashun Gobi and Taklamakan deserts towered on either side of the road, poised to link the two immense wastelands. In some places, drifting fingers of deep sand had cut across the road, forcing us to halt and extract ourselves with planks and shovels.

We were heading for the second largest city of Korla where, at the time of General Ma Chung-yin's revolution, Hedin was put under house arrest for months. Before going to Korla, however, I wanted to visit Aksupe, upstream from the junction point of the Kuruk and Konche Daria rivers at Tomenpu, which had played such an important part in the movement of the 'wandering' lake of Lop Nur. I hoped that I might find some old greybeard who remembered Hedin's visit in 1934, when he canoed down Kuruk Daria and into the recently resuscitated lake with four boatmen recruited in Aksupe.

After a lengthy and bone-shaking journey, we branched off the yellow-brick road near Regiment 34 and followed a track through a green corridor of irrigated fields. Unexpectedly, we came across a huge dam, the Dashi Hazi. This was the dam that cut off water from entering the Konche Daria and the Kuruk Daria rivers. The dead and dying remains of mature desert poplars which lined either side of the yellow-brick road were a depressing testimony to the dam's contribution to desertification further south. The severing of seasonal water flow to these rivers was the sole reason why both the ancient lake beds of Lop Nur were now totally dry. Once again, under the leadership of our ebullient Professor, we stripped off like children and washed away the desert dust before driving on to Aksupe.

The headman of Aksupe, a gauche young non-Uighur-speaking Chinese with thick-rimmed spectacles, a wisp of a beard and pimples, greeted us with deference. He was very different in outlook and demeanour from the autonomous 'big, burly and dignified' Uighur headman, Sali Bek, who administered village life in Hedin's day. The language barrier and his ignorance of Islam and Uighur customs had clearly isolated him from the local villagers. He seemed a typical imposed stooge, cut off from the people, lonely and anxious, and was clearly delighted to have visitors from the outside world to relieve the daily tensions of his mundane existence.

'He was elected by democratic means,' commented Professor Yuan when I queried his credentials. 'There were four candidates selected by the government. The people had a good choice.'

'Were any of the candidates Uighurs?' I asked.

'Oh, no,' said the Professor, looking askance at my question, 'they were all Chinese.'

At our request, the headman assembled a group of worthy Uighur oldies in the communal village hall. As soon as I broached the subject of Hedin and his staff recruited at Aksupe, a fierce argument broke out.

'I remember a Russian who came here at that time,' said one sightless old man. 'He gave me money.'

'Nonsense,' asserted another. 'What a lie. You're only a youngster. You weren't even born. I was ten years old at the time. I remember my father saying. . .'

'You! What are you talking about?' Another ancient with a finely chiselled face, embroidered skull-cap, flowing gown and pointed beard shook a finger at the sightless one. 'My uncle was a boatman for the European, and the white man wasn't a Russian, he was from another tribe.'

The argument blazed. It became impossible to sift fact from fiction. But I did learn that they remembered Ordek, the man who at the turn of the century went to look for Hedin's lost spade and was instrumental in discovering Lou Lan. He had become a village hero and was buried nearby. They also recalled the names of Hedin's four boatmen.

I kept overhearing the name Lou Lan reverberating through the animated chatter. It was during this conversation with the old men of Aksupe that a new idea began to germinate and my dormant interest in the lost city and the hostile trackless desert that lay to the west was awakened. Hedin had referred to wild camels patrolling the deserted city streets. I wanted to visit the long-abandoned city, not from the west along routes followed by Hedin and Stein, but from the east, where no known foreigner had trekked before.

We later visited the Aksupe dam with the headman and some of the old men. Smaller than Dashi Hazi, the water smelt foul and leaked from the dam walls in countless places.

'When I was a boy,' said the man whose uncle had been Sven Hedin's boatman, 'it didn't get as hot as it does today. The Bengal tiger was found near here, there were wild pig and plenty of gazelles. Nowadays, except for a very few gazelles, they've all disappeared.'

'We didn't have the diseases that we get today,' another ancient worthy interjected. 'When the water was flowing down the Konche Daria, it was clean and fresh. Look at this.' He extended his arm towards the dam. 'It's filthy. This is our drinking water.'

I stared at the stagnant, murky water and understood why hepatitis, a disease unknown to them before, was common now.

★ ★ ★

Hedin wouldn't recognise Korla today. Surrounded by haphazardly sited industrial flotsam, the old walled city has long since been bulldozed to make way for a large, concrete people's square surrounded by tiled buildings at once garish and nondescript, and the occasional high-rise office block. The Tien Shan mountains form an impressive snow-capped backdrop, when they can be glimpsed through industrial smog. In the people's square, children frolicked like spring lambs or crashed into each other in battery-powered kiddie-cars. A squatting Uighur policeman, the first one that I'd seen, proudly showed me a naked lady displayed on the back of a crumpled playing card which he kept screwed up in his tightly clenched fist.

We had just completed a 360-kilometre, two-day, there-and-back dash down a new oil road into the Taklamakan desert. This had revealed nothing other than four dead wild camel skeletons, a great deal of sand, a huge amount of oil activity and the certain knowledge that the camel herds in the Tarim river basin are doomed to extinction on account of the discovery of oil.

Driver Song was mercifully off tea-filled newspaper and back on nicotine. I had discovered the delicious baked Uighur mutton dumpling. The sun shone through the yellow haze and, as we were heading home, spirits were high. Taking me to one side, the Professor suddenly became conspiratorial.

'We can go back to Urumqi via Turfan by the normal route,' he said, his eyes glinting behind his specs, 'or we can take another, more interesting road which goes over the Tien Shan. It's very beautiful and it's quicker.'

'Let's take it. I've been to Turfan.'

'There is a slight problem. It's closed to foreigners. However, if you would like to dress as a Uighur we could try . . .'

I laughed. 'Of course, Professor. I'll dress up as a Uighur, Mongol or Kazak. Whatever you advise.'

'I suggest that you pretend to be sick so we'll wrap you in a blanket and put you in the back of the jeep. When we come to a check-point, cover your face and groan.' Professor Yuan reached in his pocket and pulled out a Uighur Muslim skull-cap. 'Here, I think you ought to wear this.'

I tried it on and it was a perfect fit.

'You knew all the time that I'd opt to go back over the Tien Shan,' I said with a smile.

'After forty-five days travelling with you, I think I know you well enough by now,' he replied. We shook hands. Not for the first time, I thanked my stars.

★　★　★

'Groan, go on, groan.'

I groaned in a suitable manner.

The slightly dishevelled, dumpy woman in military uniform peered inside the jeep. Unusually, she wasn't wearing a hat.

'He's sick. Very sick,' the Professor explained. 'We're rushing him to hospital in Urumqi. It's a very urgent case.'

What if she asks for my papers? I thought. I can hardly give her a British passport. I groaned again. But she didn't. For once we'd met a soldier who was not officious and was not even smartly dressed. She gave a wave of her hand and the wooden road barrier was lifted.

We climbed higher and higher into the Tien Shan. Apparently, Mao had decreed that military installations and industrial units should be tucked away in these mountains for security. And when we reached the steel works and industrial town of Balguntay, it contrasted starkly with the surrounding snow-covered peaks where Mongol drovers were driving flocks to summer pastures, just freed from winter snows. As we wound upwards, first to 4,000 metres and then to 4,500, we passed domestic yaks grazing on the steep-sided slopes and ever-curious marmots popping in and out of their holes. Finally, at 5,100 metres, we came to a dramatic pass, cut through a huge, slab of black rock, framed by two monumental glaciers. The snows were melting and the road doubled as a river.

We looked down in awe to the road below as it looped unnervingly down the mountain side.

Driver Song became fractious. Whether it was the altitude or the fact that he had, yet again, run out of cigarettes, I do not know, but as we began our descent he accelerated. The track was narrow, rough, wet and slippery. There was a sheer drop to a gorge down many thousands of metres and for half the crazed descent my heart was in my mouth. Then, like the jeep, I boiled over.

We stopped. I would walk, I proclaimed, even if it took a week. But no further would I go at this speed and with this driver.

The Professor, bold and brave in the desert, was remarkably weak in team management. But for once I had an unusual ally. 'Botanist' Li, the presumed Party official, agreed with my complaint. He verbally abused the unrepentant Song, produced a licence to drive and for the rest of our journey guided us safely down the mountainside. Not far from the bottom we came to a gorge of stunning beauty, its sheer-sided slopes covered in evergreens. Having passed through this gorge, we came to the blackest, vilest, most polluted settlement that I have seen in Xinjiang – another steel manufacturing settlement, with four tall, slender brick chimneys that under a bright blue, cloudless sky, poured thick black smoke into pure mountain air. The Professor insisted on a lunch stop and we ate sooty noodles in a café of indescribable squalor. Driver Song, once again tetchy and surly, refused to join us and sat in his jeep manicuring his fingernails. Every inhabitant and building in this overwhelmingly depressing town, only two hours' drive from Xinjiang's capital city, appeared to be covered in coal dust.

After a few days' rest and refurbishment in Urumqi we set off to investigate the area south of the Mongolian Great Gobi Reserve A. In the northern tip of Gansu Province, which borders the reserve, we saw the results of legal, illegal and military mining. In one area, a crudely-painted notice warned that the land was so badly contaminated with potassium cyanide, used for processing gold, that herdsmen must not graze there. We saw a year-old hybrid camel, the offspring of a wild bull that had ranged 100 kilometres in a desperate search for a domestic mate. The Mongol owner informed us that he would kill it for meat as it would soon become too difficult to handle.

We heard tales of a 1992 sighting of three more Gobi bears in the Dacaotan spring, fifteen kilometres from the international border, but our efforts to get to the border area ended in frustration at the hands of the military at Ming Shui. Our papers for the Gansu border area were not complete and we were turned away. However, I'd seen enough to know that when the camel wandered over the international border from the Great Gobi Reserve A in Mongolia, it headed south to disaster. Contaminated land, hordes of illegally armed miners, military mines with armed guards and indiscriminate blasting in camps of unbelievable squalor, ensured that there was no chance of survival for the wild Bactrian camel. It was only in the Gashun Gobi, where the hostile nature of that forbidding terrain discouraged man's intrusion, that the wild camel had a chance of survival, provided that we could establish the sanctuary in time.

* * *

On 4 June, having travelled just over 5,500 kilometres during the previous five weeks, I was ready to leave Urumqi, but Xinjiang Airways wasn't. After warm farewells, promises to return and renewed commitments of sanctuary support from Professor Yuan and my Urumqi friends, I found that my favourite airline was subject to a ten-hour delay. During this imposed wait, I was unwillingly picked up by a dapper, tweedy, gentleman with a General Zia profile and a Bertie Wooster accent who turned out to be Tarak, the Chief Magistrate of Islamabad. Freed from my self-imposed embargo on politics while in China, we discussed everything from Islamic fundamentalism and the current Afghan situation to the Uighur liberation movement. I was surprised to learn from him that six activists in the last-named cause had recently been shot in Urumqi. When we finally became airborne after surviving the sweaty, pushy Pakistan traders and the stony-faced Chinese bureaucrats, I soon discovered that my new-found Muslim VIP companion fancied a drink.

'Can you turn that way, old man, while I raise my coat lapel to have a swig of this,' he whispered with a conspiratorial grin as he produced a half-bottle of Red Label from his inside pocket. 'I don't want these people to see me knocking back dear old Johnny. It really wouldn't do in my position.' He gave me an oily smile and I inclined to the right. Whereupon, on the pretext of brushing something or other off his immaculately creased, white linen trousers he took a slug from the bottle.

'Can I offer you a nip?'

'No thanks, I'll stick to beer.'

He put his hand rather disconcertingly on my knee. 'The moment I clapped eyes on you, I knew that you were an Englishman of the old school,' he said patronisingly. 'Your jacket told me all.'

I looked at my battered old tweed jacket with its rips and tears and patches sewn on by the leather workers in Dun Huang market-place, now hanging loose and revealing years of wear.

'Oh, thanks.'

'And your baggage, those old, green, travel-stained canvas bags covered in dust. I can't begin to imagine what you are . . .'

'I'm just a traveller.'

'Do tell me . . .'

I didn't want to but I did.

He stared in amazement. 'But, good heavens, we have camels in Pakistan. Why go all the way to China and that terrible desert in Xinjiang to see camels? Surely . . .'

'These ones are wild, the ancestors of . . .'

But something useful did come out of our chance meeting. I was swept through immigration and customs in very, very VIP style. A Mercedes carried me to my lodgings and the Chief Magistrate of Islamabad, whose business or other interests in Urumqi remain a mystery, asked no favours.

7

Tu-ying and Lou Lan

For lust of knowing what should not be known
James Elroy Flecker

It must have been four o' clock in the morning when Xiao Yuan let out his heartfelt cry. I struggled out of my sleeping-bag, fumbled for a torch, pulled on sand shoes, unzipped the Kenya canvas tent flap and wriggled outside into the soft sand. It was cold, well below freezing. A stiff wind was blowing and there was a full moon. I ran over to the Professor's son who was standing shivering outside his tent, dressed only in an expedition 'camel' sweater and pale blue underpants.

'Are you all right?'

Loud snores came from the direction of Lao Zhao and Professor Yuan's tent.

'Yes, I'm okay. Don't worry about me. It's nothing, only a dream.'

'Did she come again?'

He hesitated, not wanting to sound foolish. 'Yes,' he said softly glancing over his shoulder towards his father's tent. 'I could see her just as clearly as last night.' He shuddered. 'She appeared like a black and white picture on the side of my tent. She was old, very old, with deep, sunken eyes and grey, tangled hair. She begged me to come outside with her, beckoning with the finger of her right hand and calling me by name.' He laughed nervously and repeated, 'It's nothing, only a bad dream.' He paused. 'The strange thing is that I really did want to follow her. I had to force myself not to take hold of her hand and go out with her into the desert.' He bent down to crawl back into his tent. 'Go back to sleep, John, I'm fine. Thanks for checking up on me.'

On two successive nights Xiao Yuan had dreamt that an old woman was trying to lure him into the desert. When I'd told him that Gobi travellers down the centuries, including Marco Polo, had told tales of lost souls who wandered the desert wastes inveigling travellers to follow them, he had laughed. 'That's just crazy superstition,' he had said. But I sensed that after this second visitation, he was not quite so sure.

I, too, had had my share of exotic desert dreams that included escaping from hostile, red ochre-coloured Masai, seeing my house in flames in England, and watching a friend run berserk with a shotgun. The ochre, fire and blood provided continuity in the form of a vivid, red backdrop, but as yet, thank goodness, there had been no invitation to follow an outcast soul into the wilderness.

At least this isn't a dream, I thought to myself as I crawled back inside my new Arctic sleeping-bag. I really am back in the Gobi again.

On my return from the 1995 expedition I'd put in a strong plea to UNEP to continue their support for research into the habits and habitat of the wild camel. In particular, I wanted to establish their exact migration route from the winter grazing area south of Lop Nur, to the summer grazing in the foothills of the Arjin Shan mountains. It was imperative that this route, which we knew existed, be properly surveyed so that it could be firmly included within the boundary of the proposed Lop Nur Nature Sanctuary. Through UNEP, a new avenue of expedition finance, a grant from the Global Environment Facility (GEF) was tapped, and on 24 March 1996, I was back once again on my favourite airline, surrounded by Uighur companions and mountains of their cardboard boxes and plastic bags. As in 1995, the seat-belt rule was universally ignored, but this time there was no charmer from the Kazak cat-walk and heavy, thick cloud concealed both mountain and desert from view.

On my return to Urumqi it was the two expedition vehicles that concerned me. Although I had managed to squeeze out of GEF slightly more dollars than in the previous year, the truck that stood mournfully in front of the Xinjiang Environmental Protection Institute looked, if anything, even more dilapidated than its prede-cessor with the faulty springs.

'It's better, much better,' said the Professor breezily, making light of my concern. 'It's a very good vehicle.'

I looked gloomily at the rusting, pale blue, wooden-sided truck with its two bald tyres and sagging exhaust. Even my unmechani-cal eye could see that it hovered on the brink of permanent consignment to a scrap heap.

'And this is Mr Li, our hired driver.'

Mr Li, of indeterminate age and provenance, had a crumpled look and a crooked smile. He also had very dirty clothes.

'His father disappeared in the Gashun Gobi in the early 1980s,' continued the Professor airily. 'They never found him or his truck. Who knows? We may even find him ourselves, ha, ha! He's very superstitious. That's why he's bringing his good-luck mascot.'

I looked at the white pigeon in a wire cage perched on top of the truck's bonnet. 'Is it coming with us into the desert?' I asked in amazement.

Driver Li nodded vigorously and then went over to the pigeon, took it out of its cage, and placed it in the glove compartment of his cab.

'He's demonstrating how it will travel,' said the Professor. 'He says that it will bring us good luck. I don't believe it, but it will of course provide us with meat if we get hungry.'

'And Mr Song? I hope that he . . .'

'Oh no,' said the Professor forcefully, 'Mr Song is *not* driving us anywhere this year.' I sighed with relief. 'And "Botanist" Li cannot accompany us,' he continued. I waggled my head sadly in an attempt to conceal my delight. The Professor pointed out another man dressed in khaki trousers and a denim top. 'This is the Institute jeep driver, Mr Liu.'

I clasped the hand of Driver Song's replacement. He was squat, pear-shaped and sported a long wisp of black hair that had been allowed to grow down one side, so that it could be meticulously plastered over a balding pate. In the weeks ahead, the howling desert winds frequently dislodged this vanity piece and it would flap above his head like an unsecured jib. He seemed just a trifle too self-assured and cocksure, but anyone was an improvement on the temperamental Driver Song.

'Good jeep. Very strong,' said the Professor, proudly patting the shiny bonnet. I had already taken note that it had done over 160,000 km. 'As for Lao Zhao over there, he hasn't been very well. He's had to have all his blood changed by a doctor in Korla.'

Lao Zhao and I greeted each other warmly. He looked much the same to me, the roguish smile (and, doubtless, the same itching trigger finger). But it wasn't until I was alone later that night in the Scientific Academic Hotel that it struck me that the blood transfusion could be linked to an excessive dose of radiation. After all, he'd been wandering in the Gashun Gobi since the 1970s, and in those days, nuclear tests weren't carried out underground.

There was one other new member of the team, Xiao Zhao, a member of the Institute who specialised in environmental impact assessment. He spoke good English and assailed me with endless personal assessment questions such as, 'How old are you? Are you a Christian? What are the ages of your daughters? What colour is your wife's hair?' and comments like, 'You look much younger in your passport photograph then you are in real life.'

At first I bridled and suspected that he had been put up to this intensive cross-examination, but later I realised that he had an inbuilt, insatiable curiosity and couldn't resist asking, 'Why? How? What?' In the prevailing climate of religious tolerance, his young wife had been swept off her feet into the Baptists' camp. Poor Xiao Zhao agonised daily as to whether he should follow her in or drag her out, and continually sought my advice. Fortunately, our adventures during the next few weeks concentrated his mind on more immediate matters.

There were deep, dirty black mounds of frozen snow on either side of the streets as we drove out of Urumqi. We paused to buy vegetables in an open air market, wading through a sea of soot-flecked sludge before beginning a protracted haggle over sacks of onions, tomatoes and potatoes. As my presence was not conducive to price control, I kept out of sight when we moved on to the stands of the sharp-eyed Uighur butchers. A glimpse of a foreign devil in the meat market could up the price by twenty per cent. After half an hour of gesticulation, feigned disgust and occasional shouts of despair, Xiao Yuan and his father trudged back to the jeep in the biting wind, laden with haunches of ancient mutton and dried donkey meat. We were provisioned and, much to my relief, ready to hit the road.

We had just passed the thirty-seven electricity generating wind-mills to the left of the Urumqi–Beijing highway, whose flailing sails reminded me of young girls doing unending, athletic back-flips, when our truck broke down. By the time we reached Tikar, just before midnight, it had broken down a second time, our jeep was leaking oil and all my earlier premonitions about the vehicles were fully justified.

'Teething troubles,' said the imperturbable Professor Yuan. 'Just start-up problems. All okay now. Don't you worry.'

But I did. To reach the wild camel migration route, south of Lop Nur, meant crossing an unknown expanse of metre-high, treacherous *shor*. Even Lao Zhao had not been into that area before. In addition, there was an added thrust to our journey which could prove to be as hazardous as anything that we had risked so far. The Professor had agreed that when we got to Lop Nur, we would make an attempt, either by vehicle or on foot, to reach the ancient city of Lou Lan. Hedin, Stein and the other early explorers and archaeologists had struggled across a pitted and broken Mars-like landscape to reach the abandoned city from the west. We were planning to approach Lou Lan from the east. If we succeeded, we would be the first expedition to have done so in recorded history.

It was one thing to do this with sound and proven equipment, but quite another with vehicles that had been patched and mended to the point of redundancy. I swallowed my fears, with the thought that the sporting Professor had agreed to this diversion to Lou Lan without being strictly entitled to do so. If he could take the risk, then so could I, but it did seem to me that we were making this undertaking unnecessarily difficult.

The next day, while the drivers worked on their vehicles and the Professor and Lao Zhao set nets to catch minnows in a nearby spring, Xiao Yuan and I unearthed a Uighur Cinderella. Sadiq, our host and nephew of Hedin's guide, owned up to abandoning the discarded boots that we had come across at a salt spring the previous year.

'But I have stopped camel hunting now,' he said, giving us a knowing look. 'Last, year, three people from Tocsin [a nearby town] were imprisoned for five years for camel hunting. One of them was forced to walk through the streets with a placard round his neck.'

I took some comfort from the fact that somebody was doing something to control the Uighur hunters.

★   ★   ★

'What does Lao Zhao think he's doing?' I turned to the Professor in exasperation and pointed to a column of thick, black smoke billowing up in front of us. 'We're only twenty kilometres from the nuclear test site. Why has Lao Zhao signalled to the world that we've arrived?'

'It's good to burn old *fragmitis* grass,' said the Professor. 'It makes it grow strong the following year.'

'But don't you understand? If there are any wild camels in the area they'll be fifty kilometres away by now.'

The tall stalks were dry and brittle and the fire had quickly taken hold. Soon, the Leu Chwang salt spring, where we had pitched camp after three days of desert travel, would be encircled by the flames. It would just have to burn itself out. Yet again, I was being driven to utter exasperation by the insatiable hunting instincts of our guide. An enforced delay caused by yet another problem with the truck's mechanics had meant that we had had time on our hands. We had left Lao Zhao behind at the camp with the two drivers, and had spent hours on foot, scanning the lunar landscape for camels from hummock, hill and mountain top. We had avoided unnecessary exposure, we had used fieldcraft to good purpose, but there had not been the sniff of a wild camel. Yet on our return to camp, we had discovered that our unpredictable guide had decided to torch the grass and send up totally unnecessary smoke signals in an attempt to catch – what? A gerbil for supper? It was too much.

'He's never to do this again,' I expostulated, fuming with barely concealed anger. 'You must control him, Professor. We're supposed to be conservationists, not pyromaniacs.'

He didn't understand, but he got the message.

'Lao Zhao won't do it again,' he said.

The repairs to the truck took longer than anticipated, and we were forced to spend another night at the charred spring which was criss-crossed with wild camel tracks. It was cold, about minus five degrees centigrade, and it was on this night that Xiao Yuan experienced his second visitation from the old woman and the jeep's engine froze. Driver Liu, his hair triumphantly adrift, applied a blowlamp to the iced-up engine. Then he lit a fire under the radiator. I remembered the army colonel and what had happened to his hair, and backed away. Eventually, with the failure of flame and fire, it was a tow from the truck that freed up the engine and at midday we were at last under way.

At a spring named Aka Bulak, the truck sank up to its axles in salt sludge. This time it was the jeep's turn to do the towing. The clock ticked on. We followed a riverbed that led from Aka Bulak which gradually widened until it merged into a vast dried-up flood plain north of Lop Nur. After two hours in the flood plain, we reached an area littered with *yardangs*, a bewildering maze of ten-metre high, weird and wonderful eroded land forms. The truck's universal joint then broke. Watched by his twittering pigeon, Mr Li took an hour to replace it. We drove south in failing light for a further two hours. Still we were not out of the maze. Our truck took a wrong turning and for half an hour all contact with it was lost. We were all relieved when we finally linked up again. Trucks in the Gashun Gobi have been known to disappear completely. With the critical mechanical state of our vehicles it was important that contact was constantly maintained. At last the Professor had had enough.

'We camp here,' he called out, pointing to a *yardang* looming to our right. 'I had hoped to reach Lop Nur, but it's too late to go any further.'

It certainly was. We were frustrated by the constant hold-ups, tired and hungry. The temperature was well below freezing and a biting, bitterly cold wind was blowing from the east. We struggled to erect our unruly tents with numbed fingers, only to discover that just below the sandy surface was granite rock. Tent pegs buckled and we were forced to collect rocks to secure our guy ropes. After an imperfect meal of instant noodles and peppered donkey, I finally went to bed in a black humour. Why had the Professor hired these mechanically clapped-out vehicles when our very lives depended on them? Filled with foreboding and two tots of whisky, surrounded by sagging, flapping canvas, nursing split fingers and with ears, nose and mouth full of fine, powdered sand, I eventually fell into a troubled sleep, which was shattered at 4.00 a.m. when Mr Li revved his engine to stop it freezing.

★　★　★

'John, get up. Lao Zhao wants to show you something.' Xiao Yuan's voice had an unfamiliar sense of urgency. I was stiff with cold and the miseries of the previous evening had not yet dissipated. I had had little sleep and was reluctant to be rushed.

'All right, I'll come. In a moment.'

'Come now, please. It's important.'

'Can't I have some tea?'

'No.'

I had gone to sleep fully dressed in my corduroy trousers and tweed jacket. It was only a question of pulling on my boots.

Once outside, Xiao Yuan grasped my arm and led me to a nearby *yardang*. Lao Zhao hurried over and shook me warmly by the hand.

'You are the first, the very first. Not even Sven Hedin . . .' Xiao Yuan was very excited.

'I don't understand. What are you talking about?'

'Number one. You're number one,' said Lao Zhao, shoving his upturned thumb under my nose.

Xiao Yuan explained. 'This morning, Lao Zhao got up early and went for a walk. He discovered that we've pitched camp near Tu-ying, an ancient outpost of Lou Lan on the middle Silk Road. Zhao says that none of the early explorers discovered Tu-ying. A Chinese archaeologist came across it by chance in the 1930s, and Hedin learnt about it when he returned to Lop Nur in 1934. No one has been here since. You're the very first foreigner to reach Tu-ying in recorded history.'

I was, of course, thrilled with this news, but later research revealed that, unfortunately, it was not wholly true. For although Stein and others had certainly not been to Tu-ying, the incredible Hedin had, if only for an hour. Hedin had written of his 1934 expedition:

There was a minimum temperature of 42.4 degrees on the night of May 8–9, strangely cold for so late in the year! The scouts had been out, and when we got up in the morning they reported that they had not been able to find an arm of the river with any current, but that they had found the ruins of a fair-size house on the mainland to the north-west. Chen [Hedin's Chinese expedition scientist] suspected at once that this was the fort T'u-ken, discovered by the archaeologist Hwang Wen-pi in 1930. Just on nine we got into a double canoe and rowed to a place over open water free of reeds. It took scarcely half an hour to reach the place.

The posts of the house rose from a low mound situated on a peninsula, which had water on three sides – west, south and east. Chen had been there in the early spring of 1931 during

Horner's expedition to Lop-nor, and recognised the place at once.

Some of our boatmen had dug a hole in the middle of the house without finding anything . . . We stayed for about an hour, which I needed to make a sketch of the place with all its details. Chen took some photographs and measurements.

I suspect that our 'find' of Tu-ying was Hedin's T'u-ken. We walked briskly up to the low mound and clambered to the top. Three wooden poplar posts jutted out at various angles, the surviving corner posts of a rectangular building. There was no sign of Hedin's boatmen's excavations. At a lower level, which in 1934 must have been near the water, there was an area that was blackened and littered with shards of broken pottery. Was this where food was cooked? I rummaged with my hands in the dirty sand and pulled out a large piece of felt. A second foray revealed a piece of brittle leather. Both were well preserved, and possibly the 1,600-year-old remnants of discarded clothing.

I walked away on my own to the west for 200 metres, across an area that, sixty-two years ago, would have been covered by lake water, and found to my excitement the remains of another ancient building. Two long poplar poles were jutting from a gully concealed by two towering *yardangs*. They were just above the level of the former lake, and as Hedin makes no reference to them, I assume that he did not see them. At last, a real discovery! Even if Chen or Hwang Wen-pi had seen them, which was unlikely on account of the 1934 water level, certainly no foreigner had looked on them since Lop Nur swung to the south-east and the settlement was abandoned in about AD 330.

Meanwhile, the team were scouring an area which, in the 1930s, would have been below lake-level, and picking up beads, rings, coins, arrowheads and, in the case of Driver Li, a medallion, all of which Professor Yuan insisted be handed over to the archaeological authorities in Urumqi. Lao Zhao found three large pieces of translucent jade. The nearest jade mines lie over 200 kilometres to the south, near the oasis town of Khotan. This jade may have been brought by boat up Lop Nur, only to be mislaid at Tu-ying. It was awesome to think that we were the first visitors to the settlement since 1934, and possibly the first to disturb parts of a site that had lain unseen and untouched nearly a thousand years before Marco Polo's desert crossing further south. Only the wild camel had pottered among these ruins during the centuries that they had passed from the knowledge of man. I was thrilled to discover the fresh tracks of a female camel and her young calf.

That afternoon we left our camp near Tu-ying, driving by jeep back through the maze of eroded land formations north of the lake-bed to a vast plateau of pebble-strewn desert. For four hours we scoured the area for evidence of camels. At dusk we were at last rewarded by a clear sighting of a lone bull, and were greatly encouraged by the number of fresh camel tracks. At least the hunters and miners hadn't penetrated this far into the Gashun Gobi. On our return, with the rays of the setting sun filtering through the *yardangs*, the panorama was quite fantastic. We saw the outlines of sleeping dogs, lions, dragons, fairy castles, fortresses and towers. Xiao Zhao crowed with delight when he spotted an uncanny likeness to Chairman Mao. It was the landscape of a miraculous dream.

The following day, under a bright blue sky but in a freezing wind, we allowed ourselves one more forage around Tu-ying. We found enough brightly coloured beads to string a necklace. I pondered on their provenance. Had their owners seen the garrison march out to battle against the Huns and other barbarians? Had they seen the great trade caravans as they lumbered along the Silk Road towards Lou Lan with innumerable camels carrying bales of precious silk? Had they seen the wild camels, the sole surviving representatives from that ancient time? And surely the beads' owners had loved and had been loved . . .

At 1.00 p.m. we resumed our southward journey to the lake, and before long had reached the complex delta of the Kuruk Daria, dry by the hand of man since 1974. Here and there a tamarisk bush struggled to survive. Occasionally there was a pathetic flash of green, a signal of struggling life from among the dry, dusty, brittle clumps of reed. But it was desolate, a land of death, in striking contrast to Hedin's description sixty-two years earlier when he had canoed through this exact spot. He wrote, 'Tamarisks and reeds looked up out of the water. It was a delicious place! I sat with my sleeves rolled up and dabbled my hands in the cool, rippling water . . . With only one boat and two sturdy paddlers we worked up a good pace, and the water foamed about our bows. Fifteen yards ahead of us appeared a wild hog, swimming from the mainland to the reeds. He was timid, scented danger and swam for dear life. The water foamed around his bows too.'

Only a mirage induces notions of water today. The fish, the wild hogs and the abundant bird life which included the bittern (*Botaurus stellaris*), the osprey, the great-crested grebe, the black-winged stilt, the heron and different species of gull, 'which we saw in such numbers over the northern part of Lop Nur, in whose fresh waters they find an inexhaustible supply of fish', have long since disappeared. Only one animal remains, and we found its tracks and its droppings in the dried-up delta of the Kuruk Daria.

It was near this spot that Hedin made an interesting calculation:

Our nearest neighbours were, to the north-west, Singer [now within the nuclear test site], 88 miles from our camp; to the SSW, Miran, 120 miles away; to the WSW, Tikenlick, 133 miles; to the south-west, Charkhlick [Ruoqiang], 163 miles; to the north, Turfan [or Tikar], 164 miles; to the north-east, Hami, 235 miles; to the ESE, Dun Huang, 262 miles; and to the south-east, Bulungir-nor, 276 miles. If one connects all these places on a map by straight lines, there is a considerable slice of Central Asia, or about 78,000 square miles in which we were the only human beings. The belt of desert where we were constituted one two hundred and twentieth of the whole of Asia. If the whole continent was as thinly populated, its population would be only 22,000.

After an hour of grinding travel we reached Lop Nur. The grey, dusty surface of the lake-bed stretched to the skyline. To the east, a row of black lumps, possibly hillocks on a tongue of land, appeared to hover above the horizon. To the west, more black objects, shaped like horsemen, quivered in the vibration set up by rising currents of warm air. Other than these slightly ominous features, the prevailing colour was grey. Even the blue sky had disappeared behind the dust thrown up by the howling wind. We drove slowly down the lake for a further hour. The truck was frequently bogged down in sand, which meant arduous work with pick and shovel. At last, following a compass bearing worked out by Lao Zhao, we turned due east. We were now attempting to pioneer a route from the east to Lou Lan. After another hour of snail-like progress we hit rough *shor*. The engines of both the truck and the jeep boiled over almost every ten minutes, necessitating frequent stoppages. Travelling at a speed of no more than six kilometres an hour, we eventually crossed the *shor*. We passed a group of sentry-like *yardangs*, indicators of the western boundary of the old lake, and entered a landscape so utterly dead and barren that we all fell silent. Before us lay mound after mound of grey, soft clay, covered with scattered roots of ancient poplars and interspersed with eroded gullies lined with shale. Occasionally, the trees themselves, petrified into a rock-like hardness, would lie twisted and tangled in our path, forcing us to change direction. We snaked through these impediments, making frequent stops to cool our engines, and often resorted to picks and spades to extricate ourselves. It was another hell on earth. As dusk fell, the Professor called a halt and as my journal relates:

> We pitched camp on the surface of the moon in the middle of nowhere. Freezing wind. A rotten camp site. It did occur to me in the middle of the night that if we broke down here we would have a problem. No one knows we are here. Twenty kms. to the north is the nuclear test site. Ahead lies 400 kms. of sand. Behind us a further 400 kms. of sand, dry lake and desert. I try to banish these unwholesome thoughts.

The next day, Good Friday, 5 April 1996, I wrote in my journal:

Freezing wind. As if to confirm last night's dire thoughts the jeep will not start. A tow start again. But what if the lorry gets stuck and is unable to tow the jeep? Driver Liu is continually tinkering with it (the jeep) but without success. We are surrounded as far as the eye can see by an ocean of grey, undulating, flaky sand. Sometimes the surface is crust hard, sometimes it is soft. Treacherous for vehicles and totally unpredictable. We set off, after the jeep's tow start at 11.45 a.m. but do not get very far. Bogged down, dug out, the lorry eventually gets over a dune which we have strewn with dead tamarisk (1,600-year-old variety). We start to go in the wrong direction (east) over one of the countless and totally misleading tributaries of the Kuruk Daria. I feel that the risk of trying to reach Lou Lan with these two unpredictable and nearly clapped-out vehicles is too great. Gently persuade the Professor, whose ambition it has been to drive to Lou Lan, that it would be more prudent to walk. So, after travelling just under four kms. in three hours, we pitch camp on a windy knoll. It is planned to attack Lou Lan on foot tomorrow after making a recce today. During the four kms. drive we saw a V-shaped flock of migrating cranes fly overhead, and wild camel footprints. Can it be true? There is no water and only dried-up vegetation for many, many kilometres. Utterly amazing. Pitch camp and bed down relatively early in preparation for the morrow and all that it may bring.

Early the next morning, Professor Yuan erected a long wooden pole on the back of the truck, which we carried to extricate us from sand. He tied a light-bulb on the top, attached it to our generator, and Driver Li and his pigeon were left behind to guard our camp and given strict instructions to start the generator at dusk and keep it going until we returned.

At nine o'clock, with full water bottles, a compass, maps, torches and tummies packed with noodles, we launched ourselves into a featureless wasteland that stretched in every direction to eternity. Our plan was to try to find the main tributary of the dried-up Kuruk Daria. The river had formerly flowed quite close to the ancient city, and as long as we stuck to the main riverbed, we should eventually spot the Buddhist tower or the city watchtower, two prominent features of Lou Lan. The problem was that the river had flowed into a network of small tributaries as it neared Lop Nur, and in their dried-up state, it was difficult to pick up the main artery. After numerous false starts and dead ends, we eventually reached a wide, deep-sided riverbed which we felt must be the main tributary of the Kuruk Daria. We set off, our faces to the west, trekking along the twisting sand river, and taking turns to climb up the steep bank to see if we could spot either of the two landmarks. After four hours of trudging though soft sand, with a freezing wind blowing strongly on our backs, there was still no sign of a tower. By this time we had all realised that Lao Zhao's calculations were wrong. Lou Lan was much more than fifteen kilometres from our camp site.

'Hey, John. Look at this.' The ever-cheerful Xiao Yuan ran over to me, waving a piece of pottery. 'We must be getting nearer the city.'

Soon we were all picking up pottery shards, and I noticed with interest that a few seemingly dead tamarisk bushes by the side of the river had sprouted long, twisting roots that sprawled metres over the riverbed in a desperate attempt to find moisture. Then, at long last, there was a 'holloa' from the top of the bank. Lao Zhao had spotted the Buddhist tower. We scrambled excitedly out of the sand river and stared at a tiny triangular hump just discernible on the horizon. It was a very long way away. When the outline of the watchtower came into view, we saw to our dismay that it was a good way to the left of the triangular tower.

'The city is eight kilometres from the Buddhist tower,' said Lao Zhao, confirming our unspoken thoughts. 'Even when we reach the first tower there's still a great deal of walking to do.'

We had now entered the remains of an ancient oasis. In nearly every gully between the hummocks of decayed poplar and tamarisk roots, the ground was littered with broken pottery. Spurred on by the sight of the shards and the tower, and propelled forward by the stiffening wind which caused dust to swirl around us, we at last reached our destination. It was four o' clock, and we'd been walking non-stop since nine o'clock that morning.

'Stein was here,' muttered Lao Zhao, pointing to empty crevices on the sides of the tower and running his index finger across his throat. 'He stole everything.'

And indeed Stein had taken away many of the religious paintings that were once an integral part of the tower. Today, nothing remains there to tell of the religious habits and beliefs of the people of Lou Lan.

We were elated. It had been a walk of roughly twenty-two kilometres and we still had to reach the city itself. Nonetheless, our arrival at this man-made construction, after tramping through the very worst landscape that nature could devise, gave us all a lift. We hugged each other and took an endless succession of posed photographs, before seating ourselves on some massive timbers which had fallen from the tower to devour our meagre rations. Lao Zhao was very happy. As our guide, compass bearer and map interpreter he, after all, had borne the greatest responsibility.

After half an hour's rest we set off for the ancient city. Although the route was difficult, there was now an added spring in our step and it took us just over an hour. We headed for the awesome central tower. This watchtower, standing plumb in the middle of the city, is surrounded by the remains of houses to the east, south and west and an open square to the north. The flagstaff erected on the tower's summit by two members of Hedin's team, Chen and Horner in 1931, still remains in place and, although the steps which wind to the top have mostly worn away, the tower is still climbable. The view from the top is breathtaking. Grey desolation and decay spreads out in all directions and I gasped aloud when I saw the jigsaw puzzle of hummocks and gullies that we had managed to cross.

The dimensions of a number of the ancient houses can still be identified by the woven tamarisk and reed building material that once formed the base of their external walls. Many of the buildings could also be accurately plotted by the distance between their upright support poles. A large building near a market square had been the city's municipal centre or *yamen*, and individual rooms could quite clearly be seen within it. One building had a door lintel firmly positioned between two upright posts, while another large construction had a massive end wall which had splayed out on either side to form a huge V. Man-made square notches could also be found in a number of collapsed cross-pieces.

The early explorers had unearthed manuscripts and letters, written on paper and wooden staves, which accurately dated the abandonment of the city. These show that Lou Lan boasted an inn, a hospital, a post office building and a temple. Most of the letters dealt with routine administrative matters, but one translated into a very human and heartfelt sentiment. Upon receiving sad news, Tsi Ch'eng writes, 'Miss Yin having been without any previous illness, the misfortune that so suddenly befell her was quite beyond expectation. I received the sad news and so much greater is, therefore, my deep-felt sympathy and regret. But a deep wound cannot be endured. What then can help?'

Our team searched hard among the ruins for gems, earrings, coins, spoons, tweezers, hairpins and Roman and Syrian glass – trinkets and necessities that earlier explorers had unearthed. But apart from numerous pieces of pottery, much of which was too cumbersome to carry, only a fragment of a bronze mirror and a coin were found.

The extent of the city and the quality of its preservation is remarkable. Only in the desperately dry air of the Gobi, where measurable rainfall may occur once in a decade, can this phenomenon occur. Nevertheless, I was surprised that 1,600 years of violent sand storms had left so much for us to explore. It was not at all difficult to imagine that this was a very important centre on the longest caravan route on earth, that great highway, the Silk Road, which linked east and west. And from the top of the tower, one could almost hear the tinkling caravan bells and see the endless processions of camels, winding across the desert and through the city gates.

Aren't those flickering shadows in the square below crowds of walkers, riders, donkeys, camels and carts? Aren't those people, off-loading bales of silk from squatting camels on the far side of the square, traders from the east? And those over there, spreading their wares out before them on woven blankets of camel hair, merchants from the west? Surely those are the shouts of camel drovers, the cries of hawkers and traders, the laughter of girls and the guffaws of ribald men? Or is it only the ever-present wind, moaning around the cracks and crevices of the tower and making fools of us all? The traveller who in our time journeys over these obliterated tracks hears only in fancy the echo of the caravan bells dying away in the distance, and the camel drivers shouting at their beasts. This desert city of the dead is haunted by a multitude of ghosts.

We stayed in Lou Lan for as long as we dared. Without provisions or water it was dangerous not to return to our camp that night, especially as Lao Zhao had grossly underestimated the distance. If a sand storm sprung up and we were marooned in Lou Lan we could find ourselves in considerable difficulty. It is as dangerous to lose one's way in the maze of *yardangs* surrounding Lou Lan as in the subterranean passages of the Roman catacombs. We felt a growing sense of unease as the watery sun, half hidden by dust, started to dip towards the horizon. None of us wanted to remain in the ancient city after dark.

As Driver Liu had a bad knee, it was decided to split up into two groups. The Professor, Xiao Zhao and myself setting off in front, with Lao Zhao, Xiao Yuan and the ailing Liu following more slowly from behind. My journal again:

We set off in a setting sun which provided a spectacular back-drop for this ghostly city. We head directly for the river-bed and avoid the Buddhist tower. The sun disappears as we reach the river and our torches light up footprints left on our out-ward journey. Fortunately, as our batteries fade, a watery moon rises. If there had been no moon and if the wind had not changed direction to blow from behind us, it would have been much more difficult. Professor Yuan tires but keeps going. It's too cold to rest. If we do, we stiffen up with cold. We leave the river-bed as our torches 'die' and to our great relief see our 'star in the east', the light from the bulb on the truck. As we walk towards it, the moonlight fades away. The going becomes more and more difficult and we stumble around *yardangs* and through crumbling shale for over three hours. Suddenly, our 'star' disappeared!

At this point our situation was serious. We were looking for a needle in a sandstack with nothing to guide us. The moon had completely disappeared and the second party, who were following our footsteps, were a long way behind. If we missed the truck and carried on into the featureless wasteland, we could easily disappear for good, like so many Gobi travellers before us. We would also lead the second party to disaster.

'I suggest that we spread out in a line as far apart as possible,' I said. 'We can't be too far away from the truck because we left the riverbed three hours ago. Whatever we do, we mustn't lose contact with each other.'

We spread out as far as we dared, the Professor in the centre, Xiao Zhao on the right and myself on the left. The shadows ahead of us played constant tricks. What appeared to be a truck turned out to be yet another hummock of twisted wood. We kept constantly stopping to call out, hoping that Driver Li would hear us. There was no response. Apart from the wind, it was as silent as the tomb. And then, unexpectedly, just as our hearts were sinking into the sand, Xiao Zhao gave a great shout. He had spotted the truck. We were safe. It was 1.30 a.m. on Easter Sunday, and after walking non-stop for sixteen hours and covering fifty-five kilometres, we had risen indeed!

Our thoughts were for the party behind us. Professor Yuan roused Driver Li from his slumbers in his cab, gave him a dressing-down (Li had thought that we would not be returning that night and so had put out the light), and restarted the generator. I was nearly asleep on my feet. After two steaming bowls of porridge oats, I stumbled into my tent and collapsed in an insensible heap. I was woken at 7.20 a.m. by stirring shouts, announcing the arrival of the rest of our team. They had walked slowly, nursing Driver Liu, and had seen the light when it was switched back on. Uncertain of the distance to the camp, however, they had decided to light a fire, get some sleep and continue at daybreak. To their utter astonishment, they woke to find that they had camped only 500 metres away.

It was a joyful Easter, even though the day meant nothing to my companions. We celebrated with the Professor's firecrackers and the last of my carefully hoarded whisky. We rested, secure in the knowledge that we had reached Lou Lan from the east, the first expedition in recorded history to have done so. That night I lay awake for many hours, listening to the mysterious spirit voices of the night.

Later in the year, when word spread of our successful attempt to reach Lou Lan from the east, a Chinese 'explorer' based in Shanghai tried to follow our tracks. He was transported in a massive oil exploration vehicle to the place where we had abandoned our vehicles, but had insisted on walking to the city by himself. Two days later, twenty kilometres from Lou Lan, he had been found dead from dehydration.

Let Professor Yuan Guoying have the last word on our incredible journey to Lou Lan. In 1997, he published a paper in Chinese on our discoveries at both Lou Lan and Tu-ying. The quaint English translation reads like a piece of prose from the seventeenth century, yet in its final three descriptive sentences, it poignantly captures the hazards of our momentous trek: 'Former archaeological and touring teams have to start at the March bridge on the bank of the Konche Daria and walk 27km to the Lou Lan town from the west. We initiated a new eastern route and also walked 25km to get to Lou Lan because it was hard for automobile to travel. The rode [sic] is so rugged and rough, and so wriggling tortuous for walk, with no fresh water for camel and horse, that it is terriblly [sic] hard to make tour of Lou Lan town from the east for archaeology.'

★ ★ ★

The next day, back on the lake-bed of Lop Nur, we concentrated on our main objective, the plotting of the migration route of the wild camels. So far we had only seen one lone bull, north of the lake, but to find and explore their winter grazing area we had to head due south. We were once again governed by the wretched condition of our vehicles. By five o'clock in the afternoon we had reached the vast expanse of *shor* that surrounds the western, eastern and southern sides of the lake. But our lorry had developed a serious problem; it was burning engine oil as rapidly as it was consuming petrol. We had brought with us ample supplies of both, but not enough oil to cope with this emergency. And there was yet another problem: Lao Zhao was in unknown territory, and had never attempted to penetrate south of the lake. We found the vehicle tracks of scientists who had undertaken research in the area some years ago and tried to follow them, but one by one they petered out. So Lao Zhao set a south-easterly route. He was confident that it would eventually lead us into the Aqike valley, the winter grazing grounds of the wild camel. The *shor* grew taller and taller. The vehicles were now covering only two to three kilometres an hour. Frequently, we had to get out of the jeep to break down great slabs of rock-salt which threatened to split the vehicle's oil sump. After three and a half hours on this fearful terrain, the Professor called a halt. It was 8.30 p.m.; the light was fading fast and the truck was billowing thick black smoke as it burnt up a mixture of oil and petrol. The jeep was running on three cylinders.

We somehow managed to secure the kitchen tent to the back of the truck, but found it impossible to erect our own tents on the brittle, spiky terrain. While the two drivers sucked on a succession of cigarettes and succeeded in dampening each other's spirits still further, Xiao Yuan, Xiao Zhao and I prepared supper: noodles, dried donkey meat with sugared tomatoes, peppers and limp onion tops. Then we bedded down as best we could. It was cold, well below freezing, and I shivered in my Arctic sleeping-bag.

There's always a low point on any expedition, and I hit it then. 'What on earth am I doing here?' I asked myself. 'I have a comfortable house and a warm bed. I don't have to look for wild camels for a living, and am not earning a penny for doing so. Is there any sense at all in risking my neck in one of the most dangerous, unpleasant and uncomfortable places in the world?'

Finding it impossible to sleep, I groped for my battered, shortwave wireless in an attempt to dispel the gloom. The aerial had long since snapped, and I cast the makeshift copper wire replacement over the rock-salt and attached one end to the broken, metallic aerial stub.

'. . . And they're lining up for the start . . .' I perked up, and clamped my Afghan fur hat firmly on my head. Could it be? 'And they're off.' Yes! Commentary from the 1996 Grand National. Quick, place a mental bet. Good-bye Gobi; hello Aintree. I revelled in twenty minutes of bliss. My horse finished, though not among the leaders, and I drifted happily off to sleep.

The next day dawned cold, bright and clear. Our party rose early, woken by the alarming bangs from our expanding drums of petrol, caused by the rapid rise in temperature. We couldn't wait to get moving and, after a hasty breakfast, quite literally 'bashed' on through the *shor* for another kilometre. But the slabs of brittle rock salt grew even higher. We were forced to stop, and the Professor and his son set off on a foot reconnaissance to see if they could discover any end to this tortuous terrain, which was now beginning to shred rubber from our tyres. Driver Li had sunk into despair, convinced that he was about to suffer the same fate as his father. He chatted endlessly to his pigeon, looking to this remarkable feathered pioneer for salvation. Driver Liu's spirits were equally low. Unfortunately, he manifested his depression in shows of truculent surliness and hot-headed chatter. He'd long since stopped worrying about his hairpiece and seemed preoccupied with picking an argument with any member of the team who went near him. Lao Zhao was also at a very low ebb. He was our guide, recognised nationally as highly experienced. Yet here we were, lost on the fringe of Lop Nur, uncertain of both our route and direction. As we settled to wait for the return of the Professor and his son, we presented a sorry picture of desolation and despair. They eventually returned at eight o'clock, having made a round trip of twenty kilometres.

'It goes on for ever,' said the Professor gloomily.

Lao Zhao unrolled his satellite map and poked a stubby, nicotine-stained finger at a large expanse of white.

'There are only eighteen more kilometres to cross,' he said.

No one believed him.

I thought for a moment. To travel eighteen kilometres would take five hours, maybe six. We had shredded tyres, a truck on the point of collapse and our guide was uncertain of the way. It was clear that we were going to have to abandon the attempt to reach the Aqike valley by this route. The only alternative was to return to Tikar. Once the vehicles were repaired or replaced, we could drive to Dun Huang via Hami and attempt to enter the Aqike valley from the east. It was a lot of extra driving, and we might not penetrate to the south of the lake, but it seemed the height of folly to attempt to go forward in our present state. I put forward these views. For once there was no protracted discussion.

'We all agree with you,' said the Professor immediately. 'We will head back tomorrow.' There was really no alternative.

Lao Zhao did, however, make one bright suggestion. He advised Driver Li to mix gear-box oil with our vegetable cooking oil in order to eke out the rapidly dwindling supplies of engine oil. He said that he'd seen it done before and it had worked. No one argued with this, and the two drivers started to blend this seemingly incompatible mixture.

We spent another uncomfortable night on the needle-sharp *shor*. Next morning, Driver Liu said that he was so worried that he didn't sleep all night. Driver Li said that he didn't sleep because Driver Liu stank. They glowered at each other over their morning noodles as Driver Li stroked Tweet-tweet, the name I had given to the admirable bird who never complained and seemed to sleep soundly every night.

When we set off, Xiao Yuan, Xiao Zhao and I walked in front of the jeep, pulling any lumps of *shor* out of the way that could have caused damage.

'You're road-building for China,' shouted the Professor as we slowly negotiated a passage through a particularly treacherous area of rock-salt.

The truck began to smell like a mobile kebab shop as cooking oil circulated in its vitals. But no matter, this unusual form of lubrication was clearly working. The engine hadn't seized up and we were making progress. We reached the lake-bed and started to move more quickly, stopping every half an hour to top up the engine with the cooking-oil mix.

By late afternoon we had reached the Kuruk Daria delta without a major incident, and then followed our tracks past Tu-ying and through the myriad of fantastically shaped *yardangs*. Our spirits rose. Late that night we arrived at the Aka Bulak spring. We pitched camp, exhausted but immensely relieved. Driver Li no longer looked as though he was preparing to follow his father to death and destruction. Driver Liu had forgotten about his knee, his bad dreams and his fractious disputes. The Professor, unshaven and baggy-eyed, had shed some of his concerns for our ultimate safety. His greatest relief was that we were now clear of an area that we had not had permission to enter. And Tweet-tweet, as calm and imperturbable as ever, emerged unruffled from her cramped quarters and pecked away at her seed by the light of her owner's torch.

The next day, the disasters and tensions of the last few days abruptly returned. We had only covered forty-five kilometres when a piston-ring broke on the truck, bringing it to a grinding halt. And to add to our woes, the temperature dropped and Lao Zhao was yet again uncertain of our position. Driver Liu lost his temper with our guide and Zhao went into a major decline. However, both drivers worked on the truck until well after midnight. They stripped the engine into so many pieces that I wondered whether they would be able to put them together again. Next morning, when I awoke cold and stiff, the desert was covered in an inch and a half of gleaming white snow, topped by a sky of brilliant blue. While an oil-besmirched Driver Li continued his efforts to turn a six-cylinder truck into one of five cylinders, Driver Liu attempted to thaw out his radiator over a fire, with assistance from his blow-lamp. By 11.00 a.m., twenty-four hours after the collapse of the cylinder, a double miracle occurred. Both engines were running.

Lao Zhao, who had lost considerable face over his faulty interpretation of our satellite maps, recovered some of his self-esteem by finding the way. However, on closer inspection of the maps, I couldn't help wondering if our wrong turns and dead ends were entirely the fault of our guide. One or two prominent hills appeared to have wandered or gone missing altogether. Valleys seemed to have completely disappeared. Are satellite maps deliberately fudged in sensitive areas?

We drove through a landscape which had been lit by thawing snow to a surreal brilliance. Even the drabbest hill and mountain stood dressed in newly revealed colours. The sharp, clear atmosphere, coupled with unaccustomed moisture, highlighted colours in the rocks of unimaginable complexity. In the centre of a stunning arena of lights we spotted a lone bull camel. It stared at us momentarily from a gleaming hillside, took fright at the slam of our jeep door and disappeared over a snow-capped hill. We arrived at Wanwan Quen (Twisting Spring) and stopped to eat lunch.

'Look at that. Just look at that,' I exclaimed.

The mountains to the north of the spring appeared to have been daubed with a painter's brush that had been dipped in alternating shades of green, yellow and brown. As the sun rose higher, these primary colours blended into increasingly subtle variants of the original. It was breathtaking.

'It's lunchtime,' said Xiao Yuan. 'Come and eat with us.'

'But can't you see what I'm looking at?'

I was throwing words away. My travelling companions were hungry and it was time to eat. They couldn't understand why I wanted to stand and stare at mountains. I yearned for a comprehending companion.

Later, pottering about in the reed-beds near the spring, I was struck yet again by the strange after-effects of snow in the desert. The dusty, dead fronds of dried reed had been transformed into stems of glistening, golden yellow. The salt sludge that harboured ticks gleamed with the brilliance of powdered snow. Everything was utterly transformed, except the perception of my colleagues.

Two hours later we reached an outlying iron-ore mine. In stark contrast to the majestic scenery that we had just crossed, it was covered in mounds of rubbish, pieces of discarded machinery and the inevitable mass of plastic waste. Even the magical light could do little to improve this eyesore. Indeed, it emphasised man's desecration of the environment. The miners were as grimy as their surroundings, but they gave us some much-needed engine oil. During social chit-chat they told stories of sophisticated hunters, even government officials, coming in four-wheel-drive Toyotas from as far afield as Urumqi and Hami in order to shoot camels. We learnt that a miner from their own mine had recently blown off an arm and a leg at the Aka Bulak spring while trying to set landmines to blow up camels for 'sport'. And why? To find a variant for his diet. I recalled the memorable description by Hedin of a camel that had been shot by one of the Uighurs in his party when he was making a crossing of the Taklamakan at the turn of the century: 'She sank into a posture in which camels usually rest. We hurried to her and I made a few sketches while she was still alive. She did not look at us but seemed to be in despair at having to part forever with her otherwise inviolate desert land. Before she died, she opened her mouth and bit into the sand. I forbade any more shooting.'

If only I could be instrumental, nearly 100 years later, in forbidding any more shooting. All this grim news brought home to me forcibly the extreme urgency of establishing the proposed Lop Nur Nature Sanctuary. With the winds of economic change blowing more strongly every year, even in the remotest parts of Xinjiang, the camel is coming under ever-increasing threat. If those intent on its destruction have already penetrated to the Aka Bulak spring, how much further into the desert will they dare to go next year, or the year after? Will there be any wild camels left at all in five years' time? We had seen two lone bulls north of Lop Nur, a not unnatural occurrence after the mating season. How long before both they and their harem of females are totally destroyed?

8

The Valley of the
Shadow of Death

*Something lost beyond the Ranges. Lost and waiting for
you. Go!*

Rudyard Kipling

'I dare you to ask that one,' Xiao Yuan said with a huge grin, nod-
ding his head at a pretty Uighur girl seated at a table on the far side
of the dance hall. She sat next to an unsmiling older woman, staring blankly at the young dancers circling in front of her. Long
slender fingers toyed aimlessly with a glass of orange juice. No
one had asked her to dance.

Our team, minus Lao Zhao who was resting and Xiao Zhao
who had returned to Urumqi, were huddled, seeing yet unseen, in
a smoke-filled, dimly-lit, VIP snuggery in the Shanshan Municipal
Dance Hall. The Professor sat stock still, staring straight ahead of
him, eyes glinting with suppressed excitement behind his metal-
rimmed spectacles. His son, whose idea it had been to attend the
Saturday night Shanshan hop, was animated, ticking away like a
metronome. The scene took me straight back to the 1950s and
Saturday nights in rural Warwickshire, where girls preened and
giggled on one side of the hall while boys gawped and 'dare-doed'
in mock bravado from the other. Even the music – the fox-trots,
the quicksteps and the waltzes – sounded the same. And likewise
the dancers, by no means confined to the under-thirties, who were

all kitted out in their number ones. Clad in our dusty, patched and worn expedition gear we were clearly under-dressed, but in spite of our sartorial disadvantage, we nevertheless indulged in our own juvenile game of 'dare do' and the dare was now on me. I walked stiffly across the dance floor and up to the poor, unsuspecting Uighur girl.

'May I have the pleasure of this dance?' This may sound a trifle old-fashioned, but that was how it was done in Sutton-under-Brailes village hall, and it had worked in those dim and distant days.

The girl was dressed in black and wore a red and white flowered headscarf which toned in perfectly with her blood-red lips, rouged cheeks and white, powdered face. She smiled nervously and was clearly teetering on the brink of a refusal when the older woman, with a sharp knowing look, pulled her to her feet.

The woman whispered something which I suspect could be translated as 'there may be dollars in it', and moments later the girl and I were twirling to the 'Invitation Waltz' thumped out by a black bow-tied, three-piece band.

She was tall, lithe and supple and smiled as I chatted away. Not a word passed her lips and she danced like a regular and much practised devotee of the Shanshan scene. She was enveloped in cheap scent. I closed my eyes and breathed deeply on the intoxicating, sticky-sweet smell of 'Bint el Sudan' which mingled tantalisingly with face powder and feminine allure. It was a heady and welcome change from the odour of socks, sweat and soup stains.

When the music stopped, I bowed, said goodbye to my Uighur lovely and melted back into the cigarette-filled smog of the snug. The Professor studiously avoided my look and stared in front of him with a face as black as night. What had I done? What huge social gaffe had I committed? After all these weeks of vicissitude, what was my ultimate sin?

'What's wrong with your father?' I asked Xiao Yuan. 'What have I done to upset him?'

Xiao Yuan drew me to one side. 'It's not you,' he whispered. 'You've done nothing wrong at all. When he saw you get up to dance he followed you. He asked a girl to dance with him and she refused. He has lost tremendous face.'

'Should we go back to our hotel?'

'No, no. That will make it even worse. He'll feel that we had to leave because of him. Don't worry, by tomorrow he'll have forgotten all about it.'

I could see that Driver Li was also looking mortified.

'And Li? Did the same thing happen to him?'

'Yes, but it was much worse. A girl started to dance with him and then went and sat down. She told him that she didn't like his smell.'

A disco record had been put on and immediately the mood in the dance hall changed. Xiao Yuan and I jumped to our feet. He indulged in self-centred exhibitionism with his earlier partner while I inhaled deeply on another draught of my Uighur fix. We returned to the snug, proud of our pluck and panting from the exertion of gyrating in heavy humidity.

'And now for the highlight of the evening,' cried the dance organiser. 'Musical chairs!'

This announcement was greeted with huge applause. It was audience participation time, and the face-losers forgot their damaged self-esteem. I gawped now as chairs were set in the middle of the floor and adult dancers played out the children's party game in boisterous style to a frenzy of encouraging cheers.

And then, on the stroke of eleven-thirty, Saturday evening's entertainment in Shanshan came to an abrupt end.

★ ★ ★

Journal entry, Shanshan, 15 April 1996 (Shanshan is a medium-sized town, 500 kilometres north-east of Tikar):

The vehicles are, I hope, repaired. After refuelling with beer and petrol we set off at 12.00 p.m. for Hami. Having been frustrated in our attempt to enter the Aqike valley from the south of Lop Nur, we now propose to travel by road via Hami and the oasis of Dun Huang and attempt to enter the Gashun

Gobi and the Aqike Valley from the east. A journey of a mere 1,700 kilometres. No such luck. Half way to Hami the universal joint on the jeep explodes under my feet. A few weeks ago I didn't know what a universal joint was. I certainly do now. It affected the radiator and we are stuck yet again with a non-runner. The 'joint' is repaired by the side of the road but the turbulent radiator necessitates frequent stops for water and a cool off. Eventually at dusk, we pull into Sandouling, a coal mining town 75 kilometres from Hami. A howling gale blows sand and indescribable filth everywhere. After endless searching we at last find someone to repair the radiator. During repairs, we shape up in a begrimed eating-house to noodles covered in soot, under a flickering, blue neon light. I nearly choke on the coal-fired cooker's smoke. We eventually reach Hami well after midnight. In spite of the so-called repairs, the jeep's engine is still on the boil. Professor says that he will telephone Urumqi to ask for a replacement vehicle. About time too. We doss down in a quarter-star hotel. I am lightly partitioned off from the Prof. and a TV set, which vies with a disco outside my window to keep me awake all night.

[Next morning:] I was screamed at by a cleaning woman who slammed the loo door in my face. She was collecting up the used 'bottom' paper deposited in the wire wastepaper baskets positioned beside the squats. No squatting or peeing allowed until she's finished. When the flies buzz around during the summer this place of abomination will surely forfeit its quarter star. I was bursting. I couldn't wait. Nothing to be done but to return to my cot and empty out into a glass which I tip merrily out of the window. Three tumbler-fulls splash on to the steps in front of the disco. There were no screams or shouts. I have taken my revenge on the disco. The TV will have to wait.

★　★　★

Hami, renowned throughout China for the quality of its melons, had been the headquarters of an ancient Khanate. The last ruler was Maksud Shah, whose ancient lineage stretched back to Jagatai, the son of Genghis Khan. But when Maksud Shah died in 1930, the Chinese authorities in Urumqi abolished the Khanate and imprisoned Nazir, the heir to the throne. The subsequent turbulence gave rise to warlords such as Ma Chung-yin and resulted in years of strife and anarchy. In spite of the sack of the city, the palace remained virtually untouched until the Cultural Revolution, when it was destroyed and houses were built over the site.

During our enforced stay in Hami, waiting for our replacement vehicle to arrive, I determined to try to discover the site of the old palace. In particular, I wanted to find the palace well which had been used as a reserve treasury vault and into which the last ruler had tipped masses of gold and silver when he realised that his regime was threatened with extinction. Even during the reign of Maksud Shah, the exact location of the well was a closely guarded secret. But I felt certain that someone in Hami must know of its whereabouts.

A section of the old Uighur quarter of Hami still stands, although I doubted if it would stand for much longer. The juggernaut of Chinese modernism, with its wide roads and sterile, lavatory-tiled buildings, has pushed from the east to the very fringe of the mediaeval remains of the quaint, old township of mud buildings and narrow, twisting lanes. It seemed sensible to begin the quest at the tombs of the Khans of Hami, even though these lay outside the old city walls. The pillow-shaped tombs, locked away in a crypt under the towering, turquoise-tiled cupola of the royal mausoleum, had miraculously survived the turbulent revolts of the 1930s and the mindless desecrations of the 1960s perpetrated by the Red Guards. The nearby multi-pillared and exquisitely painted Friday mosque had also remained untouched, but when Xiao Yuan asked the ancient caretaker where the palace of Maksud Shah had stood, he was met with a blank stare of incomprehension.

'But he must know,' I said to Xiao Yuan. 'He's old enough to have been alive when Maksud died.'

Xiao Yuan and I were on our own. His father had made it quite clear that he thought the search for historical remains was a futile waste of time. And anyway, there was a good war film on television.

Fear showed in the caretaker's rheumy eyes when the question was pressed a second time. He'd lived through too much turmoil and strife, and had witnessed what happened to people who talked too much. The authorities in Xinjiang had recently cracked down on a movement that was agitating for Uighur independence. It was dangerous to answer questions like this, especially when foreigners were involved. He shrugged his shoulders, shook his head and turned away.

'We're not going to learn anything from him,' I said, as we walked out of the mausoleum and into the surrounding residential area.

'Over there, try over there.' The portly Uighur trader in a black peaked cap waved airily towards a muddle of partly dilapidated mud-brick buildings. 'Ask for Sharif. He knows where the palace was, his father used to work there.'

We threaded our way through the narrow streets. Children stared and taunted Xiao Yuan, who began to look uncomfortable. One of them threw a stone. In certain parts of Uighurland, the Han Chinese are not popular, and it is not surprising that one of the leaders of the Tiananmen Square demonstrations was Wuer Kaixi, a Xinjiang Uighur. Prior to the demonstration, he humiliated the then Prime Minister during a television interview. He has since fled China.

We stopped to ask directions from two ancients who were squatting by the roadside. 'That's Sharif's house over there,' they said.

I noticed a low mound of mud which stretched about twenty metres to the east. Xiao Yuan had seen it too and confirmed my unspoken thoughts. 'That looks like the remains of the palace wall,' he said.

We eventually found Sharif, a dour man whose house was guarded by a large black Tibetan mastiff hooked up to a long chain. Sharif was prepared to talk to us and confirmed that his house had been built within the walls surrounding the old palace. 'And this was the palace well,' he said, pointing to the remains of a huge circular well that was stuffed up with mud and rubbish. 'Our water comes out of a tap nowadays,' he added proudly.

'Is the well still full of gold and jewels?' I asked with a smile.

'Oh, no,' Sharif replied gloomily, 'the palace treasure was looted a long time ago.'

As we walked towards the well, the guard dog curled its upper lip, snarled, and began barking ferociously. A young child started to scream and I hastily checked that the restraining chain was secure. It was unusual to see dogs anywhere in Xinjiang and particularly in a Muslim quarter. They were either eaten or considered taboo.

'He's a good watchdog,' I commented after looking at what remained of the well.

'So he should be,' Sharif replied. 'He's a descendant of the guard dogs of the Shah. My father used to look after them. He guards me well. It's in his blood.'

The glory of the Kings of the Gobi had indeed, long since, departed. All that remained of the royal palace that had been 'sumptuously furnished with divans and soft carpets and many beautiful things', and the 'Chinese landscape gardens with slender camel-back bridges thrown over running streams where peacocks swept their trains regally and paraded their magnificence among the winding paths', was a ferocious dog, a dirty, disused well, a screaming snotty-nosed child and a morose old man.

★ ★ ★

Halfway along the road from Hami to Dun Huang, the team stopped for a hawk, chew, spit and a drag near the ancient city of Qiaowan. And just for once, it wasn't an enforced vehicle repair stop. Before squeezing back into our vehicles, we stretched our legs along the top of the well-preserved Qiaowan city walls and looked in on a soberly dressed Chinese Mrs Danvers, who rather haughtily informed us that she was the sole custodian of some rather unusual relics. She told us that in about AD 1600, the then Tang dynasty Chinese Emperor had had a vivid dream of a fertile oasis surrounded by waving willows that lay far to the west of his empire.

Much impressed by the beauty of this vision, he had ordered his senior minister to set off in search of the green and pleasant land.

After a lengthy and difficult journey across the intervening desert, the minister eventually lighted upon the source of his master's dream, the unoccupied oasis of Qiaowan. It was so beautiful that he decided to set up house there himself, and constructed a superior establishment with the help of his master's money. He then sent word back to the Emperor that he had found nothing of import, but that he would continue the search if he was sent more cash. The Emperor duly obliged and the corrupt official immediately extended the size of his house and household.

There then followed a period of lengthy silence which so exasperated the Emperor that he decided to find out for himself just what his minister was getting up to. When the Emperor eventually found his official, ensconced in luxury in a land of milk and honey, he promptly ordered him to be skinned alive, his bones wrapped up in the flayed skin, and the top of his head converted into a superior drinking vessel for the Emperor's personal use.

Before we embarked for Dun Huang we were privileged to see the skin, bones and scalp of the former occupant of Qiaowan. They were lovingly cared for by the unsmiling, ultra-serious lady caretaker, who delighted in showing a foreign devil just what happens to those who don't obey the central authority in China.

★　★　★

The Professor had set up a meeting in the Hall of the People in Dun Huang to try and gain the support of the local authority for the proposed Nature Sanctuary. It was chaired by Mr Wang, the Vice-Mayor, and attended by Mr Wang, the Head of Forestry; Mr Wang, the Assistant Head of Forestry; and Mr Wang, the driver to the three other Wangs. I wondered idly whether there was just the faintest whiff of nepotism in the air. Had Abbot Wang of the Caves of a Thousand Buddhas fame hidden away something other than old manuscripts in one of the many ancient caves under his care? When I brought up the Abbot's name later in the evening, there was clear evidence of nomenclature solidarity. In striking contrast to Lao Zhao, Wang senior's opinion of the holy man was not in the slightest bit rancorous.

'He was duped by Stein,' the Vice-Mayor opined. 'He did nothing wrong. Stein was a thief and Abbot Wang was a simpleton.'

The three official Wangs and their driver were seated on one side of a long, rectangular table, and we sat opposite them. Three ceiling fans revolved slowly overhead. One fan had come adrift from its moorings and the Wang team looked to be in imminent danger of decapitation. Green tea, bottled water and biscuits were set in front of us by an office flunkey and, when this ceremony was complete, Professor Yuan explained to the meeting exactly what we were about. The Wangs conferred, and Vice-Mayor Wang scribbled something in a tattered notebook. He was a trifle tattered himself. Black bags bulged under narrow, rheumy eyes. His hair had receded from the front of his head and, by way of compensation, stood bolt upright up at the back. I had never seen anything quite like it. Dyed bright blue, yellow or green it would have made a novel punk hairdo; longitudinal Mohican. His shirt tails were too short and parted midway down his front to reveal a tummy which hung over the top of his black, plastic belt.

'We support your plan for the sanctuary,' intoned Number One Wang after a prolonged study of his notes. The Wang clan nodded their heads in collective agreement.

'May I put that in the official report to NEPA?' I asked.

'Yes, you may.'

I smiled and thanked the senior Wang with a hearty shake of his soft hand.

I clearly provided a good excuse for an evening on the local authority expense account for, with a lavish sweep of his arm, he announced that he would like to invite us all to an early dinner in the best hotel in Dun Huang.

'Even our leader Deng has stayed there,' he added expansively.

Later that afternoon, settled and seated around a circular dining-table, it soon became apparent that the whole Wang clan chain-smoked when not on official parade and that *maotai* had made a major contribution to the size of Wang senior's tummy.

'Let us throw politics out of the window,' announced our ebullient and unorthodox host after the third toast. He pointed to a serving girl in a long red dress with a thigh-length slit. 'Do you think that girl is beautiful?'

'Definitely,' I replied, wondering what would follow next. 'Very beautiful.'

Mr Wang puffed low-grade tobacco smoke in my face.

'I think so, too,' he pronounced, following it up with a roar of laughter which so startled the poor girl that she fled from the room, her face crimson with embarrassment.

The atmosphere thickened and the toasts grew more feverish and frequent. We toasted the success of future expeditions, nature sanctuaries, London, wives, children, eternal friendship, and then, horror of horrors, I was obliged to nibble at another hind leg of dog.

But in spite of this, and the depressing fact that the exchange four-wheel-drive vehicle that we had picked up in Hami had developed engine trouble, I was well pleased. As we were driven back to our two-star lodgings by Driver Wang in a black, tinted-window, VIP Santana, I reflected that we now had the written support for the proposed Lop Nur Nature Sanctuary from the local authorities in Korla, Hami, Turfan and Dun Huang. Only Ruoqiang remained, a hard nut to crack because of their mining interests, but crackable nonetheless. I thought that NEPA ought to be impressed with this growing evidence of local government support.

Later that evening, as if bent on ensuring that we didn't lose touch with reality, the Gobi threw a sand storm at Dun Huang. The market closed and I spent the remainder of our waking hours teaching the lads how to play liar dice to the accompaniment of a steady splatter of sand on the bedroom window. It was difficult enough to get into the Aqike valley without the additional hazard of driving sand, so we decided to wait until the wind had completely died down before we set off. By the time we eventually left Dun Huang forty-eight hours later, Xiao Yuan was out on his own in the master class of liar-dice players.

Heading west from Dun Huang, we followed the same route, in reverse, as we had followed the previous year. After having passed Devil City and crossing the north–south sand barrier, I was alarmed to discover that illegal mining activity had greatly increased during the previous twelve months. Vehicle tracks criss-crossed the desert and we came to two new gold mines where wild-eyed, unkempt miners lived like troglodytes in deep, underground holes.

'They'll all have left in two years' time,' commented Lao Zhao. 'They aren't finding enough gold to make it worth while for them to stay.'

But I wasn't so sure. Their set-up looked pretty permanent to me, and a good deal of money appeared to have been put into an expanding enterprise. And meanwhile, the noise from the constant blasting must be driving the wild camel deeper and deeper into the inhospitable heartland of the Gashun Gobi, where the supply of rough vegetation and salt water was rapidly diminishing.

We drove through improbably beautiful pebble-strewn coloured hillocks and passed two more mining camps before we at last reached the Aqike valley. An unending 'sea' of sand and *shor* stretched to the south. But unlike two weeks earlier, when we had attempted to cross the *shor* from the lake-bed of Lop Nur, we could now see our goal on the distant horizon, the shimmering sand barrier of the Kum Tagh.

Journal entry, 21 April 1996:

On entering the Aqike valley, the truck immediately becomes bogged down in soft sand and Mr Chen, the replacement driver of the 'new' jeep, gave us a remarkable exhibition of his total lack of expertise in desert conditions. After the truck gets stuck a fourth time, the Professor calls a halt. He decides to set off in the jeep with myself and his son to scout out a route. The sand gives way to *shor*, and Xiao Yuan and I walk ahead in an attempt to break up the more prominent pieces of rock salt before they break the sump. We spot recent traces of three wild camels that have rested on an old tamarisk hummock. It's always an encouragement to discover that the camel has been there first, even if we don't catch a glimpse of the beast itself. The jeep gets very stuck in some treacherous *shor* that is underpinned with wet salt sludge. This could be extremely dangerous. If the jeep sinks up to its axles into the sludge we'll never get it out. Fortunately, after two worrying hours with spade and shovel, we manage to extricate it. We are forced to return, weary, despondent and dispirited, to our base camp. On our arrival, we discover that Driver Li has spent half the day trying to straighten the running-board of the truck with a sledge hammer, much to the alarm of his pigeon. Just after our arrival and before we have had time to eat, a sand storm gets up and blows hard until 2.00 a.m. Its strength must be force seven. Xiao Yuan's tent is blown away and we help him to scavenge for his kit as best we can. Just after midnight my tent collapsed and slid down the upright tent poles. Fortunately, the guy ropes hold and I look on impotently under a welter of flapping canvas as sand piles up, covering cameras, clothes and valuables. I concentrate on ensuring that my tent does not follow Xiao Yuan's into the night. Next morning, the wind drops and I manage to repair splits in the canvas near the uprights with the bottom halves of plastic water bottles. Tweet-tweet, Driver Li's pigeon, had survived the turbulent night without so much as a single ruffled feather.

23 April 1996:

We are yet again attempting to cross the Aqike valley. We only take the jeep as we are convinced that the truck will never make it. We carry as much water and provisions as we can for five people; the Professor, Lao Zhao, Xiao Yuan, Driver Chen and myself. If we manage to cross the *shor* in the jeep, we will then follow the wild camels' migration route for as long as our supplies hold out. The new driver, Chen, is really irritating. He is clumsy, slightly simple and cannot speak without shouting. And as for his personal habits! We set off on a new line three kilometres to the east of where we attempted yesterday's crossing. There is more sand further east and less *shor*. Hopefully, this will make it easier for us to cross to the sand dunes. We get stuck twice in sand but manage to dig ourselves out after an hour and a quarter of hard, sweated labour. We then reach the *shor* and after three hours of tortuous and nerve-wracking travel manage, at long last and at the seventh attempt, to reach the Kum Tagh. Hooray! All the sweat, tears and frustration have been worthwhile. We discover the skeleton of a fourteen-year-old adult camel which, for a refreshing change, appears to have died from natural causes.

In 1981, Professor Penjiamu of the Xinjiang Environmental Protection Institute had led a team of scientists into the area to the north of the Kum Tagh. When they reached the sand dunes, they ran out of drinking water and the Professor set out on foot in an attempt to discover a short-cut across the rock-salt. He never returned. Although comprehensive air and land searches were made, the Professor's body was never found, and a stone memorial had been erected near the Kum Tagh in his memory. Lao Zhao had worked with Professor Penjiamu, as had Professor Yuan, and they were both greatly attached to his memory. Lao Zhao had brought with him a small tin of pillar-box red paint to touch up the faded Chinese characters that were inscribed on one side of the obelisk.

Having carefully repainted the faded inscription, Lao Zhao burnt newspaper to let Professor Penjiamu know that we had arrived, poured a bottle of beer around the wooden railings surrounding the memorial to cheer him up and left some food for him to enjoy after we'd left. Then he sat and meditated for a full hour, staring as if transfixed at the characters on the memorial plinth. It was an eerie and somewhat awesome sight to see the old rascal so deeply affected by the memorial to his dead colleague.

That evening, as we followed the deeply rutted track of the migrating wild camels, the placated spirit of the deceased Professor must have come to our aid. We spotted a bull camel perched high on a sand dune, then another and then, in the fading light, three females and two young calves. We camped in a blissfully remote spot, far from the machinations of men, under a startlingly star-lit sky. The rolling outlines of the massive dunes to the south were illuminated by the light of a full moon, and for once there was not a breath of wind. I climbed to the top of a towering dune and looked away to the north beyond our camp, to the *shor* and the edge of the great lake-bed of Lop Nur.

I reflected that the food, fuel and water that we had packed into the jeep would not allow us more than twenty-four hours in the Kum Tagh. Tomorrow we would have to return to our truck and make our way back across the Gashun Gobi and eventually to Urumqi. The task of surveying the wild camels' seasonal migration route between the south of Lop Nur and the Arjin Shan mountains and, in particular, discovering the precise spot where the camels migrated over the sand dunes, would remain undone, the mystery unsolved. To the best of my knowledge, the Kum Tagh had only been crossed in recorded history by Sven Hedin, just before the turn of the century. I badly wanted to attempt a crossing myself, but the journey would have to have a purpose and a meaningful end result.

As I was musing on all this, I turned towards the Kum Tagh and, in the milky light of the full moon, thought that I saw a string of camels wending their way over the dunes. For a fleeting moment, they appeared to have substance. I shook my head and looked again. The camels faded away as mysteriously as they had appeared. My eyes had played tricks on me in the moonlight but they had inspired an interesting idea. I got up and walked briskly back to our camp. I'd thought of another way to solve the riddle of the camel migration and I wanted to discuss it with Professor Yuan while the idea, and the vision, were still fresh in my mind.

I found the Professor some distance from our tents, humming to himself and hopping up and down from one foot to the other. Good, I thought to myself. He's at peace with the world. He's placated the spirit of his friend Professor Penjiamu, we've at last managed to cross the Aqike valley and we've seen seven wild camels. This is a good moment to talk to him about the future.

'We must complete this survey,' I began.

The Professor nodded in agreement and continued with his jig. 'I agree, but it's impossible for us to go any further without our supply truck. We'll have to return tomorrow or we'll run out of water.'

'I understand, so we'll have to try to come back next year.'

'Our vehicles will always have difficulty crossing the *shor*. Just look at the trouble that we've already experienced. It's been very dangerous at times, and we are still in a potentially dangerous situation.'

'Exactly, and that's why I'm proposing that next year we undertake the survey using domestic camels to carry our kit, food, water. Let's do away with the vehicles and all their problems. Domestic camels don't have universal joints and carburettors. If their wild cousins can cross the Kum Tagh, then so can they.' I paused and noted that he had stopped jigging and was listening intently. 'I think that we should attempt to make the crossing from the south. We can survey the foothills of the Arjin Shan in an attempt to pick up the migration route. When we have found it, we can follow it through the Desert of Lop and over the Kum Tagh. The wild camels have been migrating for centuries. They must have discovered an easy crossing point. It should be a much easier route than attempting to cross that terrible *shor* from the north.'

The Professor smiled. 'Whether we travel south–north or north–south we're going to have problems. Whether we use jeeps or camels we're still attempting to go off the map into unknown and virtually unmapped country, with all that that implies.'

Xiao Yuan and Lao Zhao had joined us and the Professor's son had explained to our guide the gist of our conversation.

'What do you think about it, Lao Zhao?' I asked.

Lao Zhao was game for anything, especially if there was a whiff of foreign exchange in the air. He nodded, smiled and said, 'Good.'

'Can you find us a team of strong camels?'

Lao Zhao nodded a second time and muttered something in Chinese. Xiao Yuan translated, 'Lao Zhao says that we'll need two camels per person. If we have a team of eight people we'll need sixteen camels.'

'And herdsmen?'

'We'll need at least three.'

'Can Lao Zhao arrange this?'

'Certainly, if he's given the money in time. The camels will have to be fattened up before we set off. They'll lose condition very quickly in the desert and we'll need to purchase them at least three months in advance.'

By midnight we had a date, a budget, a tentative route, and an expedition plan to put up to the Environmental Institute in Urumqi. All we needed was $30,000, and that was a problem that the Professor and Lao Zhao were quite happy to leave me to solve.

After the conclusion of our discussion, the unpredictable Professor let off a string of firecrackers which must have scattered any remaining wild camels to the far-flung reaches of the Gashun Gobi. He was celebrating the end of our current expedition and the hatching of a plot for another.

★　★　★

Three days later we arrived at the scruffy, polluted and unbelievably ugly iron-ore mining town of Yamansu. The mine bustled with unceasing activity. It was as though we had arrived at a human ant-hill. We were unheeded and unwanted. Even the weather had changed; it was very cold.

Earlier, we had quit the Aqike valley and crossed back over the *shor* without undue difficulty. We had then followed a new route to the north-east, in an attempt to hit a midway point on the Hami–Dun Huang road. We had crossed an amazing magnetic field that had set our compasses spinning, a vast salt lake where miners were excavating blocks of crude salt, and kilometre after kilometre of barren stone Gobi.

Our abrupt stop at Yamansu, just south-west of the main high-way, was not premeditated. It was brought about by yet more mechanical trouble; the snapping in the township's main street of one of the truck's steering rods.

We were standing on the edge of a huge man-made crater, wait-ing for the arrival of a replacement spare part, when the ground suddenly shook with the force of a large explosion. Smoked billowed upwards as small rocks splattered round about us. Massive mechanical diggers, reduced to the size of toys by the enormity of the open-cast mine, scurried forward to scoop up piles of black rock and load them into waiting dumper trucks. Relays of these trucks snaked up the sides of the mine and roared past us, filling the air with grit and dust. A bitterly cold wind whipped up piles of discarded rubbish and wrapped a strip of plastic sheeting around Professor Yuan Guoying.

'This was wild camel country twenty years ago,' the Professor said, as he struggled to free himself, 'now it's the biggest iron-ore mine in China. There aren't any wild camels within 150 kilometres of here.'

My mood of recent optimism had radically changed. The size of the iron-ore mine was depressing. Raw reality had pushed aside romantic dreams of camels wending their way over rolling sand dunes. If Yamansu, with its rail link and human population in excess of 2,500, had developed from empty desert in just twenty years, what would happen to the other areas we had visited, where gold and iron-ore mining, much of it illegal, had just got under way? As I stood shivering with cold on the brink of the vast mine, I began to think that maybe the odds against establishing the sanctuary in time to save the wild camel were impossibly high. As I gazed down into the black abyss, I wondered gloomily whether we were all just spitting hopelessly into the freezing wind.

9

Men Are Unwise and Curiously Planned

Away, for we are ready to a man! Lead on, O Master of the Caravan . . .

James Elroy Flecker

Exactly eleven months later, Jasper Evans threaded his way through hordes of jostling, gesticulating, exuberant, white-robed, Haj-returning pilgrims at Islamabad airport. He looked like a hangman's bag carrier. His kit-bag and canvas hold-all were covered with many metres of neatly coiled rope.

'I brought some rope along just in case the Chinese don't have enough of it,' Jasper said in his slow, emphatic way. 'The Africans often bring pieces of old rope on safari that break as soon as you tighten a load. Maybe the Chinese are more practical, but anyway,' he shrugged his shoulders, 'I thought I'd bring some along with me just in case.'

The rope was made from hand-woven coir, not manufactured plastic, 'which slips through your fingers and cuts your hands'. It was typical of Jasper to have had the foresight to bring rope all the way from Kenya. I didn't want to set off into the desert of Lop with seventeen domestic Bactrians, the Professor, his son, Lao Zhao and three or four untried and untested herdsmen. For all their expertise in Gobi conditions, the three previous expedition members had little practical experience of working with camels. I wanted a

188

knowledgeable camel man. Someone who was used to hardship, who could live on the smell of an oily rag and who wouldn't complain if he found sand in his sandwiches. In spite of his seventy-two years and what he described as 'a bit of a creaky knee', there was no one better suited than Jasper Evans, rancher from Kenya, camel-breeder, owner of over 500 single-humped Dromedaries and one of life's true originals.

Two days later we duly boarded Xinjiang Airways at Islamabad and arrived at Urumqi airport. It was clear that nothing had changed for the better. Our papers were scrutinised by an official holding up a cigarette lighter so that he could read the small print more clearly. An expressionless girl studied a computer screen for all of five minutes as she checked and re-checked our entry visas. Maybe recent Uighur agitation for self-rule, which had resulted in a number of deaths, was the reason for this heightened security. But that didn't explain why an unsmiling, unapologetic, X-ray machine operator deliberately concealed one of Jasper's bags in the bowels of his machine in the hope that he had overlooked it.

This rather inauspicious start to Jasper's first visit to China continued when we met the Professor, his son and Driver Liu, who were waiting outside to meet us. I immediately sensed that something was wrong. Our reception was muted. Their smiles were forced. My heart sank.

As we drove along Beijing Road North to our lodging, I asked Xiao Yuan what was the matter.

'Lao Zhao has disappeared,' he replied.

'Disappeared?'

'Yes, he should have been back in Urumqi two days ago, but we've heard nothing from him for a week. He telephoned from Korla and told my father that he hadn't been able to buy the camels. He's going to have to hire them.'

'Hire them? But that will be much more expensive. I thought that we'd agreed to buy them and sell them on for cash at the end of the expedition. And anyway,' I added rather heatedly, 'your father has been sent the money to buy them.'

Xiao Yuan looked embarrassed. It wasn't his responsibility and it was unfair of me to question him too closely. 'We're waiting to hear from Lao Zhao,' he said.

After we were deposited in the Scientific Academic Hotel, another problem surfaced. 'There's not enough money for the expedition,' the Professor said pointedly. He handed me the agreed budget. A number of additional headings such as, 'team management fees', 'Institute management fees', 'insurance', 'postal/telephone fees' had been inserted.

'But we've agreed the budget,' I expostulated. 'That budget was sent to Shell, China. They've already agreed to sponsor our expedition for that amount. They're not going to give us more money.'

'It's no good. It's not enough,' the Professor intoned gloomily.

I didn't resent the fact that the Institute were trying to pick up some foreign exchange for both the team and themselves. After all, they were hiring out the Professor's expertise and could rightly expect reimbursement. But they should have thought of it earlier. If Lao Zhao was now hiring camels, the budget that we'd painstakingly finalised before I left Urumqi last year would be blown apart. I'd done my bit and found a sponsor, these monetary afterthoughts could sabotage the whole trip. I was extremely disgruntled.

It took five frustrating days to solve the various problems. Lao Zhao eventually turned up, having bought camels after all. Shell promised to ante up with half of the Professor's new-found requirement. But although this was a depressing time for both Jasper and me, it did give my leg a chance to perk up after an ill-timed attack of shingles and Jasper time to iron out the creak in his knee.

And so, on Easter Sunday, 30 March 1997, with matters more or less under control, we headed south, this time for a domestic camel rendezvous in the Hongliugou valley. We were joined at the last minute by a young zoologist from the Institute, yet another Mr Li, who had helped to identify a new species of hamster that lived high in the Tien Shan mountains. Surprisingly, he had been detailed to join us as the team's cook. This position had been unanimously vetoed months previously on the grounds of cost, but nevertheless it was deemed necessary by functionaries in the Institute that we take along a cook. I suspected that he might have a more political function and was somewhat apprehensive when he first appeared. But I needn't have worried because Mr Li turned out to be one of the best and most able members of the team. He was constantly cheerful, unfailingly helpful and a remarkably good cook.

Over 1,500 kilometres of roads partly covered with sand, and Driver Liu at the wheel of a low-slung Italian mini-bus, does not make for the most relaxing of journeys. Liu, hair firmly plastered down and eyebrows bristling, was in an authoritarian mood from the start. The bus was grossly overloaded and totally unsuitable for the journey, which didn't help, but it was laughable that in a land of chain-smokers, Driver Liu insisted that Jasper stub out his Kenyan Sportsman cigarette as soon as we were under way. And when we finally hit the yellow-brick road south of Korla, he displayed, with an unerring predictability, just how inept he was at negotiating drifting sand. By the time we reached Ruoqiang we had dug ourselves out at least seven times, Jasper had seriously upgraded his opinion of African drivers *vis-à-vis* Chinese, and collective frustration had peaked. Thank goodness this was an expedition to be undertaken with camels, leaving Driver Liu, his inadequate vehicle and our jeep back at base.

Halfway along the deeply rutted road between Regiment 36 and the Hongliugou valley, in howling wind and driving sand, we came across two of our camels being ridden at a hectic pace by Uighur herdsman Yusuf and Chinese herdsman Dum Dum. We had been further delayed when our jeep developed engine trouble in Ruoqiang and this, coupled with the Urumqi problems, had set the two camel-minders fast-trotting 200 kilometres to Regiment 36 in search of food. Mutual joy and relief mingled with Jasper's delight at being reunited with camels.

The next two days were spent in the lower reaches of the Hongliugou valley, setting up a base camp and preparing for the expedition. Sacks were stuffed with dry *fragmitis* grass to prevent our loads chafing the backs of the camels. Old Ahun, an Uighur with a finely chiselled face and a goatee beard, the senior of the four herdsmen, sat patiently plaiting camel-hair ropes. Jasper had been prescient. The ropes that the herdsmen had brought were old, frayed and totally inadequate. But there was one thing that Jasper didn't agree with. He needed to explain a technique that had stood him in good stead on many previous occasions.

'I think that the sacks should be tied on like this, so that the weight of the load does not press on the spine and so that . . .'

Xiao Yuan tried hard to follow. Herdsmen Yusuf and Wang gazed in utter incomprehension. Lao Zhao gave a crooked smile.

'Because if you don't . . .' Jasper gave the 'don't' a particularly heavy emphasis. It carried the necessary impact to impress his message on the mind of the most obstinate African. But this was China. No one agreed. They weren't even listening. Lao Zhao smirked.

'You want to put it on like that.' Xiao Yuan was being polite. He spread the stuffed sack vertically over the withers of the squatting camel.

'Yes, I want to put it just like that so that it takes the weight off the spinal column and spreads it evenly over . . .'

Yusuf had grabbed the sack and placed it horizontally along the camel's left side. He smiled at Jasper, the smile of a knowledgeable father to an uncomprehending and rather stupid child.

'Yusuf says that this is the way to do it. If you place a stick on the sack like so, and tie it to the end of a stick on the camel's other side like so, then . . .'

'Yes, but what I'm trying to tell you is that . . .'

'We've always tied them this way, so that the . . .'

Jasper looked at the faces of the three men who were grouped around the ever-patient, cud-chewing, camel.

'Okay, that's fine,' he said with a resigned shrug of his shoulders, having realised that the conversation was a total waste of time. In Africa, Jasper's way would have prevailed, even if the African camel-handler had secretly believed that his way was best. But this was China.

Lao Zhao walked away. Old Ahun hadn't even looked up from his rope-plaiting. There wasn't the slightest chance that the camel sacks wouldn't be tied on as they had always tied them: horizontally and using two sticks.

'It seems to me,' said Jasper when we were on our own later that day, 'that there's not much point in advising the Chinese. They think that they have all the answers. They're not interested in any advice.'

'Unless they ask for it,' I said, remembering the lessons I'd learnt from the two previous expeditions. 'If they ask for advice, then they'll listen. But it's absolutely no use telling them anything if they haven't asked for it.'

It was a hard lesson for Jasper to learn, and not something that Africa had prepared him for.

Having swapped the low-slung Italian bus for a Chinese truck in Ruoqiang, we had planned to cross the Arjin Shan mountains by vehicle. We were to drive up the frozen Hongliugou riverbed to the old nationalist fort of Bashkagun, where I had lodged in considerable squalor in 1995, follow a track to a prominent pass at the head of Chashkan Sayi (Many Mice) valley, and then drive down that valley over another frozen riverbed to a freshwater spring called Honliu. The camels were to have taken a less arduous short-cut through the Arjin Shan foothills which was, supposedly, impassable to vehicles. Both parties were then scheduled to meet up at Honliu spring, where we would set up a base camp that would provide a convenient springboard for our crossing of the Desert of Lop and the Kum Tagh by camel.

But the spring thaw had set in earlier than anticipated. On its first dummy run to test the strength of the ice, our supply truck sank up to its wheel-tops after half a kilometre of slither and slide. After a further two hours of pushing, shoving, digging and cursing, sloshing about up to our knees in half-frozen slush, we finally managed to get the truck back on to a weight-bearing surface. By that time it was clear to all of us that it was quite impossible to follow the riverbed by vehicle, and a meeting was called which resulted in a plan change, the first of many. The Professor decided that the camels would take the route that the vehicles should have followed. This meant establishing a base camp for our vehicles at our present camp-site in the Hongliugou valley and taking the camels over the Chashkan Sayi valley pass at 4,000 metres. A daunting prospect for the camels but, as we were later to discover, the correct decision. Even if the river-ice had held, the vehicles would never have been able to drive down the Chashkan Sayi valley. The route was much too narrow and treacherous, and I quietly welcomed the Professor's decision. The less we all had to do with Chinese machines and mechanics the better, especially after our experiences on the two previous expeditions.

On the eve of our departure we lit a great fire. One of the two sheep we had brought with us was slaughtered and barbecued, its head cooked by the fearsome blast of a petrol-fired blow-lamp. Before settling down to a farewell feast, the Professor gathered us together and lectured us all on the route, the purpose of our expedition and the need for rigorous self-discipline over water consumption. The latter was particularly important as our route change had increased the number of days on the march and nights in the field. Duly impressed, we squatted on our hunkers to do justice to a banquet in the bush. There were no spoons or forks and Jasper struggled with 'these damned Chinese sticks'. Later that night, songs of three nationalities, pitched excruciatingly off-key as a consequence of too much *maotai*, floated down the valley to a backdrop of the Professor's celebratory firecrackers. Next morning, after numerous adjustments to our kit and feeling slightly the worse for wear, we set off.

The camels were plump and fit. The hiring hiccough with Lao Zhao was never fully explained. There were still a number of unanswered questions in my mind, but there seemed little point in rummaging about in the mind of Lao Zhao. We owned, indubitably, fifteen fine adult camels and two untrained teenagers who had been included as part of an overall package. The adults varied in colour from white to dark brown. Jasper had been allocated a ginger biscuit-coloured, well-trained, shaggy-haired stalwart, and I possessed a dark-brown veteran of many desert treks. My camel looked faintly ridiculous rear-view on, as he was rapidly shedding a thick winter coat. By the end of the expedition he looked as though he had mislaid a pair of woolly trousers. Bactrian camels seemed, according to Jasper, more intelligent than their one-humped relatives. After six weeks working with our pair, they had both mastered English words of command.

We called the two teenagers Bill and Ben. Bill had an upright tuft of black hair on the top of his head that turned him into a desert punk. Ben, eyes constantly moving from side to side, lived in a state of permanent agitation. Every day poor Ben was confronted with a new and alarming experience. His teeth were set on edge. He ground them ferociously.

'Lo, lo, lo, lo, lo, lo, lo,' Dum Dum called out to collect up the camels for their evening meal. We had pitched camp at Smir Bulak spring, twenty kilometres beyond Bashkagun. Our GPS (Global Positioning System), my one gesture to the twentieth century, and presented to the team by an old established Anglo-Chinese trading house, informed us that we had pitched camp at 3,334 metres. It felt like it. At 6.00 p.m. the temperature was minus six centigrade and dropping rapidly.

'Lo, lo, lo, lo, lo, lo, lo, lo.'

The camels ignored Dum Dum and raced towards the tent that Jasper and I had just erected.

'Hey, go away. Go over there.'

'Go on, get along, will you?'

They wouldn't hear of it. They milled around Jasper and me, pulling out tent pegs and tripping over guy ropes. What was going on?

Suddenly we realised. Jasper had brought a bright yellow plastic groundsheet from Kenya and had spread it out neatly in front of our tent. The camels, seeing the colour and associating it with food, had ignored their dried maize kernels spread on the herdsmen's grey canvas sheet and homed in on our tent like wasps to a jam pot as soon as they heard their cook-house call. Pandemonium continued until we had hidden the groundsheet.

We also had a major problem with our accommodation. The Kenya canvas tent, stalwart of previous expeditions, was too weighty for camel carrying. So I had brought with me a design and a fabric fit for the space-age.

'You can stick it on the side of Everest. When a wind gets up all you'll have to do is adjust the guy ropes,' the salesman had said. 'It will stand for ever when other tents have been blown to the ends of the earth.'

That sales patter went down well in Holloway. But Jasper and I soon realised that one needed at least a second-class engineering degree to work out how to erect the wretched thing. And at minus six degrees centigrade we didn't have the inclination to hang about. Tent pegs buckled at the first blow and were clearly more suited to a back garden in Surbiton than the Gobi desert. Having jointly struggled in vain, Jasper dived under twisted tentage and entangled guy ropes in a valiant attempt to impose order. He emerged, minutes later, having successfully disentangled three layers of mosquito netting and internal lining.

'It's just like grappling under a Victorian lady's underwear.'

'You should know,' I said.

By the end of the expedition we had just about got the hang of it and the tent had indeed stood when others had fallen, but as Jasper rightly said, 'It's much too complex a bit of kit to take on safari.'

Next day we reached the mountain pass, but not without difficulty. We were still struggling to overcome the problem of balanced load positioning. Bags and sacks had slipped, camels had panicked. Two camels carrying water had got hooked up to each other and bellowed and fought as water containers banged against their sides. If we wanted to ride a camel we had to ensure that the inadequate piece of felt which served as a saddle prevented our more tender regions from becoming chafed with rope. This all took time to work out, and meanwhile the camel train plodded on at five kilometres an hour.

At one point I turned back to help Lao Zhao with a slippage problem. No sooner had I done so than my kit slithered down one side of my camel. By the time I had struggled to control my camel, persuaded him to sit and re-tied the loads, Lao Zhao had disappeared over the horizon. Fortunately, Jasper had seen the problem and turned back to lend a hand. Meanwhile, light rain turned to sleet and then snow. Just after we crossed the pass, a blizzard set in.

'I haven't seen falling snow since 1944, when I was dropping depth charges on German submarines,' Jasper said. It clearly wasn't a climatic experience he was eager to rediscover.

As we crossed over the pass and on to a frozen river, the blizzard intensified. The woolly-headed camels looked like load-carrying polar bears.

'And I thought that we were going into a desert,' groaned poor Jasper. It was no joke for him, coming from fifty years in the tropics into the bitter cold of Central Asia. On we trudged, adjusting slipping loads with freezing fingers. Then disaster struck. A camel put its foot in an ice crevasse and disappeared up to its shoulder. It bellowed in protest as two herdsmen hacked away with picks to try to free it from the ice. We had no spare camel carrying capacity. The last thing we needed was a camel with a broken leg.

An hour later it was freed intact, we regrouped and continued on down the valley. The wind freshened as dusk fell and the combination of driving snow and intense cold creased our faces and cracked our lips. We pitched camp at dusk, struggling once more with unfamiliar tentage in the freezing cold. Instant noodles sent us to sleep and next morning the inside of the wonder tent's 'underwear' was covered in five-centimetre-long icicles, formed from our condensed and frozen breath.

We woke up in fairyland, albeit the fairies' winter quarters. The light was translucent and the early morning sun picked out in glorious detail the cracks and crevasses on the sides of the majestic mountains that surrounded us. Dum Dum had lit a fire and brewed tea. I filled up my mug and placed it outside our tent. Then I picked up Jasper's mug and walked back to the fire to fill it up and take it back to Jasper. By the time I had returned to our tent, my tea was covered in a thin film of ice. Even our cameras froze and ceased to function.

Packing our loads on the camels in temperatures well below freezing took time. Not only were we stiff with cold but we were still unpractised at loading and positioning our kit. In spite of knitted gloves, our fingers were split and frozen and our hands were chapped. This resulted in a late morning start but, once under way, we made good progress, synchronised to the rhythmic clunk-clunk of two wooden Somali camel bells that Jasper had brought with him from his ranch in Kenya. All at once, the valley abruptly narrowed and the trail sheered down the side of a waterfall. Our hearts sank – there was no visible foothold for the camels. Only relatively fresh droppings and tufts of snagged hair made us realise that if wild camels could negotiate this slippery corridor then their domestic cousins should be able to do so as well, in spite of their 180-kilo burdens.

The next three hours were spent constructing a step-ladder of rocks and stones so that our camels' feet could grip on the side of the slippery slope. When we had at last finished and the camels were put to it, they scrambled down remarkably well. The herdsmen had tied them nose to tail. Jasper had pleaded in vain for them to be freed, so that they could negotiate the track at their own pace without the encumbrance of being roped to an unpredictable team-mate. Not for the last time he was proven right. A camel slipped and fell. As the camel in front of it carried on down the slope, its nose-peg was abruptly ripped out through the sensitive membrane of its nose. The poor animal's face was immediately covered in blood and the pain must have been excruciating. This inability on our part to insist that a particular course of action be taken, especially with regard to camel welfare, was one of the most frustrating and ultimately distressing parts of the expedition. The camel's nose would never recover. Its nostrils would be for ever split asunder. Understandably, it became head-shy and rebellious until the very end of our trek. Jasper, whose camels in Africa were all controlled with head-collars, was particularly upset. Only Bill and Ben were free from the tyranny of the nose-peg. They were deemed too young for it to be inserted, but their time would come.

Many people, worldwide, hold the view that camels are bad-tempered, vicious animals that kick, bite, regurgitate and blow the partially digested contents of their stomachs over any human being within spitting distance. All these things they assuredly do. But it's usually only because they have been ill-treated. A horse is head-shy if beaten over the head. It will also kick and bite out if it senses that you are a threat. So it is with the camel. If a riding camel is exhausted and the rider beats the creature with a stick, tugs repeatedly on the painful nose-peg or throws stones at his mount's neck at point-blank range, the camel responds accordingly. When it later catches sight of its tormentor, it's hardly surprising that it bellows, spits and kicks out.

Over the five weeks of the expedition, the two camels that Jasper had under his charge became noticeably friendlier and more amenable. These intelligent creatures knew perfectly well which side their maize kernels were buttered. Of course there are exceptions. Some camels, as with people and horses, are born difficult and remain so all their lives. But the vast majority respond to kind and considerate handling, especially when they are young and impressionable. One only had to watch Jasper Evans talking to and caressing a camel to realise how true this is. Professor Yuan was constantly shouting at Jasper to get away from a camel's back end.

'You will be kicked, Jasper,' he would cry out. 'A camel's kick can be very serious. It can break your leg.'

No camel kicked out at Jasper. They both knew what they were about.

One other aspect of camel management that was spurned, indeed laughed at by the herdsmen, was the suggestion that the camels should be hobbled at night. Professor Yuan had said somewhat loftily, 'We never hobble our camels in China. They are too well trained.'

Jasper had begun a chapter in a book that he had published with Debbie Atkins on practical camel management by saying that if you wanted to return from the desert alive, then you should always ensure that your camels are securely tied up at night. This was nothing more than common sense and, on trek in northern Kenya, surrounded by lions, leopards, hyenas and other camel predators, one would never have dreamt of doing otherwise. There were few such predators in this part of the Gobi, wolves being mainly confined to Mongolia, but there was a hostile and violently unpredictable climate to contend with. It would be a further five days yet before the results of ignoring this all too sensible advice would become glaringly apparent.

★ ★ ★

Journal entry, Tuesday, 8 April 1997:

We complete a long, tiring trek of 26 kilometres. Once we had left the waterfall behind, the downhill going became slightly easier until we reached the mouth of the Chashkan Sayi (Many Mice) valley. It certainly lived up to its name. It was covered with rat holes and pika (*Ochotona oalasii*) scuttled about in all directions. To our great disappointment the spring water was undrinkable as it was too salty. We were therefore forced to make a second change of plan. After a lengthy discussion with Lao Zhao, the Professor decided to continue travelling on a westerly compass bearing until we reached another valley called Chukur Chap (Very Deep Gully). Lao Zhao was convinced that we will find good, drinkable water there. I certainly hope so, as we must have fresh supplies and full water containers before we enter the desert. There is no fresh water in either the Lop Desert, the Kum Tagh or near Lop Nur.

A very stiff walk over steeply undulating sandstone foothills, which the camels had great difficulty in negotiating. Dum Dum nearly had a serious mishap when he insisted on riding up a tiny, narrow ridge instead of getting off and walking. Part of the ridge collapsed under the combined weight of 180 kilos of kit, goodness knows how many kilos of portly Dum Dum and the long-suffering camel. He jumped free just in time before the poor camel slid down the side of a steep hill, bellowing in terror. Thank goodness he let go of the camel rope otherwise we might have had another camel with a bloody nose. Neither Dum Dum nor the camel was hurt. Fortunately, the incident persuaded the Professor to order that a rider must dismount when the terrain becomes too rough. I must say, I prefer walking as long as possible to avoid a sore bottom and an aching back.

We surprised seven wild Tibetan asses. There is much evidence of both asses and wild camels in these remote foothills of the Arjin Shan mountains, which is encouraging. Jasper is bearing up but he sometimes looks very tired. The recent extremely cold conditions must have been quite a shock to his system. Fortunately, we have at last managed to increase the comfort level of our so-called saddles, so he is able to ride without cutting himself to pieces. No doubt by the end of the trek, we will have perfected both the art of tying on loads and constructing a comfortable saddle out of a flea-bitten, moth-eaten piece of unwashed felt.

We eventually reach Chukur Chap at 8.00 p.m. We are all pretty exhausted but Zoologist Li quickly earns full marks from the team for cooking a delicious Uighur dish of mutton, veg and rice in no time at all. We rest content. The Chukur Chap water is sweet and clear and we experience our first tolerably warm night since we left Urumqi.

On 9 April we filled up our water containers at the picturesque spring and set off just before midday. Xiao Yuan took the lead to guide us out of the wide Chukur Chap valley. We hadn't gone far before he turned his camel and trotted back towards us.

'I've picked up what must be a wild camel migration track,' he called out excitedly. 'It's deeply rutted and runs just below the left bank of the valley. Provided we don't lose it, it could lead us over the Kum Tagh.'

This was a lucky break, especially as we had picked it up so quickly. If it merged into a well-trodden trail then the puzzle of the Kum Tagh wild camel crossing place could soon be solved.

The banks on either side of the widening valley had become smaller and we could see that they petered out completely into desert about two kilometres ahead of us. Suddenly, Lao Zhao spotted three goitered gazelles and, before I realised what he was doing, he had untied his gun, dismounted from his camel and was running at the double to the shelter of a sand bank so that he could take a shot. When I heard the sound of his rifle, my heart sank.

Fortunately, he appeared to have missed, but it was this incident that triggered my fuse and Lao Zhao's self-examination and confession in front of his party peer group. But I doubted its long-term efficacy, even though it was the last time on that trip that he fingered his trigger.

By the time we pitched camp on the evening of 9 April, we had successfully crossed nineteen kilometres of Lop desert and reached the foot of the Kum Tagh. We had followed the deeply rutted migration track of the wild camels all day, and were positioned and prepared for a crossing of those formidable sand mountains at first light.

★   ★   ★

Journal entry, Thursday, 10 April:

I had felt certain that the wild camel track would lead to a relatively easy crossing point, and so it proved. Their track meandered through a narrow cleft in the towering dunes and we managed to cross over the Kum Tagh in under three hours with surprisingly little difficulty. When one looked at the mighty sand mountains from the foothills of the Arjin Shan mountains, they appeared to present an insuperable barrier. Two young, female wild camel calves hadn't made it, though. Their skeletons, bleached white by the searing sun, lay to one side of the track. The GPS proved useful in pinpointing exactly where they had fallen. We made the actual crossing over a line of comparatively small dunes whose slopes were not steep and whose surface was firm. Had Hedin found a similar crossing point further to the east nearly a century earlier?

Once we were up and over the dunes, we entered a seemingly unending stretch of stone, flat, featureless Gobi. The wild camel migration route stretched out clearly before us. Through the field-glasses, far, far to the north, Jasper and I could just make out a glimmer of white, shimmering in a haze of heat. This, according to Lao Zhao, was a vast stretch of salt flats. Beyond them lay our destination, the rim of the dried-up Lop Nur lake basin, cut off from the desert by towering cliffs. The vegetation along the edge of the lake forms the winter grazing of the wild camels. If followed to the east, it enters the Aqike valley that we had been forced to retreat from in 1996.

When we were halfway across the stone desert, the camels started to tire and some of them began to bellow and sit down. They needed a lot of encouragement to get up and move on. Herdsman Ahun's camel in particular was a constant problem. Jasper is tiring, too, although he certainly isn't bellowing and sitting down. He rides most of the time and keeps his silence, chewing on an old piece of zebra 'biltong' that came with him from Nairobi. I remind myself that he is 72 and offer a silent prayer that I might be able to undertake such a trip in ten years time.

At one point I find myself leading a camel carrying six full water containers that weigh over 200 kilos. No wonder the poor creatures want to sit down. On and on for hour after blistering hour, over totally barren terrain, devoid of any form of life. As the sun sinks lower towards the horizon, our camels cast long shadows over the ground. We make a timeless scene, similar to faded sepia prints that depict Stein and Hedin in the Taklamakan, or earlier pen and ink images of camels plodding along the Silk Road. Three-quarters of the way across the desert, with the light failing and a long way still to go, the Professor decides to send Li and Dum Dum ahead on foot to scout out the country and light a fire from lake-side scrub to guide us in to Lop Nur. The sun sets, and both the wild camel trail and the footprints of Dum Dum and Li become almost impossible to follow. The moon is in its first quarter so there's not much light. Jasper and I think that the Professor's decision is extremely unwise. In the fast-fading light it seems to us to be folly to separate members of the team. But decisions are not ours to make and to protest would be a waste of words.

At last, in pitch dark, we reach the edge of the salt flats. Almost immediately our camels sink into wet salt slush and become very agitated, and we lose the trail of our two guides. At any moment I expect our camels to take off into the night, our kit bouncing impotently on their sides. At this point the Professor starts to argue with Lao Zhao. We are not exactly lost, but after 12 hours' arduous trekking and having covered over 42 kilometres the contours on the ground do not tally with those on the map. Lao Zhao stops yet again to peer at his bundle of wind-tossed satellite images by the light of a rapidly fading torch. After ten minutes he gets up, mutters something to our Professorial leader, flings out a right arm and strikes off in a north-easterly direction.

Ten minutes later, Xiao Yuan and I think that we see the light of our herdsmen's camp-fire. But shortly afterwards we spot another similar light and then another. The lights dance from right to left and left to right. Then as we close in on them they completely disappear. Unhappy Gobi spirits are definitely playing tricks on us again. At last, after much squinting and narrowing of eyes we catch sight of a genuine flicker of a flame which remains constant. We head towards it and at long last we move off the salt flats on to a harder, more substantial surface. By this time, both men and camels are exhausted, and the wind is blowing bitterly cold, howling mercilessly across the bleak salt marsh flats that we have just left behind us. Then, without warning, we stumble to the very edge of a massive split in the rock surface and discover that a steep chasm separates us from the fire of Li and Dum Dum. Somehow they have managed to get themselves separated from us on the far side of a huge gorge. Neither Jasper nor I can understand how they have managed to get there.

We set up camp in pitch darkness at 11.30 p.m. We put up our tent a little way away from our colleagues. Jasper and I struggle in a freezing wind and for the umpteenth time curse our tent's office-bound designer. Oh, that he were here, to suffer alongside us as we wrestle with his impossibly fractious brainchild. We have walked/ridden 43 kilometres today in very taxing conditions. Jasper is very, very tired and sore from chafing ropes. At last, and to our great relief, we crawl under the misshapen Victorian underwear which serves as a tent and down our last drop of whisky. Then, absolutely dead-beat, we snatch sleep between shivers.

★ ★ ★

'Hey, Japper, look at this.'

Jasper crawled slowly backwards out of our hyena hole.

'It's just as well I didn't have to have a pee last night,' he said, as he peered over a sheer cliff edge. 'It's the biggest long-drop I've ever seen.'

Quite inadvertently, we had pitched our tent on the edge of a cliff. To our right lay the steep side of the gorge that had separated us from our two herdsmen; in front of us, many hundreds of metres below, the dry lake-bed of Lop Nur stretched to the distant horizon. The only significant feature that we could see was the snaky outline of a salt river which flowed into the lake out of the deep gorge to our right.

'There's vegetation down there,' I said pointing to some tufts of tamarisk and saxsaul. 'If we'd been able to cross the *shor* last year, we'd have pitched up somewhere near here.'

There was a quiet satisfaction in knowing that we had finally achieved what we had tried, unsuccessfully, to do in 1996. We had reached the winter grazing area of the wild camel.

The next day, 11 April, was a rest day. Lop Nur stretched away to the north under a cloudless sky. Our camels browsed among the tangled clumps of tamarisk and saxsaul which sustained the wild camels during the winter months. They then strung out along the stream of salt water which snaked into the lake for about five kilometres before it disappeared completely in that vast arena of man-made desolation. I pottered slowly through the dry, knee-high *fragmitis* grass and saw where other animals had pioneered. Goitered gazelles, foxes and the bold prints of a wolf. Lao Zhao found the remains of two young camels which appear to have died from natural causes. My journal seems untroubled, the text complacent. 'The camels are so clever. They wander away to the east for miles. Yet they return to us instead of disappearing and settle down contentedly while we demolish a bush banquet, cooked and concocted to celebrate our success in reaching the wild camels' winter grazing. Herdsmen Yusuf, Dum Dum and Wang are terrific. Friendly, willing and cheerful. There have been no real arguments between anyone. The Professor, too, is in fine form.'

Next day we followed the migration trail due east. It meandered though tamarisk, *fragmitis* and *shor*. Then it turned abruptly to the north-east and into the great lake itself. There was no mistaking the firm line of the camels' march. Following one another in single file, they had, over the centuries, left behind then an unmistakable track that neither desert storm nor nuclear test could obliterate. Their track led us back through razor-sharp *shor* to the lakeside where *yardangs* paraded on to the lake-bed in uniform lines. When off the *shor* we saw scuffed sand where groups of up to ten camels had rested. But the total of dead young camels had by this time reached seven.

The night of 12 April was perfect. It was utterly still and myriad stars twinkled overhead. To the north-west, comet Hale-bopp displayed its vibrant tail with an astonishing brightness. We went to bed happy, well-fed and content.

But the Gobi should never be taken for granted. The line that divides success and disaster is finely tuned. The restless spirits of the desert lie constantly in wait, ever ready to pull the rug from under the feet of the complacent traveller. That night I had the most extraordinary dream. Dressed in a bright blue gown, I was guest of honour at a ceremony. I looked out at a sea of upturned and expectant faces that stretched, like the lake-bed of Lop Nur, to the far, far horizon. At first I ignored the tug on my sleeve, I was too busy staring at the gigantic gathering. But the tugging continued and, somewhat annoyed, I glanced down. A courtier was kneeling beside me, a Cheshire cat-like smile on his face. He was holding up an open tin of dead, dry fish. What was I supposed to do with them? I turned to look back at the huge crowd. Their whole manner had changed. Their faces were no longer benign. They were angry, hostile. I hadn't done what they had expected me to do. The fish! What was I supposed to do with the fish?

On 13 April my journal records that, 'A fresh wind got up on the night of the 12th. About 2.00 a.m. it developed into a powerful sand storm. The next morning, amidst a wreckage of flattened tentage and buckled tent poles, we emerged in a howling wind to discover that all but two of our camels had fled. Hyper-sensitive young Ben and an ailing elder remained, as for the rest, they had completely vanished. We are over 280 kilometres from our base camp.'

10
A Sign from Noah

And the dove came in to him in the evening
Genesis VIII: 11

It wasn't until the second day that the Professor began to worry. On the day after the disappearance of fifteen of our camels, we all set off, a fresh wind on our backs, to Kush Lanze, about ten kilometres to the east. Ahun had been sent off to seek out the missing camels and the Professor seemed quite certain that the old man would find them. Meanwhile, to fill in time, he organised a wild camel survey to the east.

Kush Lanze is a rocky promontory jutting out into the lake-bed. Professor Yuan, in relaxed mood, insisted on carving graffiti on the soft surface which advertised not only our arrival, but the fact that Shell was our sponsor. Xiao Yuan looked preoccupied. Mr Li was unusually silent. Lao Zhao wanted to return, but nothing deterred the Professor.

'Our camels will be waiting for us back at camp.' he said, cheerfully handing me his knife. 'Carve UNEP on the rock, John. Someone will come here one day, thinking that they are the first explorers, only to find that we were here before them.' He laughed and expectorated with unusual vigour.

'I expect it will be a contingent of oil-boys,' said Jasper, gloomily turning away from the spitting area which was now being worked over by Lao Zhao. 'They'll be here sooner than you think. I've already seen the tracks of one of their exploration vehicles.'

So had we all. I prayed fervently that the 'oil-boys' wouldn't discover oil in the area. If it was discovered in marketable quantities then we could all say goodbye to wild camels, nature sanctuaries, winter grazing areas and highly endangered species. Our efforts would be consigned to the scrap-heap. Nothing ecological, environmental or ethical would count against the ruthless financial logic of oil extraction. It was ironic. We were only here by courtesy of Shell. We were all oil-boys now!

The wind grew stronger and whipped up the sand.

'Shouldn't we go back?' queried the Professor's son.

'No, no. We must finish the sign writing,' his father insisted.

I struggled feebly in a limp attempt to carve UNEP.

'Here, let me do it.' The Prof retrieved his knife and deftly transformed my half-hearted and cack-handed effort.

'There,' he said with pride as he pointed to the capital letters gouged deep into the sandstone, 'Shell and UNEP, Wild Camel Expedition, 1997'.

We applauded his effort, but he still wasn't ready to return to our camp. All our thoughts were centred on the missing camels. The Professor appeared to be completely unconcerned, convinced that they would soon be found.

'Photos, photos,' he called out.

And so we posed, singly, in pairs and in groups, while Mr Li took our pictures. The increasing strength of the wind and driving sand brought the photo opportunity to an abrupt halt, even the Professor reluctantly agreeing that it was time to return.

'The camels will be waiting for us,' he called out optimistically as we set off. 'Don't worry. You'll see for yourself.'

But the Professor was wrong. The journey back against the fierce wind took twice as long as our outward journey. We found a dead adult camel, but the homeward trudge was hard and we didn't have the energy to examine it for long. It took five hours for us to reach camp, and we soon saw that one tent had been blown to shreds and most of the others flattened. Only our hyena hole had somehow managed to remain upright, its undergarments flapping uselessly in the howling wind.

Ahun looked grim. He told the Professor that in spite of his efforts he had seen nothing. He hadn't even found the camels' tracks. He was promptly re-equipped for a further solo forage, this time with four days' food rations, and the one fit adult camel that hadn't taken off with the others. Once again, Jasper and I had major doubts. Ahun was being sent out on his own in gale-force conditions, which made camel-tracking extremely difficult. Would it not have been better for him to have set off with a colleague, the much younger Yusuf, Dum Dum or Wang? It was no use either of us making the suggestion. The Professor was adamant. A decision had been made.

On Monday 14 April we took stock. We had water for nine and a half days and ample food. Our nearest supply of fresh water was the spring at Chukur Chap, which, without camels, was three days' march away. If the camels weren't rounded up in six days we would have to abandon camp and set out for the spring on Sunday morning, 20 April. Everything would have to be left behind except for absolute essentials and food and water for the return journey. The food taken would have to last for the three-day onward trek from Chukur Chap.

Jasper was suffering from intermittent nose bleeds, probably caused by the flying sand which gets into everything. To walk back to Chukur Chap would be tough on us all. For Jasper, with his gammy knee, it would be hell. He was becoming increasingly conscious of this and starting to worry that his slower walking pace would cause us extra delay.

'If I croak on the walk back I don't want you to fuss around with my body,' he said to me in all seriousness. 'Just dig a hole and cover me up with sand, I'd much prefer it that way.'

I wouldn't discuss the subject with him. I firmly believed that, one way or another, we would make it back to the vehicles.

That evening, having climbed back up the cliff from his tamarisk squat, Jasper handed a mess-tin to the Professor that was half-full of water.

'I think that you ought to taste this, Prof.'

'It's salt. Not good to drink,' said the Professor, wrinkling his nose in disgust. 'If we drink it, we will all get a bad belly-ache.'

'I know, but it's good enough to use for washing,' said Jasper. 'Both on our own bodies and the dishes.'

The Professor considered for a moment and then nodded in agreement. 'Good, idea. You're right, Japper.' He gave the necessary instructions. Jasper sighed with relief. At long last, a piece of unsolicited advice had been accepted.

That night, Lao Zhao set fire to the *fragmitis* grass in the lake-bed. We'd spent the afternoon and evening hauling bundles of parched, dry wood up on to a kneel which would underpin a fiery beacon for Ahun. But why the needless conflagration? I sometimes despaired of Lao Zhao.

Just before midnight Ahun, the old Uighur herdsman, returned. His trip had been a disaster. He hadn't found the missing camel tracks. He'd consumed four days' rations in twenty-four hours but far, far worse, he'd totally exhausted our one good camel. Great raw weals stood out on its hind legs, which graphically highlighted where he had lashed it forward. After Ahun had dismounted, the camel absolutely refused to move. It just sat there, moaning softly to itself. Ahun had found nothing, achieved nothing and totally wrecked our only reliable means of transport.

* * *

Journal entry, Tuesday, 15 April:

The Professor and the team have sent Ahun to Coventry. They hardly speak to him, ignore him at meal times and generally behave as though he no longer exists. They say that he's old, stupid and an ignorant Uighur. Little wonder that there's a flourishing Uighur independence movement. For all his sins, he doesn't deserve that treatment and Jasper makes a point of keeping an eye on him. At long last, the Professor makes an overdue decision and instructs Yusuf and Dum Dum to set off to look for the missing camels. During a solo desert scout, Yusuf had picked up our camels' tracks from the ropes attached to their nose pegs. They trail behind the camels like snakes and seem to indicate that the camels have headed back towards the Arjin Shan mountains. Who can blame them? In the Arjin Shan there is fresh vegetation and drinkable water. Here there is only salt water, dry *fragmitis* and a howling wind from which there is no shelter. Jasper boils up camel maize to soften it so that we can drench the sick camel. The poor animal is totally exhausted and refuses to eat on its own. We attempt to pour the maize kernels down its throat through an adapted plastic water bottle. In spite of rumbling, angry protests and attempts at regurgitation, quite a bit of the warm, soggy mash reaches its stomach.

In order to try to win favour, Ahun makes a huge *nan* bread in the glowing ashes of last night's beacon fire. Later that afternoon, the camel struggles to its feet and we manage to guide it down the steep, lake-side cliff and into the parched *fragmitis* grass. It nibbles, not over-enthusiastically, at a few dry, dusty spikes, but at least it's making an attempt to eat. Jasper feels that his time doctoring the poor animal has been well spent.

★   ★   ★

'Hey, John, Japper, come over here. Chang has something interesting to tell you.' Xiao Yuan was standing by the kitchen tent and calling out to us excitedly.

'What is it?'

'Come on over, he'll tell you himself.'

Jasper and I bent our heads into the driving wind and made our way over to the sagging kitchen tent. The wind had freshened and the canvas flapped noisily as we squeezed inside. Herdsman Chang was squatting in a corner, sucking on a cigarette. He looked relaxed and happy.

'Chang's mother was a "shaman" who could see into the future,' Xiao Yuan explained. 'He's inherited her gift and can do exactly the same thing. He's quite famous for doing it in Ruoqiang. Herdsmen come from all over the place to consult him.'

Chang looked totally detached. He couldn't be more than thirty-five years old, yet his face was deeply lined and there were large black bags under his eyes. Jasper had been long enough in Africa not to be sceptical. He'd had his own experiences of the power of an old African shaman woman.

'Tell them what you have just told me,' Xiao Yuan instructed.

Mr Chang hugged his knees, half-closed his eyes and rocked slowly back and forth. 'Last night I had a dream,' he said. 'I saw the camels come back into our camp.' He opened his eyes and looked up at Jasper and me. 'They'll return on Saturday morning, between 12.00 p.m. and 3.00 a.m. One will be missing but Yusuf and Dum Dum will have found all the others. They'll all be tired and thin but they won't be sick. Don't worry, they'll return and will get us back to our vehicles. We'll be all right.'

I turned towards Xiao Yuan. 'Do you believe him?' I asked rather stupidly.

Xiao Yuan smiled and shrugged his shoulders. 'I don't know. But it helps,' he said. 'My father says that he doesn't believe him, but even for him, it helps.'

Later that evening, after a good supper of filling rice, the Professor organised a class of relaxation exercises for the whole team. We stood on a windy ridge, grouped in a semi-circle around the Professor and imitated him as he pulled, rubbed and flexed parts of his body, especially his face and head. He punctuated the exercises with inhalations of three deep breaths which, the Professor told us, 'pulls the good air through your head and expels bad fumes through your feet'. We pushed, pulled and prodded until our whole frames, from top to toe, had been thoroughly worked over. At the end of the forty-minute session we certainly felt relaxed, and retired to our tents with our heads full of Chang's encouraging forecast and our feet having gratefully expelled the last of our body's bad odours. Things were looking up. The

Professors last words tó us were, 'Don't bother to get up too early, it saves food!'

★ ★ ★

Journal entry, Wednesday, 16 April:

We are on two meals a day now and having to watch both food and water. If only the wind would die down. It's tiring having to struggle with one's head down and makes the daily task of collecting bundles of firewood for the nightly beacon doubly difficult. Jasper has taken up residence in a tamarisk bush conveniently placed by the side of the dry lake. He moves from time to time in a clockwise direction to keep shaded from the sun and is keeping a diary, called 'Observations Made During Days Spent in a Tamarisk Bush in the Gobi Desert'.

I teach Xiao Yuan, Chang and Mr Li to play backgammon. Xiao Yuan has learnt it so well that he beats me with a frequency which is monotonous and bordering on the embarrassing. Jasper drenches our camel with softened maize twice daily. It's picking up and starting to move around but still hasn't got the energy to go too far. It certainly won't run off!

I wash my smalls in the salt pools left by the river which flows into Lop Nur. I don't enjoy doing it and know that I don't make a good job of it. There's not much of an end reward when everything ends up looking as though it has been starched with salt. Everyone else washes their clothes so much better than I do, especially Jasper. I concentrate hard on my socks and try to make a good job of them. I'm very conscious that they might be needed for an extended and unwelcome bit of walking.

In the evening, went out from camp to look for stones as Jasper and I both think that we should try to grind up some of the camel food for human porridge to eke out our dwindling food supply. Unknown to me, Jasper has crawled out òf his tamarisk bush to do the same thing. We travel our separate ways and he returns with a good flat, smooth stone for a base and I seem to have found a reasonable grinder.

During my walk I pick up the trail left by our camels. The track from the lead rope which trails behind them sticks out like a bicycle wheel's track. How Ahun missed this I can't begin to make out. Did he deliberately return because he didn't want to follow the camels back to the mountains on his own? If so, why did he eat up four days' supply of rations? And why did the Professor consider sending just one of our herdsmen after the camels when there are four of them? It is extremely difficult for Jasper and me to get involved in the decision making. The Professor feels that our welfare is his personal responsibility and spends his time in discussion with Lao Zhao. For example, we were to have waited here until Sunday morning before we abandoned camp. Now it has been decided that we must leave on Saturday the 19th. No doubt our dwindling food and water supply situation has dictated this decision. Fine, but Jasper and I only learn about it through Xiao Yuan. It can be most frustrating.

That evening, Jasper and I boycott the Professor's exercise session. Not because we are mean-spirited but because our bellies are full of rice and maize porridge. Listened to the news and learn that 200 Haj pilgrims were killed when their tents caught fire during their pilgrimage in Saudi Arabia. It's sobering to realise that other people living in deserts are facing bigger problems than us.

Journal entry, Thursday, 17 April:

We breakfast on Ahun's *nan* and powdered milk. The camel maize porridge is also available for the strong of heart and stomach. After breakfast it is firewood beacon-hauling time. When pulling at the dried tamarisk bushes for wood, clouds of white mosquitoes are activated. They were not around when we first arrived here, but word seems to have spread around the lake that there is some good, fresh blood on offer, some of it very special and encased in a white skin. I hope the mossies enjoy sucking on old West and East African, malaria-strewn red blood corpuscles. Jasper and I have both been laid low with malaria from time to time. Relieved when I have completed my quota of firewood. Jasper manages to bring up an immaculately tied bundle while I appear over the cliff top with ropes flapping, inadequate knots and branches of tamarisk trailing behind me. It's a stiff climb up to the beacon point but mercifully the wind has dropped. Maybe that's why the mossies are so dreadful.

Mr Li finds the complete carcass of a young camel down by the side of the lake. I bring back the skull tied haphazardly on top of a bundle of wood. So far we have found eight dead camels, seven of whom are young. The young must have a very high mortality rate, and Jasper speculates whether it could be due to radiation. Perhaps if I get the skull back to England we'll find out!

Later, find Lao Zhao slumped in a corner of the kitchen tent looking like an opium addict and sucking on a small glass bottle of ginseng. He has brought a stack of them with him packed in red cardboard boxes. I remember that he has had to have his blood changed twice over the last two years. He looks pretty grim and I wonder once again about his radiation levels. We're quite a team. Jasper is 72, Ahun must be 66, Lao Zhao is 64, I'm 62 and the Prof is 59. Life begins about sixty!

Jasper retires to his tamarisk bush having repaired the aerial of my wireless by using the thin strip of metal which he peels off from a sardine tin. He's fashioned the tin's key into a tool for threading a strip of elastic through his Chinese army underpants. I can reveal a serious defect in Chinese military equipment. Their army underpants have no elastic in them to hold them up. Jasper bought six pairs of military undergarments in Urumqi market and not one of them has elastic around the waist. The underpants fitted him at the beginning of the expedition but by now he has lost weight. Resourceful at all times, he brought with him a packet of 'lackey', as he describes it. But if the Chinese infantry lose or put on weight, they are faced with a very serious problem. How can they possibly shoot straight if their underpants are falling down? Military planners of the world take note! Wars can be won or lost, depending on whether your army is equipped with sufficient 'lackey'.

Chang painstakingly makes noodles in the kitchen tent. Great heaps of noodles, using up our remaining bags of flour. Jasper grinds away at the camel's corn in one corner while Lao Zhao sits slumped in another corner sucking at his ginseng. The rest of the camp retires to improvised shelters. I write this journal propped up in the fourth corner and surrounded by the select remains of previous days' meals. At supper time, the mossies are hell. Every mossie in the Gashun Gobi appears to have been given an invitation to the feast. They are white and so easy to see, but boy can they bite. They come when there's no wind, but on balance, we wouldn't want the wind back so we have to endure the millions of winged tormentors.

★ ★ ★

The night of Friday, 18 April was remarkably windless. 'I hope it's not the calm before the storm,' commented Jasper drily. Each of us was moving about more slowly, preoccupied with his own thoughts and steeling himself for the walk which lay ahead. We got up late. Jasper put on socks and gym shoes and said that he was going for a walk to 'test them out'.

Wood collection, backgammon, noodles, evening exercises. The days settled into a routine but we were all preparing ourselves mentally for Saturday. The Professor and his son laid out supplies – water to enable us to get to Chukur Chap, food to take us on the extra three days to our base camp. There is little margin for error. For example, a two-day sand storm halfway to Chukur Chap could be a major problem. We will have to leave almost everything behind. My cameras, including the BBC video camera, must come with us, but the video has only three batteries left and each one lasts for only about ten minutes. We had considered bringing a solar panel which could be fitted to a camel and which would charge up the batteries. But we decided against it, and I'm glad that we did. Slipping loads on journeys through narrow gullies would have caused endless problems and I'm sure that the panels wouldn't have remained intact.

That evening, as the sun was setting, Jasper and I set about drenching the ailing camel. It was definitely better and starting to eat maize of its own accord. The horrible weals had begun to heal and it had put on a little weight, but we both knew that it was sadly out of condition and its ability to carry water for any distance was questionable.

The rest of the team were standing out on the beacon point just behind us, peering into the featureless expanse of flat, stony desert which stretched away to the horizon. They strained, willing to see movement.

'Hey, Japper, look at that.'

A lone swallow had suddenly swooped down and practically brushed my clothing. It veered sharply away and then zoomed in and encircled Jasper.

'I've never seen anything like it,' he said in amazement.

The bird did a perfect figure of eight around us, brushing our sweaters as it did so. We both stared at it transfixed.

'Swallows are flock birds. I've never seen one on its own like this. I can't believe it.'

We watched it as it continued to swoop down and circle round about us. Suddenly a cheer broke out behind us, hesitant at first and then swelling into something loud and confident. Applause broke out, followed by excited chatter. Xiao Yuan ran over towards us.

'Japper, John! Look over there! Look!'

We stared at the distant horizon. I saw nothing. My field-glasses were near by. I unstrapped them from the case, fumbling and cursing as I did so. At last I raised them to my eyes.

'Yes, Japper. Look, look. Our camels!'

We forgot about the swallow. On the horizon, tiny black specks had appeared. They were some of our camels. Then further to the east another line of camels appeared.

'That's Yusuf over there. And look, over there. It's Dum Dum.'

The rest of the team had run over to our ridge. We were all hugging each other and cheering.

Soon the distant dots became clearer. The two herdsmen drew near, and half an hour later Dum Dum arrived, exhausted but triumphant. Then Yusuf appeared. Each of them led in seven camels.

Dum Dum prised off the top of a bottle of beer. 'We found them in a valley of the Arjin Shan,' he said, between long slugs at the bottle. 'We've brought them all, except for one. It wouldn't come. It just sat down and refused to move no matter how hard we tried.'

'But we've got them,' said Yusuf.

Indeed they had. The camels were desperately thin and they had lost a great deal of their woolly winter coats. They were wild-eyed and unsettled, but they were back.

'I hope that you hobble them securely tonight,' said Jasper. 'It wouldn't be much of a joke if they ran off again.'

Dum Dum nodded vigorously. 'We'll hobble them,' he said between extended slurps of Beijing beer. 'Don't worry about that.'

Chang said quietly, 'I got the timing a bit wrong, but I told you that they'd find them. I knew they would and that we'd be all right.'

I shook hands with Chang, Dum Dum, Yusuf, the Professor – with everyone. We were all mightily relieved not to have to set out on foot the next day.

'What do you make of that swallow?' I asked Jasper, as we settled for the night. 'I suppose that a scientist would tell us that it was a migrant bird, blown off course, which suddenly saw life in the desert and homed in on us. I've seen one or two dead swallows in previous years. Birds that have lost their way and perished in the desert.'

'It was a sign from Noah,' said Jasper calmly as the Professor let off a string of celebratory firecrackers outside our tent.

★　★　★

Next morning we headed back with our camels towards the Arjin Shan, the same mountains to which they had fled. After six days of inactivity our team couldn't wait to get under way, which no doubt accounted for my filling my water bottle with salt instead of fresh water. It certainly shortened and enlivened my mid-morning tipple. However, the poor camels had not the slightest enthusiasm for the long walk ahead of them. They tried trick after trick. Some got up and then sat down, making it as difficult as possible for loads to be tied on their backs. Ben, of the nervous, teeth-grinding disposition, who had been earmarked to carry the camels' maize, would have absolutely none of it. He ran off and successfully managed to evade all attempts at recapture. He ended up following us, at a very discreet distance, all the way back to the mountains. My camel got up just as I swung my leg over his back in a vain attempt to mount him. This ensured that I ended upside-down in a sand dune on more than one occasion, and acquired not only a camera full of sand but also an added incentive to walk. Exactly, no doubt, as my perceptive camel had intended.

We made light work of the long haul over the great expanse of stone Gobi which stretched away from the lake. The hours seemed to pass twice as quickly as on the outward journey. We hummed and sang to ourselves or each other. Even Ahun was allowed back from Coventry and chatted happily away to his fellow Uighur, Yusuf. Our spirits were high and we felt good. But this euphoria was abruptly clouded when the camel that had been exhausted by Ahun suddenly sank to the ground and refused to move. It was only carrying empty water containers, which were no burden, but it had quite clearly said to itself, 'enough is enough'.

For nearly an hour we cajoled, cursed, pushed and prodded. We strung a rope round its hind legs and pulled at its forelegs. The camel would not move and adamantly refused to rise to its feet. There was nothing, absolutely nothing that we could do – except, of course, kill it. We had a shotgun, which would have needed more than one cartridge, or a sharp knife, which would have been a messy way of doing the deed but decidedly more humane. After a few moments of heated debate it was decided to leave the poor beast sitting where it was, in the hope that it would eventually get up and make its way back to the Arjin Shan mountains. There it might find fresh vegetation and water and hopefully develop a will to survive.

It was a difficult decision to make and there were sound arguments for and against. Not least powerful was the argument that if we were in an area where wild camels were untainted by pairing with domestic stock, then wasn't it the height of irresponsibility to leave a live, domestic female in their midst? I didn't think so. Personally, I thought that the camel would die where we left it. It was so weak and feeble that the chance of it surviving until the next breeding season in eight months' time was highly remote. I couldn't bring myself to see it slaughtered after what it had endured. Others will argue that that would have been the most sensible and humane thing to do. All I can say is that we were there and made the decision on the spot. So, rightly or wrongly, we left the poor creature where it was. As we walked further and further away from it, it presented a pitiable sight. After thirty minutes or so I could no longer look back at the pathetic black blob, staring silently at our retreating caravan and surrounded by the vast empty expanse of pitiless desert.

That night it was windless and warmer, and Jasper and I dispensed with our high-tech tent and slept under the comet. We had covered thirty miles and were sore and stiff. We slept fitfully. The memory of our camel left to die in the desert haunted my dreams.

Next morning we crossed the Kum Tagh. Once again it was not a difficult crossing-place, and a sounding from the GPS made sure that we put the correct grid reference on the proposed sanctuary map. It was another long, tough day of travel, totalling twelve hours in all. We didn't reach the Chukur Chap spring until 10.30 p.m., where we pitched camp in the dark. But it wasn't just dark. As we approached the mountains in a fading light, a strange mist came down. It was distinctly eerie. Although there was not a breath of wind, the mist was not formed by moisture but by dust. It seemed to float down from above, causing the temperature to drop rapidly. It also reduced visibility down to about twenty metres.

It wasn't until the next morning that I learnt from Xiao Yuan just how fortunate we had been. The dust mist had been caused by a huge sand storm in the desert that we had just crossed. Had the storm hit us on the march both we and the camels would have been in the greatest difficulty. And if we had been attempting to cross the desert without our camels then I think it's fairly certain that not all of us would have made it to Chukur Chap. It could so easily have been a very different story.

★　★　★

We wallowed in the Chukur Chap spring. The cold, clear, bright water which gurgled over the rocks was an indescribable treat. Lop Nur grime and the pungent smell of unwashed feet was sponged away. The camels, too, were given a break and wandered off to find the tender green shoots of fresh vegetation. But we couldn't afford to spend a whole day at Chukur Chap and left shortly after our midday meal. The Professor wisely decided not to attempt to follow a short-cut over the Arjin Shan. A great deal of the stuffing had been knocked out of our camels during their double trek from Lop Nur to the Arjin Shan and back again; to have attempted to go back over the mountains was asking for trouble, and we'd had quite enough trouble for one trip.

We trekked through stunning country. The ominous mist of dust and sand had lifted, and the light was crystal clear. The crevasses and gullies which gouged the sides of the Arjin Shan mountains stood out in unbelievably sharp relief. The slanting late afternoon sun revealed every precipice, buttress and fissure in these huge battlements. As the sun sank lower, they were clarified further and then, in the evening haze, they gradually lost their detail until, thickening, they vanished completely in an all-conquering indigo. We wound our way up and over sandstone foothills which stretched in a seemingly unending line ahead of us. There were droppings of wild ass and wild camel strewn along every winding track that we followed. The picturesque scene was marred by the unceasing bellowing of Lao Zhao's camel, the poor creature who had had its nose peg ripped through its nostrils when we led it down the man-made ladder of stones on our outward journey. Lao Zhao showed little sympathy for it in its all too obvious distress, and at times beat it forward unfeelingly. Both Jasper and I saw the hard and unyielding side of Lao Zhao's nature. He was certainly no lover of animals.

Our camp that evening was pitched in an utterly remote valley of great beauty. It seemed as though no human being had ever set foot in the sheltered paradise that we entered. Ancient poplar trees were just breaking into flower. This had a great effect on Jasper and myself as we hadn't seen a tree for weeks. There was a freshwater spring hidden among some tall *fragmitis* grass and the tracks of gazelles, asses and numerous wild camels criss-crossed the soft, sandy surface. Later that evening, Dum Dum and Chang took a perverse delight in burning every piece of dry wood in sight. Some of it must have lain untouched for centuries. Jasper watched in horror as they hacked at the huge trunk of a fallen poplar.

'In the desert, you should always use the bare minimum of fire-wood,' he said with great feeling. 'When wood is a rarity, it should be treated like gold.' Jasper was acutely aware that the cutting down of trees was an immediate cause of a desert's advance. It seemed as though Chang and Dum Dum were setting fire to the Garden of Eden.

Two days later, at just on eight o'clock at night, we wound our way up and over a final barrier of sandstone and into the Hongliugou valley. Xiao Yuan and Mr Li forged on ahead up-river to find our vehicles and alert them to our return. We had covered sixty kilometres from Chukur Chap spring, seen ten wild camels shimmering in a heat haze near the Kum Tagh and passed up and over foothills of outstanding beauty. We were six days overdue and on this last leg, with only the map as a guide, we had been impeded by numerous culs-de-sac which had forced us to retrace our tracks. Tired and footsore, we were nevertheless exhilarated. In spite of our adventures and near disasters we had achieved our objective. The survey of the wild camel migration route had been made. We knew precisely where they crossed the Kum Tagh and exactly where some of the camels from the Gashun Gobi wintered near the lake and summered in the mountain valleys. Just how many of the wild camels undertook the migration was not clear. But although we were disappointed at not having seen more of them, it was clear from their tracks that a considerable number, possibly well over sixty, followed the migration route. Only the seven young dead animals that we found on the lake shore gave us cause for concern. A full moon rose over our camp fire, outlining the huge tamarisk bushes of Hongliugou.

'We've come back from the dead,' said the Professor later that evening. 'For four weeks we walked off the map. If we had had to walk back without our camels then Jasper, Lao Zhao and Ahun would have died.'

I looked up in amazement. 'What about me, Professor? Don't you think I would have died as well?'

'No,' said the imperturbable Professor Yuan Guoying. 'You are a good walker. You would have made it. But Jasper and Ahun are too old and Lao Zhao is too sick. We would have had to cover them all with sand.'

Having spoken his mind, he went off to ignite some firecrackers to celebrate our safe return. Later, he sang patriotic songs to the mountains.

'Japper, I've got a confession to make,' I said as I groped in my kit bag.

'That's unlike you,' said Jasper.

I held up a rather battered Book of Common Prayer.

'I thought that if you croaked in the desert you wouldn't want some fancy, new burial service, so I brought this along so that you could have the full-blown King James version. I would have made certain that you had the works, dust to dust, the lot.'

Jasper was speechless. 'You cheeky so and so,' he said eventually. 'And what if you'd croaked first?'

★ ★ ★

There was a mild sensation when our two drivers pitched up at 10.00 a.m. They were of course delighted to see us. When we were three days overdue, one of them had driven back to Regiment 36 and telephoned Urumqi. At any moment a red alert would be sent out and planes and vehicles would set off to find us. They just might have set off already. We had to let Urumqi know that we were all right. After we'd slaughtered and eaten our remaining sheep, it was imperative that we packed up and left for Regiment 36 as quickly as we could.

The excited chatter subsided for a moment, then one of the driver's said, 'I've seen wild man.'

'You've seen what?'

'Wild man. I was driving up the Hongliugou riverbed three days ago. It was getting dark and I had just switched on my headlights. All of a sudden, a naked, hairy man ran across the riverbed and dived into some reeds. I stopped the truck but I couldn't find him. But I did see his footprint.' He stooped down and drew the outline of a footprint in the sand. 'It had a large toe like this.' He drew an oversize big toe. 'There's no doubt at all. It was wild man. I've seen him before.'

'What?'

'Yes, in 1992, when I was driving in the Kunlun mountains I had a similar experience. Wild man ran across the road just in front of my truck. I found the same-sized footprint.'

Lao Zhao and the Professor had joined us.

'What do you think about it, Lao Zhao?'

'I believe in wild man,' he said slowly. 'Once when we were camping over the border in Tibet, someone entered our camp at night and stole some tins of food. At first I thought it must be thieves, but then I saw the footprint. It was exactly the same size as the one that the driver has outlined in the sand.'

'These mountains are vast,' said the Professor. 'There are many valleys where no man has ever penetrated. We may even have been to one or two of them on our trip. One could spend a whole lifetime in the Kunlun or Arjin Shan mountains and still not know them properly. I've never seen wild man, but I do believe that he exists. There could well be a large primate that has adapted to life in remote mountain areas. He's been seen in Tibet, North America and Siberia. Why not here? New species are still being found. One day, someone will find wild man.'

I would have loved to go off with the driver to look for the footprint, but there was no time. We had to stop the air search and all the subsequent embarrassment that it would cause. Wild man would have to wait. Meanwhile, we had to get to Regiment 36 as quickly as we could.

That afternoon we said goodbye to our camels. Bill and Ben were more subdued now, and our faithful pair, like all the others, were thin and very tired. In spite of our tribulations, they had done us proud. They had carried us, with all our kit, up and over mountains and across some of the harshest desert landscape in the world. In all they had covered nearly 300 kilometres. We patted them with real affection and watched with feeling as they walked stiffly away to graze on huge swathes of young *fragmitis* grass.

Later that evening we set off on the 180-kilometre journey to Regiment 36. Just outside Miran we came across two trucks that had set out from Ruoqiang to find us. It was just as well that they had. Our jeep was bogged down in sand and we were finding it extremely difficult to extract ourselves. There was also a secondary problem. Xiao Yuan's tummy was in turmoil, having lost a battle to hold down a huge quantity of mutton and beer that he'd gulped down in Hongliugou. This meant that Jasper, the Professor and I had struggled with the jeep alone under a starless sky before the trucks appeared and eventually pulled us free. When we finally reached the establishment of Mama Feng at Regiment 36, the Professor rushed to the telephone. He spoke urgently and hectically for a few minutes, then reappeared looking mightily relieved.

'Is everything all right, Professor?'

'Yes, but only just. At daybreak two planes were setting off to find us. And those two trucks from Ruoqiang had already travelled a good distance. We stopped them just in time.'

I thought of how it would have been reported on the radio news and in the papers, 'Foreign scientists lost in trackless Gobi. Massive air and land search under way.' The embassy would have been informed. My wife would have been contacted. The embarrassment would have been unending.

But in spite of our brush with disaster, I didn't regret not having tried to stay in radio contact with Urumqi. In this respect I am in full agreement with explorer and mountaineer Eric Shipman's friend, Bill Tilman, who wrote, 'In my view every herring should hang by its own tail . . . anyone venturing into unfrequented and possibly dangerous waters does so with his eyes open, should be willing to depend on his own exertions and should neither expect nor ask for help. The confidence that is placed, and successfully placed, in being rescued fosters carelessness or even foolishness, and condones ignorance.'

Quite. Judging from the state of our vehicles, the radio wouldn't have worked any way.

★ ★ ★

'Hey, come and eat our noodles. They're good. Plenty of pepper and vinegar. Lots of mutton. All made just for you.'

The delightful Mama Feng took my arm and led Jasper and me into the dining-room of her primitive but exceedingly warm and friendly caravanserai. The TV was switched on. The Professor was already surfing the channels.

'No police will come here tonight. It's too late. They're asleep.'

It was nearly midnight. Once again I marvelled at the ability of the Chinese peasant to produce a delicious meal, without a grumble, at any time of the day or night. It was abundantly clear that Mama Feng was delighted to see us all again and we rewarded her by saying that we would stay for two nights to enable us to sort out ourselves and our kit.

Mama Feng's giggly daughter lugged a battered, electric twin-tub washing machine into the compound and set about rejuvenating our mounds of smelly, salt-starched, sand-filled clothing. After breakfast we discovered that the caravanserai had no long-drop. When we asked where we should go to squat she waved her arm towards the distant fields and then, just to make sure that we understood, squatted on her hunkers and pointed at her bottom.

'I suppose it'll improve the village onions,' commented Jasper as he wandered off towards the farm land.

Later that morning, Jasper and I tracked down the Regimental barber in his one-room mud hut. He shaved us, cut our hair and completed the blissful half-hour session by providing an ultra-relaxing head and face massage. Heaven!

On 26 April, thirteen days after our camels had abandoned us, we set off on the long and tedious drive for Urumqi. Our camels, with Ahun, Dum Dum, Chang and Yusuf in attendance, would make their way slowly back to Ruoqiang where they were to be fattened up and sold. Driver Liu was back at the wheel of his Italian bus for this final sector of our journey. Once again, we were pitched inexpertly into sand dunes on the yellow-brick road. Jasper was itching to drive the vehicle himself, but knew that that was impossible. I noted with growing unease that the 'oil-boys' had been making many surveys to the east of the road. I uttered a silent prayer that they wouldn't find what they were looking for.

We reached Regiment 34 at midnight, and once again a piping-hot meal was produced at the roadside guest house without a thought for the time. We slept like babies on wooden boards in a crumbling out-house. When we reached Korla, the noisy doss-house was mercifully full, so we stayed, appropriately enough, at the more sumptuous Lou Lan hotel. On the outskirts of Urumqi Mr Liu subjected us to the 'wash the vehicle before we enter the city' ritual. Not that he did it himself. He employed a group of ladies, who swarmed over the vehicle like foraging bees, while we were consigned to seats outside in the freezing wind. Mr Liu's influence over the Professor was still wonderful to behold.

And then, at long last, we drove into the capital of Xinjiang and back to the Scientific Academic Hotel. Urumqi was warm and balmy. The trees carried fresh young leaves and all signs of winter snows, slush and dirt had disappeared.

'The Professor was right,' I said to Jasper. 'We've come back from off the map.'

'And from the dead,' he replied.

Afterword

To convert a former nuclear testing area that has had punitive restrictions on entry for over forty years into a nature sanctuary is news. News of worldwide interest. On 18 August 1997, the National Environment Protection Agency of China (NEPA) and the Xinjiang Environmental Protection Institute agreed to set up the Lop Nur Nature Sanctuary in the former nuclear testing area of China, provided that the necessary capital funding of $900,000 is raised. In September 1998 the Global Environment Facility in Washington pledged to provide $650,000 towards the capital costs. NEPA further agreed to pay the recurrent annual costs for the maintenance and running of the sanctuary. Earlier in 1997, the Wild Camel Protection Foundation was set up as a charitable trust to handle the fund-raising. At the same time, the renowned conservationist Jane Goodall agreed to use the sanctuary project as a pilot scheme for her Roots and Shoots programme, a successful venture which operates in over twenty countries and which is concerned with environmental awareness-raising. This educational element is crucial to the ultimate success of the sanctuary. Unless there is a coherent explanation given to prospective hunters and miners of why restrictions on their activities have been put in place, they will attempt to continue their illegal activities.

The quest for the wild camel yielded a very positive result, but, at the time of writing, much remains to be done in a very short space of time. Checkpoints need to be built, a reliable team recruited, and vehicles and a communications network put in place. Every year, as restrictions are relaxed to accommodate the new market economy ethos, ever-increasing numbers of adventurous Chinese will continue to seek their fortunes in an area which abounds in rumours of potential wealth.

The wild Bactrian camel struggles to survive. Its habitat has sharply diminished in size in the last 200 years. Although it appears to have been confined to the deserts of Central Asia, its range in the eighteenth century is thought to have extended to eastern Kazakhstan. We estimate that probably no more than 660, and possibly as few as 500, survive in China. In Mongolia there are thought to be between 300 and 400. What is quite clear is that they are all under escalating threat from hunting, illegal mining and, in the Trans-Altai Gobi in Mongolia, wolf predation. Only the wild camels in the Gashun Gobi, usually found in herds of no more than twelve, are completely isolated from domestic camels. This lack of an opportunity to hybridise is what makes their survival so important.

Even the announcement of China's suspension of nuclear testing for an indefinite period after the March 1996 underground test could prove a mixed blessing. Less exposure for the camel to nuclear radiation will inevitably mean greater exposure to the outside world. The Japanese have already sent forward a proposal to the provincial authority to stage a Great Gobi Car Rally. Unless the sanctuary is operating effectively within three years, it may be too late to save the camels in the Gashun Gobi. And these remnant Bactrian herds, possible descendants of the primordial camels which crossed the land bridge replaced by the Bering Strait sometime in the Pliocene (about four to three million years ago), are certainly worth saving.

It was the probable descendants of these early camelid pioneers that gave rise to the two camel species. Others that had gone south gave rise to the remaining four species of the zoological family of 'camelids', usually known communally as llamas (individually: the guanaco, the alpaca, the vicuna, and the llama proper).

The most obvious difference between the two camel species is the number of humps – localised fat deposits which, like fat in any other species, provides a source of energy. In the hotter climates of south-west Asia (and Africa) a 'mutant' with only one hump, the dromedary camel, became the dominant species. The dromedary camel's foetus still commences development with two humps, one of which disappears after a week. The deserts of Central Asia can be as hot as those of the Middle East; temperatures of sixty-five degrees centigrade have been recorded in the Gashun Gobi in August, yet in the same area, minus forty-one has been recorded in January. The severity of these winter temperatures has an effect on other aspects of body conformation. The Bactrian has generally a more massive body than the dromedary, is set on shorter legs and clad in longer, darker hair. All useful attributes in conserving heat during periods of extreme cold.

Both species have a long gestation period (dromedary twelve to thirteen months, Bactrian thirteen to fourteen months) and, at most, one calf is born every other year. With puberty late at four to five years and low calving rates, it is incredibly time-consuming to build up a declining camel population, domestic or wild. Compared to their domestic cousins, the wild Bactrian is greyer, slimmer and has smaller humps, but the fact that the dromedary foetus commences development with two humps but is born with only one, points to a long-term development from the Bactrian and makes these remnant wild Bactrians exceptionally important. Not least in this is their quite incredible ability to live off salt water or salt slush in areas where no other mammal, great or small, can survive.

It was Przhevalsky who, in 1877, had taken three skins and a skull of a 'wild' Bactrian home to St Petersburg and introduced the animal to a sceptical outside world. He was convinced that the camels were true wild fauna, not feral escapees. But the Petersburg zoologists could not determine whether Przhevalsky's specimens were the original wild stock, from which the two-humped Bactrian camel was bred, or animals which had escaped from caravans or survived the death of their drovers to become feral. After all, in 1997 we had lost our camels and had to leave one behind in the desert. Today there are more sophisticated methods of research to draw on. Dr George Amato, Director of Genetic Research at the New York Wildlife Conservation Society, has undertaken tests of specimens of Bactrian DNA and commented cautiously that 'the analysis is very interesting, and there is evidence that they may be distinct from their relatives'.

We believe that the 800 to 1,200 wild Bactrians that survive in China and Mongolia are not feral camel renegades, but the descendants of the original wild herds which roamed over Central Asia before they were domesticated over 4,000 years ago.

They must be saved.

Bibliography

WILD BACTRIAN CAMELS

Bannikov, A., 'Wild Camels of the Gobi', *Wildlife* 18 (New York, 1976)

Gu, J., and Gao, X., 'The Distribution of the Wild Camel', Chinese Academy of Sciences/Mammal Society of Japan (Osaka, 1985)

Hare, J., 'The Wild Bactrian Camel, *Camelus bactrianus ferus*, in China: The Need for Urgent Action', *Oryx* 31, 1 (Cambridge, 1997)

Kozlov, P., 'Proceedings of the Expedition of the Imperial Russian Geographical Society to Central Asia in 1893–1896 Under the Leadership of Roborovsky' (St Petersburg, 1899)

Littledale, S., 'Field-Notes on the Wild Camel of the Lob-Nur', *Proceedings of the Zoological Society* (London, 1894)

Tulgat, R., and Schaller, G., 'Status and Distribution of the Wild Bactrian Camels, *Camelus bactrianus ferus*', *Biological Conservation* 62 (New York, 1992)

Zhirinov, L., and Ilyinsky, V., *The Great Gobi National Park – A Refuge for Rare Animals of the Central Asian Deserts* (Moscow: Centre for International Projects, 1986)

MONGOLIA

Blunt, W., *The Golden Road to Samarkand* (London: Hamish Hamilton, 1973)

Bulstrode, B., *A Tour of Mongolia* (London: Methuen, 1920)

Carpine, J., *Histoire des Mongols*, translated by P. Schmitt (Paris: 1961)

Lamb, H., *Genghis Khan: The Emperor of All Men* (London: Thornton Butterworth, 1928)

Lattimore, O., *Mongol Journeys* (London: Travel Book Club, 1942)

Maclean, Sir F. M., *To the Back of Beyond: An Illustrated Companion to Central Asia and Mongolia* (London: Jonathan Cape, 1974)

Pozner, V., *Bloody Baron: The Story of Ungern-Sternberg* (New York: 1938)

Rossabi, M., *Kublai Khan: His Life and Times* (Berkeley, CA: University of California Press, 1988)

Rubruck, W. of, *The Journey of William of Rubruck to the Eastern Parts of the World*, translated by R. Rockhill (London: Hakluyt Society, 1900)

Severin, T., *In Search of Genghis Khan* (London: Hutchinson, 1991)

XINJIANG

Cable, M., and French, F., *The Gobi Desert* (London: Hodder & Stoughton, 1942)

Hedin, S., *Through Asia*, Vols 1 and 2 (London: Methuen, 1898)

——, *Central Asia and Tibet*, Vols 1 and 2 (London: Hurst & Blackett, 1903)

——, *My Life as an Explorer* (London: Cassell, 1926)

——, *Big Horses's Flight: The Trail of War in Central Asia* (London: Macmillan, 1936)

——, *The Wandering Lake* (London: George Routledge, 1940)

Holgate, W., *Arka Tagh: The Mysterious Mountains* (London: Ernest Press, 1994)

Hopkirk, P., *Foreign Devils on the Silk Road* (London, John Murray, 1980)

Polo, M., *The Book of Ser Marco Polo,* Vols 1 and 2, translated, edited and with notes by Sir Henry Yule (London: 1903)

Przhevalsky, N., *From Kulja Across the Tian Shan to Lob Nur* (London: Sampson, Low, Marston, Searle and Rivington, 1879)

Stein, Sir A., *Ruins of Desert Cathay*, Vols 1 and 2 (London: Macmillan, 1912)

Index

Index